I

BEYOND DILEMMA

A Memoir

To Jessie & Sterling, love from Donald & Marjorie

© Copyright 2005 Donald Maclean. All rights reserved.

No part of this publication may be reproduced, stored in a retrieval system, or transmitted, in any form or by any means, electronic, mechanical, photocopying, recording, or otherwise, without the written prior permission of the author.

Printed in Victoria, Canada

Front cover photograph is of author and his wife,
taken by Connie L. Swanson

National Library of Canada Cataloguing in Publication Data

A cataloguing record for this book that includes the U.S. Library of Congress Classification number, the Library of Congress Call number and the Dewey Decimal cataloguing code is available from the National Library of Canada. The complete cataloguing record can be obtained from the National Library's online database at: www.nlc-bnc.ca/amicus/index-e.html

ISBN 1-4120-3244-X

This book was published *on-demand* in cooperation with Trafford Publishing. On-demand publishing is a unique process and service of making a book available for retail sale to the public taking advantage of on-demand manufacturing and Internet marketing. **On-demand publishing** includes promotions, retail sales, manufacturing, order fulfilment, accounting and collecting royalties on behalf of the author.

Suite 6E, 2333 Government St., Victoria, B.C. V8T 4P4, CANADA
Phone   250-383-6864   Toll-free   1-888-232-4444 (Canada & US)
Fax   250-383-6804   E-mail   sales@trafford.com
Web site www.trafford.com   TRAFFORD PUBLISHING IS A DIVISION OF TRAFFORD HOLDINGS LTD.
Trafford Catalogue #04-1071 www.trafford.com/robots/04-1071.html

1   0   9

Hark:

If you be shorn of your ego right from the onset of your life, you will be neither here nor there.

Whoever writes does write through his mind and ego. Forsake your ego. Then you find you are in tune with Infinity.

Dadaji

* * *

A sharp blow to my solar plexus startled me out of my closed-eyes reverie, I sat up smartly, knowing the blow was from the flat of Dadaji's hand, knowing it wasn't designed to hurt, but rather to get my attention, and He got it.

What's the matter with you? Are you in a coma? Who do you think you are? You'll never recapture the time you allow, in your indolence, to slip away from you. Have you no clue as to why you are in this world? What do you want? Do you want to stay blind? Surely you know by now who you are! Don't you know anything?

I gazed into Dadaji's eyes, and, to be sure, He was looking directly into mine, from no more than six inches away from me, then a woman said. "You don't know who he is."

"Yes, I do," Dadaji said, "but he does not know who I am."

AUTHOR'S NOTE

This book is dedicated to my parents, who inspired me to explore, to seek an education, to travel, and to experience dilemma, and also to the memory of all my other teachers, some of whom I loved at the time, and some of whom I hated. Yes, the people I despised were also in my life to teach me! I appreciate the warm, enduring and loving friendship of the late Abhi Bhattacharya, also the unconditional support of my brother, Ian, who disagrees with some of what the book suggests, as well as support from my sister, Cathie. I am indebted to Brad Blanton, Ph.D, for his insightful comments. Others, nameless members of several writing workshops, have helped along the way, and I am grateful to each and every one of them. My wife, Marjorie, has been a constant support to me, encouraging me, inspiring me, reading each chapter, loving me. This is Marjorie's story and my story, told according to our particular perception. Someone else might remember the same events similarly or differently, would emphasize according to their particular perception, and would adopt a different story-telling style. The names and other identifying characteristics of the people written about, including those in clinical vignettes, which are composites, except when I am deliberately identifying someone, have been altered beyond recognition. The events that inspired these memories mean something to us.

ADDITIONAL NOTE

This is not a self-help book. It is not a manual. The author does not give instructions or offer methods of diagnosis or treatment of any medical/psychiatric/addiction problems. However, because of the nature of some of the material, and because the author is a retired psychiatrist, the following statement is included: No book can substitute for professional care or advice. The author and publisher are not engaging in rendering medical/psychiatric/addiction services. If medical/psychiatric/addiction problems appear or persist, the reader should consult with a physician or other qualified health-care professional. Accordingly, the author and publisher accept no responsibility for any inaccuracies or omissions and specifically disclaim any liability, loss, risk, personal or otherwise, which is incurred as a consequence, directly or indirectly, of the use and/or application of any of the contents of this book. The book is for informational purposes only.

CONTENTS

HARK 3
AUTHOR'S NOTE 4
ADDITIONAL NOTE 5

Part One - Canada
 1: Insight Deferred 11
 2: Father and Son 21
 3: Prarabda 34
 4: Dreaming 44
 5: Night Call 50
 6: Native American 56

Part Two - Scotland
 7: Breech Baby 67
 8: Iron-Poor-Blood 79
 9: The Cure 86
 10: Gossip Session 91
 11: It's A Man's Job 98
 12: Authority 108
 13: It was his Heart, You Say? . . . 115
 14: A Passionate Pursuit 120

15: Separation Anxiety 127
16: Spiritual Thirst 134
17: Pagoda 137
18: The Shack 151
19: If it wasn't for One Thing . . . 164
20: Marjorie 170
21: Fateful Anniversary 177
22: Knight in Shining Armor . . . 186
23: Queen 197

Part Three - United States of America
24: Loyalty 209
25: Medicinal Malady 215
26: What's My Secret? 227
27: Intensive Care 234
28: Respected Elder Brother . . . 241

Part Four - India
29: Dadaji 251
30: Why am I? 263
31: Manifestations of the One . . 272
32: Seeker and Sought 280
33: Dilemma 287
34: Beyond Dilemma 295
35: Vrajaleela 303

PART ONE
CANADA

1: INSIGHT DEFERRED

I was one of five family doctors serving a vigorous, action-oriented logging community in rural British Columbia, Canada; young as doctors went, but I felt I had arrived, doing what I had prepared myself for. My wife and I had left our families of origin behind, and had traveled far from our native Scotland; I was looking forward to a long career in my chosen profession, and, by way of accepting me in the community, the local men had appointed me team physician for the ice-hockey club, a position I enjoyed enormously, and something that also appealed to my wife Marjorie, as she soon became one of the team's most active and vocal fans.

One Saturday afternoon, on a house-call: The house itself was a small frame structure, painted dark green, with a low sloping roof, situated on a narrow, unpaved and little-traveled road that petered out into a dead-end in a grass-covered field. The screen door was closed, but the wooden door of the house was wide open, so that someone inside the living room could see out through the mesh on to the sunlit driveway. A peaceful-looking residence, a "retirement cottage." My knock on the frame of the screen door was greeted by a hoarse "Come in, Doc. Please walk right in." I let myself into the living room.

He was an old man and his hair was white-gray. He lay propped by pillows, one pillow beneath his thighs and one behind the small of his back, in a half-sitting position on a sofa against the far wall. It was a position in which gravity allowed him to breathe more easily, a position that encouraged his blood to circulate more readily, a position well known to physicians, but, despite the man's therapeutic posture, his lips had a blue tinge and his breathing remained labored. A faint sickroom aroma pervaded the room.

The man spoke: "Chair?" A gaunt-faced, steely-eyed man.

"Thanks, I will."

"I'm glad you came to see me, Doc."

"You're welcome. Are you alone in the house?"

"I'm alone, Doc. Yes, that's the way it is."

The man on the couch hauled in a deep breath with a massive movement of his chest wall, then let go of it as if dropping a heavy load, and at that moment he looked so tired that I didn't expect much action from him, but he raised his left arm, the one nearer to me, by way of friendly salute and makeshift handshake combined, while keeping his eyes on mine. His eyes were bright, but above, in the forehead, deep, wavy, transverse furrows, while below, a puffiness, and farther down, cheeks that were partly flushed, not with the fresh rosy color of health, but with the swollen bluish-red flush of physiological systemic failure. The effort of talking, of offering his salute, along with that of trying to sit up straight for my benefit, raised the pressure inside his already compromised neck veins, causing them to dilate visibly beneath the angle of his left lower jaw, the side closer to me. A mottled gray stubble on his chin was clear evidence that he hadn't shaved that morning.

"Please rest on your pillows, "I said. "You don't have to sit up straight."

"Right; I oughta take it easy," he said.

The skin over the triceps muscle of his raised arm sagged loosely, and vein lines and lean sinews popped up on his shrunken forearm, but his fingers were still thick and the joint at the base of his thumb was prominent, suggesting that here was the hand and arm of a man who had done hard physical work in his time, a man who had once been strong and able in his body. Once, perhaps, in the right place at the right time, in harmony with his work, a productive member of some aggressive team, he had lived his dharma in whole or in part, unknown to him.

But what did I know of that? Of his dharma? Or of mine? Or of individual life drama as the unfolding of ineffable destiny that, in my ignorance, I struggled against, trying to control what is beyond mind by mental acrobatics.

Outside, on the road, a little boy showed up next to my parked car and began doing doughnuts with his bicycle, by pedaling furiously, then jamming on the brakes while yanking the handlebars sharply to one side, causing the rear wheel to skid on the loose dry gravel. The boy's happy playful cries were musical in the quiet country air; the sound of his bicycle bell was crystal-clear; the rubbered rear wheel occasionally sliding upon gravel sounded like episodic showers of hail hitting tarpaulin.

I drew my chair up close to where the man rested, laid my medical bag on the floor, and said, "Please tell me how you're feeling."

"I want you to doctor me at home," he said, speaking rapidly, as if wanting to get the words out as quickly as possible before anything happened that might interfere with what he had to say. This was not what I had expected: I had expected him, approaching me as a new patient would, to begin telling me how he felt, what symptoms he was having, how he was coping; I had expected him to allow me to conduct a physical examination; I had expected him to hear me out as I gave a diagnosis and a professional recommendation. I made a quick visual evaluation of his condition.

"Doctor you at home! Maybe you should be in the hospital. I'd be willing to admit you."

"I knew it. I knew that's what you were going to say. Now you listen to me. I've been to the hospital before, several times. I've never seen you. I ain't seen your associate. I'm not going back to the hospital."

"Is that why you want to change doctors?"

"He and I don't see eye to eye. No, Sir. Well, enough of that. I don't want him to doctor me no more. No way. I won't do as he says."

The man coughed. He coughed three times; long hacking coughs, each followed by deep inhalations, and when the coughing spell subsided, he dropped his gaze to his middle and he slapped his belly with the flat of his right hand as if rebuking it for being out of shape, for indeed it was protruding like a giant gray jelly fish under his half-open shirt, but then again, maybe he slapped it for emphasis, to let me know he knew what was wrong, or maybe he slapped his belly for both rebuke and emphasis. Yes, that was probably it. At least, that's what the expression on his face suggested, for it changed from one of stern self-rebuke to one of intelligent demonstration.

"I ain't changing my mind on this, Doc," he said.

"Who will nurse you? What if the unexpected happens? What if an emergency situation develops while you're alone here?"

"Please answer me one question. Will you doctor me at home?"

As the youngest doctor in town, I got unusual requests from time to time, but thankfully not too often, such as for performing delicate procedures in unsuitable surroundings, such as for intervention in matters that were not properly my domain, but in this man I detected no hidden agenda, and his request was simple enough, although unusual and, from one perspective at least, unwise. I made my decision.

"OK, I'll doctor you at home."

"Good," he said, and immediately he began tugging at his shirt and wriggling around so as to expose his body for examination, and what a tired-looking, worn-out body it was. I felt the swollen neck veins, I felt the swollen liver, I felt the engorgement in the abdomen; I felt the swollen ankles where the pressure of my fingers left five indentation marks; I placed the cup of my stethoscope over the front of his chest, whereupon I heard the irregular beat of an enlarged heart struggling like the engine of an ancient chug-chug truck from a bye-gone era laboring up a steep hill; I placed my stethoscope over the bases of his lungs on the back of his chest wall and listened.

Along with the expansion and contraction of his lungs, I heard the unmistakable crepitating sound of moisture and air.

"Fluid in the lungs again, Doctor?" he asked.

"Yes, there's fluid in the lungs; there's fluid in other parts of your body too," I said. "It's your heart. The muscle in your heart wall is pumping as hard as it can, but it's no longer up to the task of pumping your blood briskly through your arteries. It's no longer strong enough to suck up and redistribute all the blood returning to it from your veins, so fluid backs up in your tissues."

"I know pumps."

"I want to give you some injections," I said. "The first medicine will strengthen your heart muscle. As soon as it begins to work, your heart will pump better. You'll feel the effect in a few minutes. The second medicine will make your kidneys put out excess water, so you'll be going to the bathroom. Once your body is drained of backed-up water, you'll breathe more easily. The third medicine is a sedative. It will take away the fear that invariably goes with this condition. It'll help you relax. The more relaxed you are, the better you'll recover. A calm inner state helps. You need all three. OK if I give you injections?"

"Certainly, Doctor, go ahead. You know what you're doing."

I injected the medications into his buttock, we both waited a few minutes in a silence broken only by the man's occasional coughing, then I asked him, "Why didn't you call me sooner?"

"I knew you'd be free on Saturday afternoon. That's why I called on Saturday morning."

"Well, you caught me just in time. A few more minutes and I'd have been gone. Anyway, please tell me something. Are you afraid of the hospital?"

"No, I ain't scared of the hospital."

"Most people are glad to enter the hospital when they need it, and to be sure, you could use the hospital today if anybody could. Of course, it won't cost you anything. Did you have a bad experience in the hospital the last time you were there?"

"No, I didn't have a bad experience. Actually, I improved while I was in there."

"Some people are afraid that if they enter a hospital, they'll never walk out."

"I've walked out of more dangerous places. That ain't it. It's just this. I want to be in charge of my life. It's my time. I want to do it alone."

Soon the medicines I had injected into his body were working, reinvigorating his cardiovascular system, transforming neurological chemicals, reducing anxiety, encouraging self-confidence, and so he was no longer fighting for his life, his eyes became quieter, softer, his facial muscles relaxed, the furrows in his forehead smoothed over, he was breathing more easily, and so was I, pleased to observe such a rapid transformation in so sick a man.

"Well, is there anyone who might help you out?" I asked. "Is there anyone I should get in touch with? a relative or even a close friend?"

"I'm alone in the world. My marriage failed a long time ago. I don't blame her for leaving."

"I see. Would you like to tell me why she left?"

"I was a logger...out in the forest. It was hard work, but I loved it. I loved the work, I loved the fresh air, I loved the winter cold, I loved the snow, I loved the trees, but I was no good with people. Being a foreigner, I couldn't talk good; it got me into fights. I'm ornery...I don't take no crap."

"Yes, go on. I'm sure she didn't leave because of that."

Silence for a few seconds. The man on the couch was gazing at his middle, seemingly deep in contemplation, then he uttered one word: "Disgusting!"

"What? What is? What's disgusting?"

"I can't tell you how many times I've stayed up all night with the boys, drinking, playing cards, shooting the breeze; then mornings we'd all fill up on steak and eggs and sausages and fried potatoes. Like beasts, we were. Disgusting! What woman would put up with that?"

"I imagine your wife didn't like it."

"I wasn't much of a husband. I wasn't ready to settle down. Annie wanted a regular life. Who could blame her for that? Who could blame her for leaving?"

"Are you blaming yourself?"

"I reckon I am at that. After she left, I deliberately forgot all about her. I pushed her out of my mind, I wouldn't even talk about her, but then again, now that I'm old, it's as if she's coming back into my life, just the way she used to be. I get to thinking about her. I can't help wondering if things could have been different. If only...."

"If only what?"

"If only I cared more. All physical, I was; no concern. I didn't care nothing about nothing. Nothing! I tell you. Come day; go day; roll on payday! That was me alright,. Now look at me. No wonder my body fails."

"Yes, go on."

"She said I broke her heart. Broke her heart. Imagine that! What was that all about? I didn't know what she was talking about. Yes, things might have been different if only I'd been different, but she married me for who I was, not for who she thought I might be, but then again, what do I know? Maybe she did believe I'd be different."

"You're a thoughtful man. Are you by any chance feeling down-hearted, sad, down in the dumps, depressed? Depression happens."

"No, Doctor, it's not that. I'm just thinking, now that I'm all alone, and much of my company comes from within myself. Have you ever heard of a poor man telling everybody he's a self-made man?"

"No, I haven't, but it's not something I've given any thought to," I said.

"It's always the wealthy, isn't it? Wealthy men love to tell the world how self-made they are. It has to do with how much money they've made. You see it in the Sunday papers. You see it in the magazines. Well, I've lived my life the only way I knew how. Think of that. I didn't know how to live any differently. Not that I haven't had my share of advice, well-meant, perhaps, perhaps not. Who knows? So what? None of that advice had any effect on me. None whatsoever! I went my own way. Does that make me a self-made man?"

"It's a loaded question. I don't have a good answer."

"I thought I made my own rules for living. I thought I never sucked up to others. I thought I was a hard man, tough and strong, but I was wrong, dead wrong. What have I ever stood up for in my life? Nothing!"

Who was I, young as I was in years, immature as I was at the time, to minister psychologically and spiritually to an old man approaching the end of his life? I had no working knowledge of a valid frame of reference in which to place the life drama I was observing, I had no working knowledge of the psychology of everyday life, I was not a man of religion, and words like karma, prarabda, destiny and moksha were unknown to me. But the role of ministering was one that was thrust upon me and I assumed it.

"There's something else on your mind. What else would you want to tell me?" I asked.

"Doctor, I ain't long for this world. You know it. I know it, but don't get me wrong, I ain't afraid to die, and I ain't feeling sorry for myself. I don't have to do anything that millions of other people haven't done before me. I have no family, so after I'm gone, I'll be forgotten."

"I'll be doing what I can for you, rest assured of that, and right now you're doing great. You'll continue to make some recovery, perhaps enough to allow you to get around so you can take care of yourself in your own house."

"I appreciate that. It's why I called you. I expect to make some recovery, but bear with me while I toss out another question, and it's this: Why did He make us this way?"

"I beg your pardon?"

"The preachers tell us we're sinners. They say we fell from

grace, or something like that, whatever that means. I've probably got that wrong, too. Anyway, God made us the way we are. He made us sinners, or at least prone to sin, but He doesn't want us to be sinners, so how come He made us sinners? It don't seem right."

"It's quite a question. I don't know the answer to it. Perhaps clergy would say He gave us freedom of choice and we're disobedient, owing to our self-centeredness, but I'm not the one to say. I can't wrap it up in an explanation."

"I say clergy have it all wrong. I say He made us the way we are. Like I told you, I've lived my life the only way I knew how. If I had my life to live over again, I wouldn't live it any differently. The whole thing pisses me off. It's as if I was meant to live the way I have lived, but then again, if I'd known....Maybe."

"Would you like someone from a church to visit you? A minister, perhaps, or a priest? Perhaps you'd like to talk things over. I can easily arrange it."

"No, not at all. I want none of that; I'm not a religious man. I don't belong to any church. I've never attended much. I've never even given much thought to God; well, that is, until now...And, yes, He does exist; I've no doubt about that. God exists."

"You're thinking it out for yourself. Maybe that's the best way."

"It's the only way....Doctor, did you hear that boy out there on his bicycle, laughing, playing?"

"Yes, I heard him."

"You listen to me; they'll take it away from him."

"Oh, you mean play?"

"No."

"I'm sorry; I don't understand."

"Maybe it just happens. Maybe we give it up. Like I said, what have I stood up for? I followed the crowd. Well, I've been doing some thinking, alone here. I lost something over the years. I feel it in me; something missing. What could it be? I lost my gentle spirit. I lost simplicity. I was angry a lot, ready to fight. I told you I hardened my heart. I lived rough....It's hard to explain. I can't get the words. I'm not a man of words anyway."

"You're a lot smarter than you give yourself credit for."

"As for smarts, I always imagined other people were smarter than I was, had more than I had, that other people had a better lot in life, better families, more love, that God blessed some people, but not others. I really believed that. Oh, I had glimpses of big shots. Now all the big shots in my world are dead, all dead and gone. Think of that, Doctor, think of that."

"I'm thinking," I said.

An experienced family physician might have had "answers" for him, a psychiatrist might have "explored" his state of mind, a clergyman might have reviewed appropriate scriptures for his benefit and prayed for him, a friend might have "agreed" with him. As a young family physician, I was none of these.

"Maybe I am afraid, after all. I told you I wasn't scared. Well, I am, and now I'm being more honest about it, but then again, what's to fear? I've always prided myself on my strength and agility, and now that's gone. I told you I can't put it into words. I've been running from my own crap all my life, when I imagined I was free like the wind. Anyway, it's all over now…and, just like the wind, it can all go. So, thanks for doctoring me; thanks for helping me out. I'm getting tired. That medicine sure works. I said more than I expected to. Now I want to go to the bathroom. My bladder's full. Please wait until I'm done, if you don't mind. After that, I want to go to sleep."

"Very well," I said, standing up. "I'll wait until you're ready, then I'll leave. I'll come back to see you again tomorrow."

2: FATHER AND SON

My first visit to my parents' home in the Scottish island of my birth since my departure abroad, finally, as an adult, a man, a real man at last.

On the radio, over the air waves, came music; there were songs; some of the music was local, some of it was from the mainland, some of it from Europe. Sadness. Love. Unrequited love. Departure. Loved ones left behind. Loss. Something unspoken, intuitively felt. My father spoke: "The old songs move me; modern songs don't. Where's the poetry in modern songs? Where's the beauty?"

I looked up sharply. What was he talking about? My father and I had never been close. Never before had he shared intimate thoughts and feelings with me. Some jokes, of course, and often, but nothing from the heart, nothing that opened up the heart, nothing that left him vulnerable, and certainly not nostalgic moments. "Maybe you're right," I said. "Maybe we've given up something."

"We hide our hearts, that's what."

My father had tears in his eyes. More surprise! He had never suggested to me in words or by his conduct that he had a deep appreciation for music or poetry, and there he was in my presence all teary-eyed. But these were not tears of sadness, nor tears of anger, they were tears of joy! no less. I could hardly contain myself. I had hit the jackpot, I knew the moment was elusive, that it wouldn't last long, and I wanted to catch it, hang on to it, enjoy it, prolong it if possible, hungry son that I was. A tingle all over; goose pimples! What else about him was I blind to? I knew I was seeing only the tip of the iceberg. My father was a naturally born comedian with his own unique style; he told humorous stories effortlessly, he converted mundane or trivial events, the expressions of human frailties, into powerfully emotive vignettes that penetrated social facades, that touched the hearts of men and women alike; vignettes that he composed easily, told skillfully, extemporaneously, that he snatched like a stage conjurer as if out of thin air from an unlimited supply. His humor worked. When he told his yarns, people laughed and laughed; they laughed until the tears flowed. They laughed the kind of laughter that stimulated the brain chemicals and made the happiness juices flow, laughter that revived and refreshed them, and no one else could reproduce his stories, for it was not what my father said, it was not the words he used, that was critical, rather it was how he expressed himself totally, including in non-verbal complexity, and how he drew out the unexpected but accurate bottom line that triggered the belly laughs. No one-liners; no wise-cracks; no puns; no worn prearranged jokes passed along by others. And whenever men and women gathered together to socialize, in any group of his peers, my father was the center of attention. His special way of telling tales kept his listeners enraptured. I was proud to be my father's son.

In the commercial market place of ideas, skills and labor, however, he was nowhere to be found, he never wrote anything down, he showed no interest in competing with others materially and he never tried to accumulate material possessions. Nor did he try to master any specific trade. He didn't have that kind of ambition. He worked when he could, or when he felt inclined: sometimes he worked as a sailor, sometimes he worked in construction, sometimes he was unemployed, and in between excursions around the country and abroad to find work, which meant that he was away from home often, he was a part-time crofter. He never took up weaving Harris Tweed, as many Island men did in those days, for after all, weaving controlled the weaver, rather than the other way around. Weaving was not a job a man could walk away from whenever he felt like it. Weavers did not have a wander-lust, but then again, most weavers didn't live in households controlled by women, and typically, weavers of Harris Tweed did not talk lovingly of poetry, nor become tearful when listening to music on the radio.

My father had been in the United States of America during the 1920s and during the early years of the depression, and I wanted to learn something about that. The music softened both of us up. "What was it like in America when you were there?" I asked him.

"Times were hard," he said; then he fell silent.

Times were hard! Is that all you're going to tell me? Isn't there more? I thought. I knew he shared some of his past with the local men because they occasionally hinted at it to me, and I wished so much he would share more of his life with me. I longed for him. I yearned for him. I wanted some of the warmth I knew he had in him. I wanted his companionship. I wanted his appreciation. I wanted a demonstration of his love. I wanted my heart to touch his heart. Why didn't he express his love for me? I knew it was there. I felt it intuitively. I continued the conversation.

"How did you make out in these hard times?" I asked him.

"We didn't suffer from obesity."

"Someone told me you made your way from San Francisco to New York. You did, didn't you?"

"Yes, I did, sometimes on railway freight cars, sometimes by walking along lonely roads; sometimes I got rides from travelers, and anytime I could, I worked. I'd work at anything, but what was there to do? Next to nothing, but I wasn't alone in that situation."

The bowl of my father's black pipe was brim full of slowly burning St. Bruno's Flake; inside the fireplace a peat fire blazed; beyond the horizon the setting sun splashed the western sky over the Atlantic Ocean with streaks of red, yellow and orange; above the fireplace, on the mantelpiece, a clock audibly ticked the seconds away, while inside the living room, where my father and I sat in front of the fire, listening to the radio, evening shadows awoke like shades from another world, across the ceiling, along the walls.

"Well, there's one photograph of you taken in Ohio. You were wearing clean slacks, a clean shirt and nice shoes."

"I bought a new outfit in Ohio, where I stayed for a few weeks. I worked there on a building project, but it didn't last long. These contracts never did. As soon as the job was finished, I picked up and left, heading east."

"My cousin told me you worked on the Holland Tunnel in New York for a while."

"I did at that."

"You must have met some interesting people along the way. How about that?"

"Yes, I certainly did. I like the Yanks. They're hospitable, and always, wherever I happened to be, we shared what we had with each other. Mulligan Stew under the bridge was great when we could get the ingredients. When we couldn't, empty bellies didn't translate into empty lives, not at all. The Yanks have a good sense of humor. They're fun. Even when we had empty bellies, we laughed.

"We took each day as a blessing. People don't laugh like that today. Nowadays, even laughter is artificial. Modern humor is prepared in advance, recorded, canned and sold for money on the radio. Sad! As if true humor could be commercialized."

"We're serious in my profession. We're don't laugh with each other."

"The war changed things for everybody. It destroyed so many lives. To be sure, the war opened up the world, but now everybody's so serious about life, striving to succeed, competing with each other, making more and more money, needing more and more materials, striving more and more. How many people enjoy life? Do professional entertainers?"

"I like my work, but that's not what you mean."

"No, it isn't. I'm not talking about fulfillment in some profession. I'm talking about a lighter side to life. Well, anyway, I liked the Yanks, I have fond memories, a great life, but I came back to Scotland to marry your mother."

What if you hadn't? I thought. Where would I be? I wouldn't exist, would I? I came into existence because of someone's decision to return to Scotland, as a result of which, in a moment of time that could never be duplicated, in a certain location, one sperm in a million met one lonely wandering egg, and out of that union I arose, and, had my father not returned home at exactly the time he did, had the marriage not taken place precisely when it did, someone else might have come into existence, comparable to a sibling, from another sperm and another egg, but not I. I kept my fantasies to myself. I wanted to hear more.

"What about the Great Depression in Scotland?" I asked him.

"Here on the Island, we had croft lands that provided us with some food, we had peat for fuel, and we had a few animals. We had some milk, potatoes, cabbage and eggs, but in the big cities people were hungry."

"All we hear about is the American version."

"Sometimes there were strikes, sometimes men became violent, and occasionally there were riots. One time, when there was a great civil disturbance, we were told that some people in government in London suggested ordering the military to turn the guns on the people. Imagine that! Would the military turn on those they were supposed to protect? How true that is, I don't know, but the story went around among working men. Of course, the government didn't do it."

"They found others to turn against."

"Men who make their living out of talking say much in the course of their lives, some of which they would change, if they got the chance, and, thankfully, much of what's said is forgotten. Politicians are rhetoricians. Consider Winston Churchill, magnificent in war, in exactly the right place at the right time, a man we couldn't have done without, but, on the other hand, when the war was over, as soon as they got a chance, the public voted him out of office. Why? What did people see in him that made them give him the 'Order of The Boot,' as someone, possibly himself, referred to it later? Despite his leadership skills, despite his bricklaying days, there was a great gulf between him and working men. And working men and women were slowly awakening."

My father was gazing into the fire, absorbed in his own thoughts, and I said nothing because I wanted him to continue. He did: "Democracy is strange. Do we really govern ourselves? We labor, we do what we're told to do. Our options are limited. Leaders seem to be in charge, they create crises, they have much to lose, although it matters little to us, then comes hatred, international name-calling, patriotic songs, flag waving, boot stamping. The tramping of boots! At the beginning of the First World War, the opposing soldiers had no quarrel with each other. They didn't know who was doing what to whom. The fighting soldiers didn't want a war."

"Well, they got it," I said.

"And old men sent young men away...Why do old men kill young men? Actually, in between wars, I liked the German sailors," my father said. "All over the world, in seaports, I found the German sailors hospitable. I used to visit them on board their own ships and I always felt welcome. On Sundays when our ships had no beer, the Germans always had plenty. They were relaxed. Many times I enjoyed myself on German ships. One time, I shared ownership of a car with a German sailor. Of course, that was before we became enemies, and bitter enemies at that."

Suddenly, silence. The conversation was over. My father arose from his chair: "It's time for me to visit the lads down the road," and I also knew that, "down the road," there would be tales, yarns and merriment galore, and I would be left out of it. That longing again. A feeling as if of a hole within my heart. It was a secret I kept to myself, a secret on the tip of my tongue, a secret I never put it into words, part of a private world within me.

In due course, my visit to my parents' home came to an end, back to Canada I went, and no sooner had I gone back to work, serving others, as I saw it, than the feeling of emptiness vanished. Yes, "curing" disease, salving the wounds of others, fixing fractured limbs, injecting vigor into the broken hearts of others, "saving" others, worked.

Then one day came a disturbing letter. While riding his pedal bicycle along a local unpaved rutted road that led to the peat banks, my father had suddenly listed to his left side and had lost control of his machine. He managed to avoid falling hard, and he slowly made his way home, which was half a mile away from where he had fallen, without help. It was a "little stroke," according to the family doctor, but, little or large, a stroke was a serious assault upon the interior of the brain, and, not surprisingly, it was soon followed by another and more serious stroke.

There was no telephone in the old family home at the time, so communication was slow and limited, but, by mail, I learned that he had weakness in his left leg and that he had trouble speaking clearly and in identifying familiar objects. I was a long way off, in Western Canada, and I feared what was coming, something I hadn't expected so soon, although he had a history of high blood pressure, for which he had been taking medication. He was approaching his sixty fifth birthday. Was that old?

"Go home and visit your father," said my associate in practice. He spoke without hesitation. "You may not get another chance. If you miss out on this, you'll regret it later. Believe me, I know about these things, I have experience." "Thank you, thank you," I said, knowing that it meant additional work for him, and inconvenience. I was grateful to him for his generosity.

Marjorie and I traveled to Scotland, where we expected to find a serious situation, but nothing as serious as the situation that greeted us upon arrival. My father wanted to be up in the living room when we arrived home, so that he could greet us in person rather than having us walk in on him as he lay in bed, and so it was that he was sitting in a chair beside the fire with his legs covered by a blanket when we walked into the house, carrying our suitcases. The moment I saw my father, I knew that he was gravely ill. Oh, how he had changed! Aged. The prognosis was written all over him. It was poor.

Over the next few days he was too weak and too ill to smoke his pipe, but occasionally he took sips of a dark Scottish alcoholic beverage called Stout or Porter that the local people believed helped the appetite, elevated the mood and provided energy in a way that was easy to assimilate. "It's very bitter," said the family doctor, referring to the rich aromatic foamy glassful, during one of his visits.

"The bitterer the better," said my father, who drank very little, and whom I never on any occasion saw in the least bit intoxicated. The family doctor was a roly-poly busily clinical-looking man, with a ruddy complexion, prominent cheekbones, loosely brushed hair, brown hands with long fingers, and the inevitable stethoscope, the symbol of professional identity, protruding from his coat pocket. An aroma of medicine followed him around wherever he went.

"Well, the beverage might help your appetite. I have no problem with you taking some. Is there anything else you would like?"

The doctor stood, looking at my father, head cocked slightly to one side. He was trying to be helpful. He was being kind. He wanted to deliver something other than a neurological diagnosis, something beyond what his knowledge of anatomy, physiology, pathology and pharmacology could deliver, something in the realm of the spiritual, perhaps.

"How about some Chop Suey? Bring it chop-chop," said my father, trying to be light-hearted, and the doctor smiled. He smiled for the wrong reason. "You want chop and eggs? Impossible! You couldn't handle that. Eggs maybe, scrambled, but not lamb chops." He shook his head. The doctor had mistaken the sound of the work "suey" for the Gaelic word for egg, which had a similar sound, a mistake that could easily be made seeing that my father could not articulate well.

On his way out of the house, the doctor turned to me. "Do you have any children?" he asked. Staring dark brown eyes. All seeing, gazing right into me. I hesitated, I froze, I said, "No, I don't." I didn't like people asking me if I had children. I felt defensive whenever someone asked me that question, I wanted to hide, but the question was there, in reality, and it scared me. I felt guilty about not having children. And angry! Why? I didn't know, I didn't want to explore it at the time; some other time, maybe, yes, to be sure, I would attend to it another day. The doctor could tell I was uncomfortable. He was a perceptive man, experienced, sensitive to hidden fear in others.

"Oh, well, you're still young enough. I'm sure you'll have plenty of children in due course. I wish you well."

I believed I was "supposed" to have children, I believed I was "supposed" to "be a man," with all that that entailed, and I strove towards an idealized image of what I imagined a man was supposed to be, and what a gap there was between that product of my imagination, that awesome fantasy, and what I was in this life! If I were to attempt to be true to that imaginary being, I'd be in a perpetual state of stress; if I were to be true to myself, I'd lose, or so I believed; I believed it because I knew so little.

Alcohol relieved the tension, it percolated into me, relaxed me, and so I drank whiskey, I drank beer, and my mother disapproved. I could tell. She let me know. She nagged me. We engaged each other in a mad, merry dance.

"Leave me alone," I snarled at her one day. "I'm not here for you. I want to be with my father. Once I leave here...."

The following day, I visited my father alone in his bedroom. "Angus lived nine months after his stroke," he said to me in his slurred speech, and I knew he was thinking of his own prognosis, that he was hoping to have another nine months of life and I imagined that nine months might seem to him like a long time. Nine months! Not long at all, but then again, long enough for human gestation. Didn't we each spend nine months inside our mother's womb prior to venturing out on to the stage of life?

I answered my father: "Yes, and they were good months too.

I remember Angus well. I remember you giving him a haircut in the chair outside the shell of the new house while you were building it. Do you remember that day?"

"Yes, I do."

After I left the bedroom where my father lay, Marjorie entered and remained with him alone for some time, and afterwards she told me what he had said to her: "Marjorie, I love you. You're a good woman; a wonderful daughter." Beautiful! Something inside me relaxed. At long last it had happened. My father had accepted Marjorie; he had accepted me as a married man, as an adult. A warm glow swept through me. I smiled. The next time I went to talk to him, I sat on the edge of his bed and held his hand:

"When are you going to have children?"

Here we go again, I thought. The question gave me the shivers. It was a question I didn't want to confront. If I said to those who mattered to me that I didn't want children, I would be exposed as a mouse, not a man, but, on the other hand, if I said that I wanted children, I would have to do something about it. I remained silent. The moment passed. My father didn't pursue it. He knew.

The three weeks I had allocated to my visit went by without my getting to know with any certainty how long my father's medical condition, his will or his destiny would allow him to live, or whether another stroke would come and take him, and finally the day came when I knew that, sadly, I would have to depart.

On the day of my departure, a chilly day in September, the sky was overcast, but the visibility was excellent, and the wind came wailing across the sea, over the beaches, across the meadows; it blew icily around the new house; it stabbed me in the middle, it thrust its daggers into my heart.

At his own request, at the time of our departure, I helped my father out of his bed and into a chair by the window, so that he could see the road outside. "I want to see you get into your car and leave," he said. I wrapped a blanket around his legs. He looked weak and wan, his face was thin, he was like a shadow of a man with skin wrapped around him, he could barely hold his false teeth in place, but, despite that, he made a valiant effort to re-energize himself, as if he wanted to be his old self for just one more day, maybe just for one more hour, or perhaps a few more minutes.

What could I say to him? How about "I will not be seeing you again, so I want you to know I love you." The thought entered my mind fleetingly, but I didn't say it. I didn't even say, "Just in case we don't see each other again, although I hope we do, I want you to know I love you." Death, the end of life as I knew it, was off limits, and so was God. Much later, I came to know I feared both, but at the time I denied any such fear to myself, I repressed it, forcing it into hiding beyond my awareness, and of course I would have denied it to others if the subject had ever come up, which it didn't, which meant that I didn't for years express my fear rationally in words, in the context of a frame of reference where I might have dealt with it.

"Watch out for the bears in Canada," he said to me. "Be sure and watch out for the bears."

"Yes," I said. "I'll be careful about the bears," and I knew he was losing contact temporarily, for I was in no danger from black bears in Canada, or from grizzly bears, but then again, there were bears and there were "bears," and if a hidden message in my father's words referred to my own psychological "bears" that followed me around wherever I went, it was right on target. Shadowed by bears. Bears as shadows. Dark shapes lurking.

Marjorie and I walked out of the house carrying our luggage, we approached our rental car that was parked in the driveway and we loaded up. Once we were seated in the vehicle, we both turned around and waved back at the window, aware of my father's presence, knowing he was watching us, knowing he was with us, although we could no longer see him.

It was with sad hearts and a profound sense of loss that we boarded our plane to Glasgow, and subsequently boarded the plane across the Atlantic Ocean to New York, on the first and second legs respectively of our long journey to British Columbia. We were high above the ocean when I felt a fluttering in my chest. What could it be? I checked my pulse. Sure enough, it was irregular. Never before had anything like that happened to me. I kept quiet about it, saying nothing to Marjorie, and the irregularity persisted all the way to New York, where we checked into a hotel. Two days in a Manhattan hotel. My sister Cathie met us there. I called the hotel doctor. He was a thoughtful man who examined me physically and also ran an electrocardiogram. "The EKG," he said, as the test was in progress, "is full of irregularities. Oh, wait a minute...the irregularities are going away...they're gone. The moment I told you about the irregularities, they vanished. Isn't that something? You're back to normal regular rhythm." He regarded me thoughtfully. He had gray eyes, wavy gray hair and brown hands, competent hands they felt like.

The doctor prescribed a mild sedative for me, and it helped, so I rested before resuming my journey, while Cathie and Marjorie toured the city, and by the time I got back to British Columbia I was ready to resume my work, but a couple of days later there came another interruption. A telegram arrived via the post office. I took its contents over the telephone from a solicitous woman operator who used a carefully modulated hushed tone of voice, like someone whispering in a funeral parlor. My father had passed away peacefully. It was all over.

"Thank you for the message," I said.

The woman seemed surprised that I didn't react emotionally to the news. Although sensitive, I didn't show emotion because I practiced "equanimity," I wanted to be strong, silent, in control, never vulnerable, a grown masculine man, a perfect man, according to my idealized image.

I didn't talk to Marjorie about my father's death, certainly not about what his death, or death itself, meant to me. She didn't say a word about it either. Death, in its profound and spiritual significance, which of course excluded clinical situations, was a closed subject, as was birth in anything but the simplest terms. Out of mind, down it went, where it lurked, along with the other taboos of life. I continued working the rest of that day, I went to work the next day, and the next, and time passed, short-term became long-term.

The next time Marjorie and I visited my mother, but not before, she told us what my father's last words had been:

"Tell the children to follow Christ."

3: PRARABDA

Whenever the car we were riding in rounded a curve on the winding road traversing the length of British Columbia's Frazer Canyon, Marjorie and I caught a glimpse of the stark beauty of black sunshine at the bottom of small-sky country, I behind the wheel of our sports car, steering the sleek machine in the silence of the mountains, meeting next to no traffic, Marjorie in the passenger seat.

As we traveled north all the way from Seattle through the beautiful Pacific North-West, we had plenty of time for conversation.

"Two years before he died," Marjorie said, "my father said to his sister who lives in California, 'Marjorie will go to British Columbia some day.' Isn't that something? I had never expressed to him or to anyone a desire to go to British Columbia, we never spoke about it, nor did I have any such desire when my father was alive. How could he have known I would come to British Columbia?"

"How do you know he said it," I asked.

"It's in writing, in a letter he wrote to his sister."

"How could your father have known? I can't explain it. It's a complete mystery to me."

"Well, we're here, and it is good," Marjorie said.

Rural practice in that place at that time clarified and identified aspects of our characters to each other, although mostly we stayed blind to our own character structures and to our habitual ways of rubbing abrasively against each other, and we did that too, few as we were, emotionally needy, regressing under stress, old fantasies coloring our relationships with each other.

What about being a physician? Was that not a noble calling? I believed so when I was a boy living on a remote island, but my ideas on that subject were changing radically. How far removed from reality was the image of the altruistic caring physician? Was it all an idealized fantasy?

We physicians loved disease. We were fascinated by disease, and the more esoteric the disease, the better we liked it. There was nothing wrong with that. Was there anything else wrong? I was aware of a chronic irritation inside myself. It was something I tried to conceal. Why cover up? Because I imagined there was something morally wrong or bad about it, or, worse yet, about myself, to the degree that I equated my emotions with myself. It never occurred to me at the time that this was something to be explored, something to be clarified, to be understood as an aspect of life, to be placed into a frame of reference that made sense, out of which would come metaphoric explanations, visual illustrations, a fresh view of the world, which in turn would lead to options out of dilemmas, options for transformation. And presumably I wasn't alone in this. In my early years in training, I had noticed that many of the "grizzled veterans," particularly the more aggressive ones, seemed overly fond of crushing and humiliating the innocent wide-eyed juniors. I didn't know why. Were they insensitive? Was I overly sensitive? How about our fantasies as juniors in the presence of Authority? How about the fantasies of those in authority about Authority? What about our secret motivations for becoming physicians? The motivations we spoke openly about were façade. I knew so little, and it was easier to project than to contemplate comprehensively, to look outside than to acknowledge the Teacher within. To be sure, the actual practice of medicine seemed to be different from what we imagined in the idealizing days of our youth, and it was easy to become disillusioned, but, although I was too young to observe astutely, I did know a few mature physicians who were comfortable in their life roles and in their professional roles, at peace with themselves.

"Marjorie," I said, "the old pioneers passionately wanted to explore this land. Look around you."

"We're here, and it's good, but I'll never forget the greeting I got from Mrs. Smith the first time we met, right after we arrived in the Country of The North. You and I had barely unpacked."

"What did she say?"

" 'Fortitude! my dear; fortitude! You need lots of fortitude,' is what she said. She looked grim. What was she talking about? I gazed at her in silence. She intimidated me."

Far below the road that the Royal Corps of Engineers had carved out of the mountains, the Frazer River splashed and spilled its narrow white-water way along the bottom of the canyon, on its long winding way to the Pacific Ocean. Men and women had carved their way through that wilderness, through vast forests, across huge mountains, up and down deep gorges, in summer heat and in winter cold. And it wasn't simply fortitude they needed, besides their guns, their bibles and their mules, not at all, although they undoubtedly had that too. What they had, and what they needed first and foremost, was a passionate desire to do what they were doing. Perhaps without their knowing it, they fulfilled their destiny, they lived their dharma.

"Why did we come up north, Donald?'

"Marjorie, you know what people say about 'going up north,' don't you? I'm more misfit than diplomat. I'm not a smooth operator."

"Who wants to be a diplomat?"

"Would I want to be one of these upper-crust English professors, posturing, talking in exaggerated affected accents, sounding ridiculous?"

"Try something else."

Sometimes, when I was alone on quiet nights, the community where we lived, with its forests and creeks, its history of adventure, its increasing prosperity, seemed as if it wasn't so far removed from the giant plains of the north that was home to the howling wolves under the ice-cold, star-bright nights, but that was only a fantasy, a pleasant one, to be sure, but a product of my imagination. The two regions were far removed from each other in that vast country.

Marjorie and I continued our conversation: "Maggie Cinnamon showed up at my office one day recently. She wasn't sick. She wanted a loan of two dollars. Wrinkled face, dress too loose, hair uncombed, wearing around her shoulders a large gray shawl. What a mess! I gave her the two dollars. A local man found out about it. Hoots of laughter. Stupid, naïve me, giving cash to an Indian! Was I just off the last boat, or what? A week later Maggie returned to repay me."

"You've made a few remarks about Indians, yourself."

True, I remembered, for whenever I saw a Native American Indian weaving his way along a dusty road, clutching a brown paper bag, I would smile inwardly with a subtle shake of my head. Was I not doing important work? Was I not a busy man? Was I not saving lives? Was I not on call for emergencies? Was not my time precious? And what were these Indians doing? They were doing what they damn well pleased. What did they care about middle class respectability? What did they care about bourgeoisie values? Or about keeping up with the Joneses? Or about saving money for the future? Or about cutting down trees? Or about mining for Molybdenum? Or about blasting tunnels through mountains?

Marjorie and I were indeed approaching a tunnel. Inside the tunnel we were out of the sunshine, inside the belly of the mountain, with the curve of the road lit by rows of glowing reflectors. A pair of large lights appeared out of nowhere, approaching rapidly, coming alongside, then came the shivering roar of a massive timber-laden truck bound for the coast, its load probably going to Japan, a progressive nation of aggressive, inscrutable men on the make. A blue light appeared, marking the end of the tunnel, expanding quickly as we approached, becoming bright daylight that snapped open around us the moment we sped out of darkness. More driving, curves, mouintains.

Finally the time came when we were out of the Canyon, approaching hill country, the sky widening, the horizons moving further away, the sky lightening up, trees, some birds, slopes.

"Marjorie," I said. "Can you hear a noise coming out of the front of the car?"

She listened in silence for a while, then she said, "No, I don't hear a thing."

"It's a soft muffled thumpa, thumpa, thumpa, like distant mallet blows. I've been hearing it for some time, maybe an hour or so."

"Well, I don't hear it; not a thing."

"I do, and I don't like it."

I swung the car over to the side of the road and scrunched to a stop on a bed of dry gravel, below an almost vertical slope where many years of falling water, winter ice, and wind had worn a giant cavity in the side of the mountain. Next to the gravel where I had parked, there stood a vertical slab of rock thirty feet high. Even on such a dry day as this was, a steady flow of water ran down the side of the rock. Where was the water coming from? Was there a massive glob of water up there above us, wanting out? A billion tons of pressure. Ominous! I looked upwards. Huge boulders. I couldn't see the top. Suddenly the mountain was moving. Adrenaline rush. No, the mountain wasn't moving after all. It was just an illusion created by white clouds racing across the sky. Head-spinning beauty. I turned my back on the giant, I looked at the car, I examined the tires and the wheels, I opened the hood, I examined the engine. Nothing out of place. I slammed the hood shut, and afterwards Marjorie and I stood in silence for a couple of minutes, fascinated by the echoing music of water splashing down the slab.

"Looks OK to me," I said. "Let's get back on the road."

"Do you want me to drive?"

"No, I'm not tired. You enjoy the ride."

In the country of the low rolling pine tree covered hills, the graying grass and the imminently barren landscape suggested waning warmth, seasonal change, dissolution, departure, loss. It startled me in its intensity, but I kept quiet about it. Instead, I said: "The noise is still there, Marjorie. I'm surprised you don't hear it."

"I don't hear a thing. I have no idea what you're hearing."

I began to listen more carefully. I imagined I was using a stethoscope. I visualized the moving parts of the engine: suction, compression, explosion, transfer of energy, exhaust, oil flowing, gear wheels moving, shafts rolling, wheels turning, and I knew there should be no alien sound coming out of that orchestra of sophisticated engineering, but there was, not all the time, mind you, and to be sure, I felt better when I didn't hear it. Indeed, it went away when I concentrated on the engineering, and then I relaxed, but no sooner had I let go than the distant muffled thumping started again. It wouldn't be pinned down, whatever it was.

"I'm puzzled," I said to Marjorie. "I want a mechanic to take a look at this car."

We passed several places before stopping at a service station. I pulled the car into the station and parked. A man in overalls approached us. He had jet black hair; he had heavily-lidded eyes. "What can I do for you?" he asked.

I wanted a qualified mechanic rather than a fuel pump operator to examine the car, and so I asked the man, "Are you an auto mechanic?"

"Some people call me a mechanic, among other things. It's one of the better things they call me."

I might have appreciated the man's sense of humor if the remark had been accompanied by a smile instead of a smirk, if he hadn't turned his back on us and walked into the garage, while gesturing with his left hand for us to follow him.

"There's a thumping sound coming out of the right front of this car," I said to the mechanic. "It's been going on for some time today. I'd like you to please take a look and find out what's wrong. Something has changed in this car. Something's causing it to sound like that."

"OK, pull over here, into this empty space, put it in park and unlock the hood. The two of you can stay inside the car."

The mechanic wiped his hands on a gray-black rag that he pulled out of his overalls, he then thrust the rag back into his back pocket, and he began examining the vehicle. The bright red car shone and gleamed and sparkled like some extraterrestrial machine, with its eight-cylinder engine as its heart, making the mechanic's grimy rag and greasy hands and dark untidy surroundings look like some error of evolution. The seats of the car were covered with Palomino leather, the gear shift was on the floor, the instrument panel was black with several chrome dials that emphasized power. It was a salesman's dream. It was a young man's fantasy come true.

"There's nothing wrong with this car. It's in excellent condition," the mechanic said after he had finished his examination.

Much relieved, I placed the receipt for service rendered into the glove compartment and the two of us drove off. I didn't hear the noise any more. Really! Sure enough, it had stopped after we received the good news about the condition of the vehicle. Good news.

"Marjorie," I said, "there's a comfy-looking inn just down the road. Let's stop and relax for a while. We've got time. Once ensconced in the bar, we talked about staying overnight. "We don't have to be home until tomorrow." We decided against staying.

I purchased a bottle of liquor for consumption in the comfort of our home, and there, in the back seat of the vehicle, the bottle nestled, cuddling itself in the Palomino leather, rocking rhythmically two and fro, gleaming, luminescent, alive, *eau-de-vie, uisge-beatha*, and, between me and you, so to speak, I might possibly have broken the seal.

Marjorie and I rolled our way royally northwards on the long open black-top ribbon of road that went all the way up into the remote northwest. The driving was easy. I felt steady, I felt comfortable, I felt in control, and I felt confident; I had not a care in the world. The road reeled under the car, dry, clear and easy to navigate. Then it happened. A crack like a rifle shot; then lights out. It was the last thing I remembered for some time. The next thing I remembered after was Marjorie and I being loaded on to an ambulance, followed by a long, painful journey to the nearest hospital. Marjorie had multiple bruises, some lacerations, and an ugly gash on her right thigh. My injuries included multiple bruises, some lacerations, a bruised and bleeding kidney, and a severe fracture of the left ankle. We were transported to Vancouver by air the following day, because I needed the kind of surgical care that was not available locally.

My ankle joint was crushed beyond repair, and after prolonged surgery I was left with a shortened, narrowed leg and an ankle joint that was more like a sock full of broken bones, held together by tissue, than a real ankle joint.

A member of the local branch of the Royal Canadian Mounted Police visited us at home. He was a young officer with a bulge over his belt, wearing a hefty holster over his hip. Lots of leather. Aromatic. Authority. "There might be charges," he said. What kind of charges? He didn't say, and I didn't ask, but I assumed that charges, if they came, would have something to do with a bottle of liquor in the back seat of the car.

"If they charge me with a serious driving offense, if I'm convicted, if I lose my driving license, I'll be out of business," I said to Marjorie.

"We'll deal with that if it happens."

"You know what the medical profession is like."

"What are they like?"

"Public image; status oriented; character conscious; competitive; possessive of patients, as if patients belonged to us, and, to be sure, much of whatever power we have to cure comes from the way the public perceives us, they 'want' their designated healers to be therapeutically powerful, and without flaws. Not much room in the medical profession for a 'hopalong' without a driving license."

"Maybe you're the one who's like that."

"What do you mean."

"Nothing; I don't mean anything."

Months went by and we didn't hear anything more from the police, then one day a Mountie showed up at our house, belted, booted, armed and in charge. Authority! He sat down on the living room couch and he took off his hat. What was this? Something about him was different. We waited. Holding his wide-brimmed hat in one hand, leaning forward, he asked in a mild, almost casual tone of voice, "Did you visit a garage along the way?"

A curtain leaped off my mind, my memory lit up, and I saw myself driving the long-nosed vehicle into the garage, guided by the mechanic, I saw myself telling the mechanic about the noise coming from the right front of the engine, I remembered the relief I felt when the mechanic told me that there was nothing wrong with the car, I saw myself driving along the road once more. I said to the officer: "Yes, we did visit a garage. There was a noise coming from the right front of the car. I pulled in for inspection. I told the mechanic about the thumping sound. He told me there was nothing wrong with the car."

The Mountie's face fell. He shook his head as if in regret at what might have been, and I knew immediately that there was something important I didn't know about. Of course, the police would have found the receipt from the garage that I had placed in the glove compartment.

According to the police, the car had narrowly missed a giant pole and rolled down a steep slope, and we had been thrown out without being crushed in the process. We had not been wearing seat belts at the time. We had worn seat belts all the way from Seattle until we got to the service station, but for some reason we neglected to fasten them afterwards. Why? I had no rational answer. The belts were waist-only belts, with no shoulder harnesses, and, had we remained inside the car, in the inadequate grip of these belts around our waists, we might have been partially expelled from the rolling car with its blasted out windows and its crushed roof. With what consequences? Again, no one could answer such a question.

The Officer watched me in silence for a few moments, then he got up from the couch, and, holding his hat in his hand, he said as he walked out of the house, "You'll be hearing from us shortly."

* * *

Later we learned that an automotive engineer had examined the car by request of the police, and that he had given them an opinion, and, although no one gave us a copy of that professional opinion, we learned that there had been a defect in the axle of the car. Marjorie and I had been riding on an axle that was destined to break in two. Destiny had permitted us a tiny hint, in the form of an intrusive sound, to which we reacted rationally by having the car examined by a qualified mechanic, but which we could interpret only in hindsight as prarabda, which is an aspect of karma, something we had to work through in our lives so as to fulfill our present life purpose. All the little pieces fit to make the whole drama. We knew nothing of that at the time, but I did know one thing:

The "crack like a rifle shot" I had heard in that split-second before the car veered off the road was the sound made by steel splitting asunder and smashing into hard road as the axle broke and the right front wheel flew off.

4: DREAMING

I had taken a major hit, physically and psychologically, but back to work I went as soon as I was able to hobble around on a pair of crutches. None of my patients would have gone back to work that soon after such a major trauma. I would not have permitted it. But I wanted to demonstrate to the world that I was hale and hearty, even if something within me didn't seem right, even if something about my actions felt phony, even as I knew deep inside myself that I was serving "another." I didn't use the word "dharma" in those days. I simply had to do as I had to do. I was trying to live the dharma of another, en route in a roundabout way to coming to myself.

All wasn't well with me, and, if life was trying to teach me something, I didn't know what, and if I didn't have anyone to talk to, at least I could dream, and dream I did:

I was half-way up a sheer cliff, gripping the cliff face tightly with both hands and sticking both feet into whatever small cavities I found in the rock. I was climbing a vertical cliff, grip after grip, inch by inch, the black face of the rock pressing against my face. Initially, I felt in control of things, but then things changed, and I began to feel afraid. It started to rain. The dry rock became less solid, then it became crumbly, finally it became moist and mushy. The rain was a fine, soft mist, of a type common in the mountains of Scotland, that swirled and furled and clung, causing drops to form on my eyebrows and on the tip of my nose. The tip of my nose became itchy. I wanted to scratch it, but I couldn't let go my grip under any circumstances. The itch intensified. Were I to let go, even for a split second, I would go tumbling and turning and screaming all the way to the bottom. Rock bottom.

A piece of rock broke off under my right foot; I teetered on the point of falling; I struggled to recover my foothold; I succeeded in getting my balance back, but then, just when I was about to regain some confidence, another piece of rock, this time the piece I was clinging to with my right hand, turned to wet powder. Once again, I reeled dizzily for several seconds before regaining my precarious balance, spread-eagled and compromised far above the jagged rocks below. For several minutes I didn't move. I didn't dare. Spread-eagled and compromised! How long could I remain in that position? Finally, I looked up. Fifty feet above me I could see the safety of the cliff top, ending in tall green grass. Hope at last. Oh, how I longed for a fistful of the green, and it wasn't American Government green I wanted.

Cold wet against my face, knees spread apart, I couldn't move upwards, and I waited. My fear intensified. Why had I undertaken this mad climb with no companion and with no equipment? What did I want? What was I trying to prove? Why had I placed myself in such a deadly trap? Why hadn't I considered my options?

The sky lowered and darkened, becoming an ominous black bag that hovered over me like an evil presence. Maybe I should try going back down. Yes, that's what I would do, I'd go back to the bottom and abandon this ridiculous adventure, undertaken for God only knew what reason. Why hadn't I thought of that before? Slowly, gingerly, inch by inch or centimeter by centimeter, I experimented with my right toe, trying to find a foothold below, but I found none. All I touched was thin air. There was no foothold there, and the attempt to find one nearly sent me crashing into the abyss. Down was out of the question. Up it must be.

The mist reduced visibility to a couple of feet, not the fifty feet I had seen a few moments previously, and, clawing at the cliff face, gasping for air, fighting with every sinew to stay secure, and then, knowing that I must climb or die a horrible death, I began to slowly negotiate my way up little by little. Once the decision to move was made, I was able to negotiate my way up regularly, until finally, through the fog, I saw again the green grass I could grab, the kind of tall strong grass that would hold and bear my weight. I'd be safe once I got my fists into it. I reached for it. Was that really grass in my right hand? It didn't feel right. It felt softer than I had expected it to feel. What now? Was the grass, which was to be my last and final hope, going to fail me, just like everything else had failed me? Was there anything in the whole universe I could depend on?

It was here that the dream ended, and, upon awakening, it took me several seconds to realize it was only a dream. What a relief! Thank God! Oh, no, I couldn't thank God, could I? After all, agnostic that I was, I refused to acknowledge the presence of God in my life, and so I suppressed the impulse to thank Him. A couple of weeks later the dream returned, and in a further couple of weeks there came a weaker and final version.

I allowed it to run its course.

I wanted to recapture some of my physical agility that I had when I was beachcombing and rock climbing and hill walking in Scotland. I mourned for my lost youth. No more would I roam the moors alone, delighting in the ocean breeze, followed by my faithful dog. A fantasy. What did I really want that was doable? I wanted my ankle bones to bind together and I knew there was only one way that could ever come about. The bones would have to be fused together surgically. Arthrodesis! One day, I would undergo ankle arthrodesis, but first things first, however, and, with that in mind, Marjorie said to me, "I'll go with you wherever you go. My place is beside you."

"I'm lucky to have you for a wife."

"You would do the same for me."

I was doing some reading in psychiatry during my convalescence, and I did lots of thinking. Contemplation came naturally to me. I thought about physicians. I visualized. We doctors wallowed in blood and we loved it. We watched the anguish and pain of others, we took control of life and death over other people, we stuck needles into people, and we cut people with knives; all in the service of others, of course, laboring in the service of others while our belief that we were needed grew, that our motives were pure, while those of certain others were...well, questionable. And our desire to be loved grew, and to be needed. Did we get vicarious pleasure out of the suffering of others? Did we soothe our own anxieties by treating others? If so, what were we so anxious about? We had secrets, secret inner lives, rarely if ever talked about, in a culture of facades. I mentioned it to Marjorie.

"Stop it! Cut it out," she snapped.

"What the hell are you so angry at, Marjorie?"

"Why is everything so secret in our lives? Why can't we just be ourselves, relaxed, without putting on some phony front? We don't associate with friends."

"What friends? We're preparing to move, that's all."

"Everything revolves around you: You; you; you!"

"Why did you marry me, anyway? We could have broken it off. It was close."

"I didn't want to be a spinster. I was afraid I wouldn't get anyone else. Yes, that's exactly why I married you. I was afraid I would never get a man. You were at the bottom of the barrel."

"Some reason for marrying! Some love. Now the truth comes out."

"Why did you marry me, Donald?"

"I was lonely the day I met you. I wanted a woman in my life, someone to fill the hole inside me, the emptiness, something to shore me up, like a crutch, but I didn't want you demanding fatherhood from me."

"What?"

"It's true."

"As for the accident," Marjorie said. "I thought about getting out of the car right in the middle of our argument. What was it we argued about? Do you remember? It's all vague to me.

All I know is I was angry. I was ready to jump out of the car and abandon you."

"We're like social lepers. We're social untouchables. Is this how the Indians feel?"

"We're not social lepers. It's you who makes it so."

"How?"

"You don't respond to people. You're remote. You're aloof. You drive people away. The minister came to see us. He took us out in his car, to help us get over fear of driving. It was his way of helping us recover. He's a good man, but you told him you were feeling fine, just fine. Nonsense! You're not fine, neither am I, but you won't let anyone get close to you. You have nothing to hide, nothing, your life is open, but it's as if you do. Physicians are just men and women, that's all. Anyway, the minister prays for us."

"Fat lot of good his prayers will do."

"You don't know. Let me tell you something. My family always went to church, we made friends there. We found comfort there."

"I don't find comfort in a church, even if you do. What you find, you like. Maybe you're better off than I am in that regard, so go by yourself. Join a group. You can all enjoy the music, the rituals."

"I might at that."

"Marjorie, one of the Mounties met me two days ago. It was a casual, unplanned meeting outside, not a business call, and he spoke to me. He said, 'There's no need for you to leave town. You don't have to go. You can stay here. We don't want you to leave.' He had a concerned, gentle expression on his face, an empathetic man, helping; my heart filled up, ready to overflow, and I knew at that moment that here was a good man, a great man, of noble mind, doing the right thing. Isn't that something? A simple brief encounter, it was, but I'll never forget it. He touched me deeply."

"They never gave us a copy of the accident report. Surely we're entitled to a report on our own accident."

"I could ask them, Marjorie, but I don't want to."

"That officer is a good man. He's very mature. I can tell whenever he's around."

"He helped me a lot by what he said. He's made a difference in my life."

I wanted to continue practicing medicine as a physician, my professional standards were high, I was full of energy, and I knew I would find a medical specialty where my physical limitations would direct me into the kind of work I was designed to do. I knew it intuitively. I used intuition in my decision making, as breakthroughs in my intellectual formulations of life, and it was at this time I noticed myself paying close attention to the psychosomatic aspects of medical practice, and also to the psychologically oriented medical practice. Certain questions occurred to me: How did your injury occur? What was the sequence of events? What do you think about it? When you left home this morning, what were your emotions? What is going on in your life at this time?

Further education was mine, beginning within, where it mattered.

5: NIGHT CALL

When the ringing of the telephone interrupted my reading one evening, I answered immediately. The caller was a woman. She wanted a house call. It was night time, and the northern winter was in full blast, the kind of night on which roads would be empty except for emergency crews.

"The Chevrolet has died on us. We don't have any transportation."

Suddenly I wanted to go. What the hell!

I was going through a phase of being scholarly and "evolved," which meant that I was reading serious stuff, written by serious-minded men and women who had access to the tenured faculty lounges of universities, some of whom wanted to show the world that, by God, they had the guts to exercise their right to free speech, come hell or high water, and I liked that, but, on the other hand, it seemed to me as if an academic belief in egalitarianism might be elitist, if not indeed effete, considering; and so it was that accepting the challenge of an atypical house call to a stranger on an extreme winter's night was more refreshing than wading further through the weighty tome I had in my hands.

The cold hit me in the dark. It was a grinning grimacing cold that twisted and tightened the muscles in my face, bit into my insides, squeezed my chest, compressed the bones in my arms and legs, while my belly tightened defensively, my belt loosened around my middle, and my breathing became shallow. A scalding feeling inside my trachea! I coughed several times: short, dry coughs. The coughing helped regulate my respiration. Then shallow silent laughter.

Fine snow blew horizontally above the ice-covered ground. Higher up, eddies whirled and curled around black cavities in mid-air, like some three-dimensional cosmic art-work. Phantom spirits danced: leaping, cavorting, diving, swooping towards each other, swerving away from each other, and not a sound did they utter. The silence was other-worldly, the whole scene as if from a parallel universe. This was not soft falling snow that would have laid a protective blanket on the face of the earth and kept it warm. It was thin semi-transparent blown snow, which meant that the cold frozen snow already on the earth reflected back into space whatever warmth it had accepted during the short winter day.

It suited me just fine. Why? I don't know. Maybe my neuro-biological juices were flowing in response; that was probably it. I felt exhilarated, elated. It was the kind of emotional high that a number of young loggers, the ones who enjoyed the forest, had described to me, and that I had had difficulty understanding, but there it was in me, the same euphoria, probably psycho-biological, at least as concomitants, just what the loggers were talking about.

I inserted the key into the lock of the car door and tried to turn the mechanism. Nothing happened. The lock on the car door was frozen. I removed my gloves, located the cigarette lighter I had in my coat pocket, and pulled it out. I flicked it into flames and allowed the flame to envelop the key I held in my other hand. In this way I warmed the key before inserting it into the lock again, and again, until finally the ice inside the lock thawed, the key turned successfully and I opened the car door.

I then unplugged the electric oil-pan warming cable from the wall socket. In the northern winter, no motor vehicle could remain functional for several hours in the cold without a pan warmer. The electric warmer consisted of a coil installed in the oil-pan, connected to an electric cord that was fitted with a three pronged plug. Electric sockets were available in all parking meters, in the outer walls of all public buildings, in the walls of private business buildings and in the walls of all private dwellings.

Once I turned the ignition, the Ford Galaxy whined in a dry, labored way for a few seconds before kicking once, hesitating, then finally catching, but the moment my breath hit the windows from within, all the glass inside the car glazed over, became opaque and impossible for me to see through. Again, nature's spontaneous art work: swirls, circles in shades of gray and green, after a time responding to the humming blower by fading away, beginning as a small black hole that gradually became an expanding transparent disc through which I could see.

Just as I expected, I met no traffic that night on the several stretches of road that led to my destination, and I found the house easily enough. It was a large frame two-storied structure that was lit up in several rooms as if something social was going on, but I knew better. There wasn't. There was a door at the front, at ground level, which I ignored. Instead, I chose the door that was situated to the side, at the top of a flight of ice-covered stairs, under which were a pile of snow, a large black sack, and a shovel. A bare electric light bulb above the door flickered and flashed through the blowing snow flakes. What a courageous inspiring light that was!, never giving up, diving momentarily out of sight, but always re-surfacing, just like a well-built boat in a storm, and always lighting up the flight of unpainted wooden stairs leading up to the door.

I hopped up the stairs easily, occasionally grabbing the rail with my right hand, using one crutch for support, dragging the other crutch and my black bag, for by this time I was so adept at maneuvering that the only thing I had difficulty doing was carrying a cup of coffee and a book across the room at the same time. Well, there were a few other things, but so what!

A woman opened the door to my knock. "Good evening folks, May I come in?" I said.

"Certainly, Doctor, please come in."

Warm well-lit living quarters, cozy looking furniture; a woman and a man; the flickering screen of a blaring television set. The man switched off the jabbering of voices. The woman spoke: "He feels so sick...."

"It started last night. It's getting worse. I've been watching him all day," the woman said.

"Are you sick in any other way? What about the rest of your body?" I asked.

"No, Doctor, he hasn't been hurt. He sure is sick, 'though."

"Ma'am, you're very helpful, but I'd like your husband to tell me how he's feeling in his own words."

"Sure thing, Doctor. He can talk."

The man looked at me, he hesitated; he then removed his shirt so that I could perform a physical examination. I went through the routine. The man's blood pressure, heart, and lungs checked out as normal and his abdomen revealed no evidence of disease. I did a more thorough examination than most physicians would have done under these circumstances, and maybe such a thorough examination was not entirely necessary, but that would be from someone else's perspective, not from mine, and so, for me, it was not only necessary but desirable.

Something wonderful was happening inside me, something affective and holistic, not intellectual. It was as if a part of me, hitherto closed, was opening up spontaneously, allowing me access, expanding my universe. I felt more liberated, more lighthearted.

All the time that I was checking out the man, the woman was hovering around, apparently anxious. Was she afraid that something might go wrong? Was she concealing something? Did she have a secret? Was something important on the tip of her tongue? A couple of times her mouth opened as if spontaneously, and I half expected words, but none came. Oh, well, maybe it was all in my imagination, all in me, but then again, maybe it wasn't.

I gave my medical opinion: a diagnosis, a prognosis, and a

suggested method of treatment.

"Do you have any allergies?" I asked the man.

"No, Doctor, he doesn't," answered the woman.

I wrote out a prescription, closed my bag, and made as if to leave, but the man showed no interest in my prescription; he didn't even glance at it; his thoughts were clearly on something else. "Now, before I leave," I asked, "is there anything else that either of you are concerned about? Is there anything else on your minds?"

"No, Doctor, there's nothing else."

It was time for me to go.

"Doctor!"

"Yes, Ma'am?"

"Thanks for helping out."

"Thank you," said the man.

"Thanks for calling me. You did the right thing. I'm glad you did."

Once more outside the house, I made my way slowly down the icy steps, crutch and bag in one hand, a second crutch in my other hand, while using the wooden rail for support. I didn't feel the cold. Maybe I created my own warmth. The light coming from the bulb above the door was adequate, the bulb itself steadier than before, and soon I was once more inside my trusty Ford Galaxy. How warm it felt sitting behind the wheel! No more tightness in my middle, nor in my face, and, as for the fog, it had practically all cleared from the car windows. To be sure, the snowflakes still flew, millions of them trapped in the headlights, whirling towards my face, madly, as if in a frenzy, but I was behind the glass, protected, in control, behind the wheel in more ways than one, which is why I smiled.

I saw clearly through the glass, I saw straight ahead, I saw where I was, I saw the road ahead, and, although phantom spirits still danced and cavorted in mid-air, they did so in a delightful, creative way, and, as I smiled at them, they performed delightfully in return, a greeting, to be sure, and I felt a surge of self-confidence flowing through my veins, a suggestion of life in abundance.

A weight had fallen off me. I actually felt lighter, a strange pleasant feeling, as of release combined with mild euphoria, my eyes felt brighter, and it wasn't because of neurobiological juices, nor from adjustment in psychobiology, whatever that might be, no, not at all at all. I felt brighter lighter because I knew I was free to make my own life decisions, free in my own life pursuit, as a responsible adult, and I knew exactly what my decision would be.

6: ANGEL

Bright, alert, eager to get up and go; that's the way I felt when I woke up the morning after my nocturnal house-call through the land of the phantom spirits, over the cold night road. Something had happened inside me. Within me, a vision was coming alive, was indeed born like new life. What kind of vision? I saw a new role for myself: In that role I'd travel beyond the frontier of normal knowledge, deep into the belly of mind's darkest caverns, to bottom line, and once there, of course, I'd see the light, and so it was that suddenly I was a psychiatrist, exactly what my nature had designed me for from the beginning! An idea that arose within me, in no way suggested by another, and genuine it was, to be sure, and yes, a vision so vivid called for action. Like what? I would make formal application to programs for postgraduate training in the profession of Psychiatry.

In a distant city there was a psychiatrist who knew about residency programs, and how they worked, and one day I found myself sitting opposite him in one of the comfortable leather chairs in his office. The doctor had black wavy hair, and a hint of a paunch behind the vest of his stylish three-piece suit, but the most memorable part of him was his expressive face that seemed to harmonize with my emotions, that helped me feel at ease with him immediately, and that relaxed me from any tension I might have had at visiting him in his office. Here was someone I would love to know better. Here was a man I would readily confide in if I had the opportunity, someone I would be happy to share the critical questions with. But I wasn't there to reveal my whole inner life, I wasn't there to unburden my conscience, so to speak, I was there simply to get information. Once he saw that I was safely seated in a chair, he removed his glasses, he squeezed his eyeballs with the fingers of his left hand for a couple of seconds, then he relaxed his fingers and looked straight at me.

"You have a lot of courage," he said.

What? Me courageous? Of all the things I expected to hear, this was the last. I didn't believe I was in the least bit courageous. On the contrary, I feared being judged and found wanting. I depreciated my own potential, in my mind, that is, and especially in the presence of others, but, at the same time, having satisfied a certain Scottish Island cultural requirement against promoting oneself,-don't think so highly of yourself-I sought out exactly what I wanted. As for my actions at the time, I was acting upon a decision that to me required no more courage than moving from one house to another. What was it the doctor saw in me? I didn't know then. It was obvious that I was injured. My left leg was in a cast. Injured I may have been, and disabled, but at least I was doing something about it. I wasn't waiting for others to come to the rescue. Anyway, I didn't ask him why he thought I was courageous.

The psychiatrist didn't try to psychoanalyze me. He didn't ask me any probing questions. He was a senior friend devoting time to help out a junior colleague, and help me he did, not only by what he said, which was considerable, but by his manner of communicating to me. I appreciated that. I did tell him towards the end of our meeting that I was interested in understanding in a compassionate comprehensive way the lives we led, essentially, the human being in action in life.

"Oh," he said, "so am I, but ...." He shrugged and spread his hands out.

"But what?" I asked.

"I see many patients, I do many consultations, I make diagnoses, I prescribe medications, and as a result, I have little time to devote to the in-depth understanding of individual men and women. It takes time. I was trained in the psychoanalytic method, and it's what I love to do, but that work, and it is detailed work, requires motivation on the part of those who seek it, it takes courage, a curiosity about the world within, and a sense of responsibility. It's for the few."

Why do you want to be a psychiatrist? A question I expected to hear, but the doctor didn't ask me why I wanted to be a psychiatrist, and if he had, I might have had difficulty in answering the question with total honesty, because, at that time, I didn't want to openly admit to having felt wiped out emotionally, devastated, guilt-ridden and shame-laden, blaming myself for the car accident, deep within me where it mattered,-although I was recovering from that-even as, on the surface, Marjorie and I spoke to each other about the broken axle as a cause. Did I hope that, by becoming a psychiatrist, I might find a cure for myself? I did, but then again, a cure for what? What could it be about me that might require a cure? Later I learned that guilt and shame were there waiting prior to the accident; that guilt and shame came out of infancy, possibly came with me into this life as issues for me to recognize, acknowledge and deal with as aspects of my personal karma, that guilt and shame would surface and attach themselves to aspects of any event that seemed to warrant it, but, at the time, I had only a vague notion of self-examination as a way to clarifying dilemmas and making decisions.

As a family doctor, I had my own notion of neurosis. It had something to do with anxiety, didn't it? I knew what anxiety was, or at least what it felt like, but beyond that I had no sophisticated knowledge of the bottom line complexity of that psychiatric term 'neurosis,' and, as for insight into myself, it wasn't that I wasn't on certain terms willing to examine myself, but I believed that any admission of vulnerability to internally generated stress would be interpreted as 'character weakness,' and I was at a stage in my career when I didn't want that on my professional record; no way! not in a profession of altruistic men and women who took an oath at graduation, whose very footsteps tramped out saintly hallowed ground.

I saw for myself that many people expressed their unresolved dilemmas through their bodies, by developing bodily symptoms that allowed them to visit us. Older and wiser physicians accepted what was; they made no effort to break through the psychological defenses of others; they made no effort to understand the anxiety, they made no effort to understand hidden motives, they supported those in distress, they advised accordingly, they prescribed accordingly. Some older physicians were genuinely empathetic and intuitively skilled in the medical-psychological work they did, and there was much of it, to be sure.

When I was a young student in Edinburgh, I demonstrated and aptitude to perceive through the facades we all utilized in our daily lives. I wanted to get some understanding of life as we lived it. I passionately wanted to know the human being. I did not, however, consciously visualize myself as a practicing psychiatrist, even although I sought out extra experience in psychiatry at the time, and it was an experience that remains with me. Yes, I wanted to know myself, I wanted to liberate myself in life, but there was a complication, an obstacle. Something was in the way. There was something else I wanted.

I wanted to please someone. Who? There was nothing unconscious about it for me at the time. It was my mother. She was the one I looked to in my secret mind. She never told me I was to do anything in particular to serve her, she never told me I was to please her, but there it was in me, powerful and persistent. How come? How come I believed I had to? I imagined that everyone wanted to be loyal to parents. Wasn't that the 'good' thing to do? I did not know that, in my version of 'being loyal,' my real motive was the wish to save my own life, rather than a desire to be altruistic, and I didn't know at the time that my methods were strategies I had created in my infancy, strategies that had embedded themselves in my way of life so deeply that they operated spontaneously, automatically, unconsciously, *rigidly*, and therefore, these were not strategies that I thought out consciously, imaginatively.

Could I have broken loose? No! Not at that time. There was no way. It was something I had to live through. Ahead of me lay an involved process, a necessary part of my unfolding life evolution, although I use the term 'evolution' here by way of rough analogy, I do not claim that I evolve in life, but from time to time my inner eye opens, and I see better.

I saw around me plenty of self-destructive behavior, such as extreme drunkenness, violence-prone behavior, wrecked careers, abandoned marriages, but I didn't know that self-destruction was not the same as self-defeatism, not at all, certainly not if the bottom line intention was to sabotage an old 'agreement' made under the duress of childhood, to get back at an old adversary imagined within, even if that required destruction of oneself in the process, somewhat like suicide bombing. Behavior directed by infantile fantasies awakening under stress.

One thing I could and did do was to think. I could and did ask myself questions I couldn't answer, questions like: What do accidents mean? Do we create our own? Is an accident to teach us, to direct us in our lives, or is it simply an isolated experience? If we 'create' our accidents, does that mean we are guilty? Do accidents happen because of bad living? Is there something inside us that directs us, something totally beyond our human ability to understand?

In the culture in which I grew up in Scotland, we laughed at people with psychiatric disorders, not directly, in their presence, of course, but covertly, not knowing that we were laughing to conceal our personal fears from ourselves. We feared the demons of the mind: we feared satanic influences, we feared our own inadequacies, we feared aspects of sexuality that threatened us, we feared our own impulses, we feared our secret fantasies, and we feared God, but, like people elsewhere, we suppressed our fears, disguised them. We had our secrets.

Interestingly enough, however, we didn't laugh at men who had come out of wars seemingly different. No, about these, when we spoke of them, we would say: "He was in the war, you know."

"Oh, och aye, he was at that, poor fellow."

Life was rigidly controlled in a Scottish Island village, no one was anonymous, gossip was ubiquitous and could go in any direction, depending on which way the wind was blowing. And the wind would blow where it would ....Of course, some people left for big cities, but whether we left or whether we stayed, we carried with us our character structures, our habitual ways of relating and perceiving, our desires, our fears, our values and our dilemmas. I certainly did. I did not know that drunkards, in their own way, were protesting their own state of coerced internalized inhibitions, and exhibiting, even if only for brief moments in time and space, breakthrough flashes of independence. Not that chronic inebriation was liberated living, only a trade-off, and even that as a part role. We Islanders laughed at the antics of the drunkards, not entirely with the laughter of contempt, although to be sure that was part of it, but rather with the laughter of covert encouragement, of vicarious enjoyment, as if we knew somewhere within us that the drunkards served as vehicles of protest for the rest of us, and also as scapegoats. It was not unusual for drunkards to "get religion" at a certain age, usually in their thirties, after which they became model citizens and pillars of the community.

As for the physician I was visiting, I thanked the him for his kindness, which was genuine, and for his supportive remarks, but I probably didn't thank him enough because it took some time for me to appreciate his true helpfulness, but, to be sure, I left his office feeling lighter than when I had entered, with the world looking brighter, the sun finally out in my life. Had I had enough wisdom, I might have thanked a certain mechanic!

* * *

It was sixty below zero on a certain day in January when I sat in the small airport, preparing to fly south, on the first leg of my journey to the United States of America, in order to interview for residency programs. Although it was daytime, the shadows were weak and long, the sun low and remote, as we waited to board the flight. The old bone-squeezing ache from the cold, the shivering and the stinging feeling from the air were familiar to me. Out on the runway, where the aircraft was parked, we passengers, and there were only a few of us, were turned back by officials who told us that there would be a further delay while the pilot warmed the machine up, and all of the ice could be removed from the wings and the fuselage. It would take another two hours. The little terminal felt like a giant freezer, and, although it was probably heated, it didn't feel like it to me.

What did it matter? Not a great deal. I was happy. A letting go of the old, and a new adventure, a fresh start, a new life awaited my wife and me. I sat in a red plastic-covered aluminum-framed chair with my left leg sticking out, encased in a plaster cast except for the toes, which were exposed, not quite to the open air, for they were covered in a woolen sock twice rolled around them. Surprising how warm that part of my body felt! My two aluminum crutches were beside me leaning against the wall.

Out of the cold a stranger appeared. She walked into the waiting room. She strolled around the room for a few moments. A Native American woman, small, with tawny skin and downcast eyes. At first I paid little attention to her. She represented society's hidden secret dark side, the side of ourselves that we of the majority suppressed in ourselves, that we feared, and that we projected upon those we assumed were different. Native Americans were not exactly the elite of Canadian society. They knew it; we knew it. Every society seemed to have certain people that the majority loved to look down upon. We did in Scotland. How did the Native American Indians think? What was their worldview? We didn't know. We were not to know, unless we examined ourselves introspectively, saw our own secret side, in which we resented our own life roles, perhaps because, somewhere inside us, we knew-we must have known-that we labored in the service of a system, a society, that enslaved us by its false egoistic values that separated us from what was permanent and true in life. We had sold ourselves into moral slavery, we were willing to die for our values,-and indeed, we did sicken ourselves-false and deceptive as these values might be. *Living a lie.* And, resenting anyone who might have escaped entrapment, we feared the leap into the unknown that escape from slavery meant.

We created our own slavery, recreating it repeatedly.

The woman approached me. She had a gray woolen blanket over her left shoulder and draped over her left arm. Suddenly I knew she was heading in my direction, seeking me out personally. What could she possibly want from me? Nothing. She didn't want anything from me. She dropped to her knees on the hard cold floor directly in front of me, she removed the blanket from herself, she wrapped the end of it over my left foot, she swept the rest of it up my leg; then she walked away. I was unable to say anything.

I felt warm all over.

PART TWO
SCOTLAND

7: BREECH BABY

Crawling along the floor, hard concrete knocking rhythmically against my bare knees, reaching for a round brown timber table leg in the corner of the kitchen-living room, two women standing on the other side of the room, two women watching me, one of the women my mother, the other my mother's older sister.

My mother cheered me on, her face beamed encouragement, her eyes aglow with pride. As a mother, she was blossoming, and her sense of fulfillment showed all over her face, but then again, there was a side to her that had never found expression, and, as she saw it, never would, for the simple reason that her clock was ticking as far as worldly ambition was concerned. Worldly ambition! My mother an ambitious woman! A crofter's wife! Could that possibly be? Yes, she was, very much so, although frustrated at the same time because, in a man's world, her ambition was blocked. It was something I came to know later in life. And if her ambition was blocked, in secular and in religious pursuits, well, then, she would express her ambition, she would seek fulfillment, through her first-born son, who happened to be me. I was the "chosen one."

My Aunt Catherine, unmarried, older than my mother, rendered deaf by a childhood infection, her communication and problem-solving skills limited, made no effort to stake an independent claim in the prospecting fields of life. Careful, lest you bite the hand that feeds you, was the order of the day. But not always. There were moments. And watching me that morning, a wide smile on her broad plain face, clapping her hands, her head flying backwards in a spontaneous gesture of delight, she was herself, no doubt about it.

Above me, folds of a bright multi-colored oil cloth fell over the edge of the table top. There were splashes of green, dark-blue, light-blue and white, there were pictures of flowers. What were flowers? I didn't know. I didn't know what a design was. I didn't know what color was, but, full of wonder and awe, I watched my little sliver of life with wide-open eyes.

The room smelled of burning peat, of heather, of wood and of old family bible. Old family bible! It was there, available, although my father read from it only occasionally. We Islanders valiantly protected our religious beliefs by living in constricted rigidly controlled ways, we encouraged our ministers of religion to be stern and dark,-valued qualities-and we were anti-Catholic, but of course, all that was according to the people of the mainland, who saw in us what they denied in themselves. Yes, they saw their own secret dark side in us, we Islanders saw ours in them, and we were suspicious of each other, which meant that we feared each other, but, when it came to the practice of religious habits, attitudes and rituals, extrapolated from the ancient Judeo-Christian scriptures, and interpreted by Calvinistic Protestant ministers, our people feared no one. None of which concerned me on the day of my great adventure.

I encircled the table leg with my right arm, and, using upwards leverage, raised my rubbery body slowly into an upright position until I was standing erect. Even then my head was below the falling flap of wax table-cloth, with its dark underside. Short I may have been, and wobbly on my feet, but I knew what I wanted that day. I wanted to be one of the two-legged masters, and to that end I let go of the wooden leg of the table, took several unsteady steps away from that temporary crutch towards the center of the room, and lo! I was one of them.

The room was warm and cozy and it was good. A peat fire blazed in a simple brick and cement fireplace, where it hummed and crackled, with occasional snapping sounds as lumps of peat split open from the heat and fell into the middle of the fire, sending cascades of sparks shooting merrily up the chimney. Up where? Ah, yes! Up into a dark mysterious region above the fire. From the dark cavity there dangled a black cast-iron chain that seemed to be suspended in space. Attached to the chain was a large black hook, also made of cast-iron, strong enough to support heavy globular pots that in the best of times were laden with stew, potatoes and porridge, and also flat round pans that occasionally toasted deliciously aromatic pancakes and scones. The pots gurgled when the stew was ready to be stirred; the pans hissed when the scones were ready to be turned; they spoke the language of the kitchen, a language known to the cook. The cook was my mother.

What else did I want on that memorable day? besides becoming a two-legged master. I wanted to explore; I wanted to learn. How much could I learn from gazing at the floor hour after hour, day after day, bare-arshed on my hands and knees? Not much. From that primitive posture, I had to twist my neck around and up so as to look into the world of walking strolling talking designing loving hating men and women, and then all I could get were fragmentary glimpses, brief skewed impressions, flashes in time and space, but then there were other times when women hoisted me on to warm breasts, when women nurtured me, when women were all around me, and so it was that my earliest view of the world, apart from breast itself, and floor, was a view from my perch on a woman's breast, a fine view to be sure, but nothing compared to the view of life I got standing up alone, or to the sense of mastery I savored.

And so it was that, on that morning, with no breast to lean on, vertical on my own two feet for the first time in my current life role, and enjoying every second of it, I saw all around the world to its wide horizons. Well, maybe not, but it felt like it to me. I was still a long way from the world of the giants. I was still a long way from striding alone outside the house, arms swinging, head flung back, wearing worn dungarees, but at least I could see through the window from my standing up position. And what a view that was! Outside the house, beyond the window, the sun was shining, a few white clouds swept merrily across a light-blue sky, two seagulls landed smoothly on the turf, dancing, going pit-a-pat with their flat webbed feet so as to deceive worms into reacting as if it was raining, which for the worms would be their final instinctive reaction; a black and white cat sat on the window-sill, and a lonely looking dark furry well-fed mongrel dog ambled down the road, its tail sweeping the air behind it, looking elegant despite its lowly origins.

How proud the two women were! I was going to be a stunning success in life. I was already performing magnificently. Oh, how I wanted them to love me. I was already loved, was I not? Or was I? Was I really loved? Well, just to make sure I was loved, just to be on the safe side, I would do it again, only next time I would walk longer and with stronger steps, and then there would be other times...

I was ten months old.

Impossible, you say. No one can remember that far back into childhood. Do you really expect us to believe that story? After all, we are intelligent readers. We are knowledgeable modern men and women. We can differentiate fact from confabulation. A learned child neurologist would say that my brain was not sufficiently developed at the age of ten months to take in, process, store and make available for later retrieval such detailed information so rationally recollected. At the age of ten months, my perception would have been infantile, I would have been unable to grasp ideas, I would have been unable to impose my mentally derived order on to a world that to human minds appeared chaotic. Why argue? My vision is clear and intact. Who knows but that my perception was as valid as an adult's in its own way?

Even so, a thoughtful psychiatrist would say that I made up the story later in life, or that I was told about it, and that I unconsciously located it in my memory so as to satisfy my own need to organize that which I didn't understand, and also to screen from my conscious awareness what was too frightening for me to endure. Hmmm! Do we, including psychiatrists, not project our hopes, desires, fears, and other aspects of our mental processes into our interpretations of the universe? Of course we do. Indeed, we are an inseparable part of the universe, we are one with all of life, but, because of our ego-centric way of thinking, we separate ourselves. We alienate ourselves. We are lonely people.

And what if I were to suggest that the chaos is only apparent, brought on by the splintering of the whole brought on by limited ego-centric human mental processes? Something I learned in India, later.

* * *

The island of my birth separated itself from the mainland by a wide windblown blue-white sea, and the mainland separated itself from the Continent of Europe and from America by even wider deeper seas.

* * *

A woman in crisp navy-blue uniform, surrounded by several other women, was ceremoniously organizing a major event in our family bedroom, and clearly the woman in blue was not a crofter's wife. A crofter's wife would be wearing a frayed dress, a cardigan and a scarf around her hair, the latter to hold her hair in place, for warmth, for modesty, and last but not least, so as to abide by the iron-clad custom of Islanders.

The Island was self-contained, and custom required local women to be an example of modesty, to be respectfully submissive in the presence of their own socially sanctioned authority figures, such as the woman in blue, to behave likewise in a house not their own, and to fear Established Authority. Men also feared Established Authority. Of course, the ultimate authority was God. No one messed with God with impunity, no one, not the poor, not the wealthy, not the godly, not the ungodly, not the sober, not the drunken, not the saintly, not the sinful, for, bottom line, everyone feared His wrath.

But the woman in blue was not preoccupied with God, at least not consciously, although the Divine Presence within her, the Atman, might well have manifested in each and every one of her actions, for she was busy, she was giving orders in her gentle Island voice, soft as the drifting mist from the moors, she was totally absorbed in what she was doing, lost in her duty, working calmly, efficiently, like one internally directed, doing exactly what she was designed to do in life.

She was living her dharma, fulfilling her destiny, an unfolding spontaneous harmonious contribution to the world, not to mention local culture.

She spoke the Gaelic language fluently with a local accent, which placed her roots squarely in the Island. She wore a stiff white collar around her neck, her hair was carefully protected with a hairnet, she wore an apron, she spoke with authority, and her eyes shone with excitement. Her shoes also shone. Polished black shoes designed both for outdoor and indoor wear, shoes that reflected class, shoes that suggested a nurturing caring authority, an authority created by and respected by the Islanders.

She had propped her bicycle against the cool stone wall of the house, and a beautiful bicycle it was too, like a magic machine out of some wonderland, a machine with rubbery parts, oily parts, and shiny parts, all of which worked together smoothly as a whole. The bicycle gave off a mild but distinctive aroma from the residues of medicines, bandages and oils. I wanted to be close to the aroma. Aroma had power; aroma fascinated me; the aroma of the nurse held me in thrall, not towards the woman, but towards the source of the aroma and all that it implied. Medicinal aroma! I wanted to inhale it. I wanted to follow it wherever it took me.

The cool rough wall of the house was built of stones containing spots of light-blue, sparkling iron-oxide deposits that nature had deposited in them, and that the weight of billions of tons of ice had secured in place during the one hundred and ten thousand years of advancing and receding ice. The large stones had a quiet gravity about them, like men who were solid and secure in their identities, pillars of society, men of substance. It was indeed a most solid, permanent-looking house, built to endure assaults from rain and wind. It had to be, just as those who lived in it had to be.

Stretching my short, wiry body on my toes, reaching up with both arms, grabbing the outside window-frame, hauling my weight up far enough to allow me to rest my elbows on the rough gray non-slip concrete of the window ledge, searching for a peephole, striving according to my given core character structure that was enriching itself as I pursued my vision.

The women in the bedroom were busy, they were assisting the woman in blue, who in turn attended to the woman on the bed, for, to be sure, that woman was more on the bed than in the bed, and she howled and she bawled.

The man of the house was nowhere to be seen. Maybe my father was away from home on some job, maybe he was at sea, or maybe he was in the kitchen-living room and out of my sight.

Our house was eighty yards from the road. Traffic on that road consisted of men on bicycles, men and women on foot, women walking alongside family cows, and occasionally of men seated or standing in horse-drawn carts that rumbled and crunched slowly along the rutted dirt gravel road that meandered the length of the community and beyond, connecting a series of smoky villages together like a string of Mermaid's Purses.

No passerby could see inside the house, not even a tall man standing in his wooden cart with his legs spread apart and the reins in his hands and his cap on his head and his pipe in his mouth, could see what the women were doing, that they were assisting one of their own in labor, but of course, the whole village knew and I knew what was going on in that room on that day, which was exactly why I struggled so mightily to get a close-up view. I wanted to see. I wanted to know.

What do you want? was not a question that villagers asked of children, expecting a serious answer, and even if someone had asked me what I wanted, I couldn't have answered logically.

I couldn't have put my passion into words, and passion it surely was.

"You're a right nosy one, you are at that. You want to see too much."

"Off with you. Don't you be loitering around this room."

"The nerve of you, peeping in on your own mother like that. Look at you; all eyes; no shame. What are you kids coming to these days? Like brats you are. In my day this would never be happening. Why, we would have been spanked on the spot, right there and then. Spanked and that would have been the end of that. Discipline is sure going to the dogs these days, I tell you."

"Wanting to see everything. Imagine that!"

"He's getting an early start, isn't he?"

"Bugger off you …I mean you…Keep your cheeky little peepers to yourself."

"When I was working as a maid in the big hotels, we had Peeping-Toms just like you: Brown-Hatters-from-the-Country, we called them."

"The Lord will blind you, Laddie."

Admonitions and banter like this got rid of me for a while, but the women had to get back indoors, and no sooner had they done so than I was at it again. There was a small fold in the sheet, to the side, alongside the wooden frame to my left as I looked in, that made an irregular sliver of shadow in the otherwise pale opaque barrier. The woman in blue did not notice my left eye zeroing in on the shadow, then my right eye. Her attention was on other matters anyway; to her perhaps the room was sealed off and secure. Inside that room, the oil lamps and the pressure-fed paraffin lamps cast a yellowish glow. The Tilley was the best of the lamps, it threw the brightest light, it illuminated the most; it sat like a queen of light, like the light of the world at the foot of the bed, flinging dancing shadows on to the pale paper-covered walls.

The women knew that I was only three and a half years old, that my physical abilities were limited, but they didn't have any idea of my perseverance, and, while they were busy working, I listened to every word they uttered, I absorbed every sound that fluttered around the room, I watched every move they made. Eagle eyes; puppy ears. The women worked in harmony. They worked with a skill and a rhythm that hadn't come from thick textbooks written in small print, or from lectures delivered by bespectacled bald headed men in white coats, or from haughty professors with faux-English accents. Some of the sounds were new to my ears, sounds of strange women's voices, of the nurse's instructions, of commands, of words of comfort, and then there were the cries and moans and sighs and wails. Occasionally, the woman in blue laughed, and whenever she did, the other women also laughed, all of them except the woman on the bed. The woman on the bed was a mess. She was half-naked, she thrashed around, her face was twisted up into an expression of misery one moment, into an expression of serenity the next moment, and in between quietly taking deep breaths, she wailed like a soul in torment.

Suddenly the quality of the moaning changed. It became louder in a purposeful kind of way, until it became a crescendo of shouts suggesting closure; then came a splashing of water, followed by the gallant cry my little brother, Ian, uttered as he gasped his first gulp of air. After that, the woman in blue seemed satisfied. She had performed well, her mission was over; a living being had crossed the great divide.

The woman in blue was the district nurse, the midwife and the medicine-woman for a community consisting of several villages, where she often worked alone. She was an intelligent woman, she had competent hands and she performed magnificently. With her fresh, rosy complexion and her ready smile, she greeted villagers along the road, riding her bicycle, on her way to comfort the sick, to deliver medicine, to clean and dress wounds, to offer support to those who needed it, when they needed it. The Medicine-Woman examined the villagers in need, she laid her warm-cool hands upon the sick, she gave her valued opinions, she instilled hope whenever mothers took their sick children, or themselves, or their husbands, to her, or when they asked her to visit their aged parents. Whenever people recovered, the Medicine-Woman got the credit, which was as it should be, for she was the socially sanctioned and designated healer for the group, she was the one with the healing touch, she knew the secrets; well, most of the secrets. Only when she reached the limits of her abilities, which were considerable, did she call the district physician, and the doctor's confidence in her was well placed.

She and the doctor had helped me exit from my curled up position inside my mother's womb-an awkward position, to be sure-and they helped me land on my feet, for that was indeed the way I came out, feet first. I was a breech baby.

According to Island mythology, a breech delivery was a harbinger of good luck in the life of the infant, and as a male breech infant, I was destined to be different from the majority, I was destined to succeed, I was destined to shine like a light, I was destined to transcend the transient allure of money, or so my mother told me; yes, she who had great expectations of me.

In my relative old age, retired psychiatrist that I am, I am a passionate observer of life, a casual free-thinking philosopher-at-large, seeking the bottom line in the complexity of human affairs, too serious a man to be a rollicking jester, not musical enough, and not enough of a poet, to be a traveling troubadour. Some might say that I am not much of a social mixer, that when I do mix, I present a pleasant façade to the world, a façade that hides a desire for approval and a tendency to criticize others, especially those in authority, that I can be self-righteous at times; or that I should join a church, that I should take up golf, join a club, and of course, they might be right, or they might be wrong, but most likely they would be no better at accepting me for what I am, or what might be in my best interests, than I might be at accepting them for what they are, or what might be in their best interests.

* * *

I was standing with my bare feet on the cool linoleum floor

of the simple room that served as kitchen and living room, and I was looking out the window. To my left was my mother, holding my hand. To my right was my grandmother, sitting on a wooden bench that passed for a sofa, her knitting needles going clickety-click. The aroma of breakfast oatmeal porridge permeated the room. Culean was on the floor, gnawing comfortably on a bone, smelling of wet dog.

It was a bright windy day, with white fluffy swiftly moving clouds and occasional short sharp flurries of rain-drops as showers sputtering against the window panes, and, yes, watery wet rain fell from their pouches in dark low slung clouds.

Outside on the road, men were walking up and down, some coming together in small groups, some in pairs, as they smoked, talked and laughed. And all the time, the steady rumble of heavy vehicles was an ominous background rhythm. Not a musical rhythm. Mysterious, it was. And the grinding of gears.

One by one the men climbed aboard the machines, and then buses, lorries, cars, vans and farm tractors all revved up their engines and moved first down into the glen, then up the far side up to the crest of the distant slope until they vanished into the next glen.

To the west side of the hill, white-caps flew across the blue half-moon of the Atlantic Ocean. How fresh and clean and clear it looked. But something was amiss. The sound of the surf was subdued that day; subdued as if from grief, subdued as if from awareness of its own hidden power about to be unleashed, subdued as if sullenly angry over betrayal.

Something awesome was happening that day, and I felt that I was a significant part of it, but not completely, I hasten to add, for, to some extent, I felt detached. Yes, that's the way I felt, detached but involved, involved but detached, perceiving without seeing.

Through the rain-drops a weak wan sun lit up a black and white calendar hanging on the wooden part of the wall to the right of the window. It was a day to remember, a bright day, cloudy, wet, rainy, menacing in its significance, a strange bright windy rainy cloudy day; war clouds over Europe. On that day men were on the march, women were crying, politicians were haranguing, preachers were praying, drunkards were chugalugging, newspapers were thundering out of the presses, and I was gripping my mother's hand, eyes fixed on the road outside that was steadily emptying of men, feeling tight as a drum, knowing that manhood carried a terrible price, and overwhelmed by one thought:

I am too young to die!

8: IRON-POOR-BLOOD

Dr. Kelly was a tall, broad-shouldered, brown-suited man with a ruddy complexion and a full head of gray hair, upon which he usually thrust a greenish-gray tweed cap, a walking cap, some people might have referred to it, as opposed to the simple cloth caps that working men sported on their craniums. The Doctor and Established Authority didn't always see eye to eye, a situation that didn't prevent Dr. Kelly from following his own inclinations. What did he care about toffee-nosed Tories and the bureaucrats who served them? What did they know? He knew what it was like to make life and death decisions alone in the dark of the chill predawn in difficult surroundings, with no modern technology to serve him, he had often enough felt driving rain in his face, he had felt biting cold wind slicing through his overcoat, but he had also felt the warmth of peat fires in crofters' homes, he had enjoyed the Islanders' gratitude and their respect, he had drunk their hot cups of tea, and their bowls of steaming broth when they had the ingredients to make it. He knew the Island people.

One day Dr. Kelly showed up at our family cottage. He knocked loudly and firmly, he waited for a few seconds, then he opened the door, and there he stood motionless in the open doorway for a couple of more seconds, during which time he seemed to take up the whole height of the available space, right up to the lintel. Bright late afternoon westerly sunshine from behind him created a rich golden aura around his frame, and lit up his flowing hair around his temples,-he had removed his tweed cap, which he held in his left hand-while leaving his front in shade. The Doctor stood in the doorway with a black bag in his right hand. God had arrived!

He didn't announce himself by name. There was no need. He was Dr. Kelly and to me he was God, or at least God's emissary. He saw inside people, he knew the secrets and we knew that he knew, and so it was with several confident strides that he strode into the living quarters without looking around, then he sat down in a chair next to his patient, my mother, who had not risen from her chair to greet him, and he began with the kind of opening question that doctors of medicine often ask: "Well, Jane, and how are you today?"

She didn't answer by saying, "Fine, I'm fine, Doctor. Thank you," as so many sick people did in answer to that preliminary question that really meant to convey to the patient that the doctor was announcing his arrival, that he acknowledged the presence of his patient, that he remembered her, that he knew her condition, that he was prepared to listen, that he cared about her, and that the professional visit was about to proceed.

"Doctor, I'm just the way you see me. I'm tired ...tired, ever so tired ...I'm all worn out ....Sometimes I feel as if I'm not going to make ...."

Her voice faltered, petered out and she shook her head ever so slightly, she then puckered up her face while holding it a little to the left side, she placed her hands in her lap, laying the right one on top of the left one, and she held her knees together, with her legs slanted to the left and crossing her ankles, the left one in front of the right one, just above the pair of worn gray floppy slippers she wore.

"Oh, come now, you have a strong heart. Rarely do I see a stronger heart. Now, please hear me. People do get better. I see it all the time in my practice. Yes, indeed, there's hope, lots of hope."

"Oh, yes, I agree that it's good to have hope, but whatever's wrong with me is something you don't see much of, although I don't mean to contradict you at all....No, contradicting a good physician would not be my place, not at all at all. I have nothing but the greatest respect for physicians, as you well know yourself...but maybe you never see in your practice the kind of disease that is wrong with me. What is it anyway? Doctor, what's wrong with me? Please tell me."

"Well, Jane, you have Iron-Poor-Blood, you know. It accounts for your weakness, your lack of energy. It's why you feel so worn-out. Iron-Poor-Blood is a diagnosis."

"Isn't that what the tonic is for?"

"Yes, indeed, it is that, Jane, I prescribed, dispensed and delivered it myself, carefully and professionally prepared as a treatment for your condition. It has proven ingredients. It's strong medicine, stronger than any store bought stuff."

"Doctor, I don't want to sound pessimistic, what with the children ...and my three children always come first in my life, and the Lord knows that, but my husband's away from home so much. It's a big responsibility for one woman who is as sick as I am. I'm just not so sure about anything...and I don't seem to be making any progress."

Dr. Kelly nodded gravely, he laid his right hand on the handle of his black bag, he was silent for a couple of seconds, and then he said, "Mmphg-hmmm-hmm." It was a complex combination of sounds conveying empathy, mystery, authority and hope, with all the therapeutic value that came from a synthesis of all that, and more, and which, if uttered by someone else would have been meaningless. Certain communications were beyond words. The doctor's demeanor was quiet, reassuring, knowing; the strong serious face, the gray hair and the wisdom.

"Doctor, are you sure there's nothing wrong with my heart? I feel so faint. I feel as if I'm fading away."

"No, Jane, you have a good, strong heart, and it'll carry you."

"Well, I can only hope you're right."

"Let's go to the room," the physician said.

With that he stood up and watched as my mother heaved

herself slowly from her sitting position until she could grab the back of the chair. She then leaned forward as if into a strong wind, and slowly she shuffled towards the bedroom. The bedroom was known as "the room." Dr. Kelly followed his patient into "the room" and he closed the door behind him.

More mystery! And I was left out of it. What did the Big Doctor do when he was alone with a patient in "the room?" Did he aspire to knowledge of all things? Did he peer into the secret of life? What were the two of them doing in there? And what was all that about Iron-Poor-Blood? Was the iron in the blood poor, like some people who had no money? Was it bad iron, maybe rusty? Or was it lacking? Maybe there wasn't enough of it. And how did Dr. Kelly see into other people's blood and hearts? Was not blood and heart hidden inside in dark secret places? I knew what blood looked like. I had seen my own. I had seen animal blood, but I had never seen any signs of iron in my own or any other blood, but then an older girl in the village had told me that a needle, being made of shiny steel, if stuck into someone, would travel in the blood to the heart and kill that person, so there must be a connection between iron, blood, and heart.

There was also the mystery of the Doctor's black bag. What did he carry around in it? He had opened it before vanishing into "the room," I had heard the click it made, I saw the instruments inside the bag, and what a fantastic sight that was! Some of the instruments were black, some were of gleaming steel, and some had strange looking dials and bags and rubber pieces attached to them. Some were sharp and claw-like and dangerous-looking. Surely it would take great skill and knowledge to operate such instruments. Not many men possessed such skill and knowledge. Dr. Kelly was a man of mystery, of power and of knowledge far beyond the ordinary. Ordinary men and women had no access to such instruments, which must have come from far-away lands across the sea. They were not at all like the rough rusty farm implements that lay around the village, nor did they resemble the hammers, chisels and wrenches of the local tradesmen.

Then there were the medicine bottles. There were bottles with pills, bottles with lotions, bottles with potions, and some of these lotions and potions were red, some were yellow, and some were brown, and always, no matter what the color, there was that mysterious complex medicinal ether-like aroma that fascinated me. Whenever it hit me, wherever I happened to be, whether at home or in a school room, I inhaled it into the depths of my being and I held it inside me for as long as I could, quietly, saying nothing about it to anyone. Even with my eyes shut, I could detect the presence of medicine in the room.

I was also fascinated by lint. Whenever I heard the sound of that word, I became all ears. The sound suggested power and mystery, just like *uisge-beathe*. Lint! When uttered by my mother, but especially when uttered by the Medicine-Woman, who wore a dark-blue uniform with a white collar and a pair of gleaming black shoes and who had the shiniest bicycle in the island, the word "lint" sounded like a door closing on a problem solved. A solution.

Not to mention the feel of lint! How soft it felt to the touch. How gentle. How cool. How warm. And when someone placed a piece of lint anywhere on my body, how different it felt from the fabrics we were accustomed to in our daily lives. Fingers sank into lint, and lint was also pink in color, as well as being aromatic, at least the Medicine-Woman's lint was, and so was the Doctor's.

But lint had its limitations. It was of no avail in the treatment of Iron-Poor-Blood. Indeed, it didn't seem to work nearly as well for grownups as it did for children, and, of course, lint was not something one could swallow so as to cure certain maladies of the insides. I knew that much. Nevertheless, despite its limitations, I loved lint. Sometimes my mother would get a small supply of lint from the district nurse, who was the Medicine Woman. She kept this supply in a drawer in "the room." I never touched that drawer under any circumstances, although I do not remember anyone ever prohibiting me from doing so. I simply understood that my mother's drawer, where she kept her private belongings, was off limits to me, and I never violated her trust. But whenever I was sick or wounded, the drawer was opened and out came the lint, and, to be sure, I didn't mind peeping into the drawer on such occasions.

Eventually, after what seemed like a long wait on my part, the door to "the room" opened and the tall doctor reappeared. He paused momentarily in the doorway, his cap by this time on his head, black bag in his left hand, with his right hand on the door knob. No blazing sun behind him this time, only the interior of "the room," which was all quiet and dim, but the way in which he paused in the doorway suggested that he anticipated something, as if he knew he wasn't quite finished, and indeed if that was so, he wasn't disappointed, for, as he turned to close the door behind him, a voice came from "the room."

"Doctor."

"Yes, Jane?"

"There's just one more thing...."

"And what is that?"

"It's just that I can't help wondering...?"

"Well, what is it?"

"It's just that...Well, what will happen to the children if...?"

The Doctor halted and his face froze into a professional expression of the kind of neutrality that could go either way depending on how the rest of the conversation went. He was a man in his middle fifties, but he looked old to me. He looked as if he had lived a long time. There were deep lines in his ruddy square-jawed face. For a moment his eyes looked inwards, into himself, then he glanced at the three of us children sitting silently and staring at him in a we-depend-on-you-so-please-don't-let-us-down kind of way. As for questions, what could we possibly ask? Dr. Kelly cleared his throat and said, "Jane, I think I'll be talking to your brother, the Doctor. We'll have a detailed consultation about your condition."

My mother's brother was indeed a prominent and a highly respected physician locally, but he served a district on the other side of the island, and my mother was not his patient, being not only out of his district but also a family member, but Dr. Kelly would seek his opinion, the two of them would put their heads together and the two heads would be better than one, especially two heads "in consultation," which was bound to be a process far beyond simple conversation in gravity, creativity and significance.

The Doctor closed the door of "the room" behind him and in four paces he was at the front door. That door opened from the inside. Outside, the sun was still shining, although this time its light seemed weaker and it was more like the late afternoon fading October sun. Dusk was not far away, and soon it would be dark and all the windows in the village would be blacked out. The Doctor yanked the front door shut behind him. Crummpp-slam! The visit was over.

I stood by the window watching the Doctor's departure. He didn't climb immediately into his car; there were preliminaries. He grabbed an iron spike that protruded from the lower front of the Austin's engine and he cranked it clockwise; the engine's crankshaft rotated, the lubricating oil flowed, the petrol and air mixture squirted into each of the four cylinders, the spark plugs fired, and the engine uttered a comforting purr-rummph-rm-mmm sound.

The beautiful black machine was alive and well, ready to carry the Doctor along the winding up and down one lane rural road, on to his next house call, on to someone else who waited for his help just as earnestly as we did.

9: THE CURE

The sound of a shuffle disturbed the quiet. It broke the still early morning. A mildly aromatic darkness. The shuffle was followed by the gentle swish-wish-swish of a furry tail sweeping across the dusty cement floor. A dog sighed.

I knew the sound well. My eyes swiveled around the room and focused on a familiar spot beneath the long wooden bench alongside the wall below the window. Culean was awake. The black and white collie pushed his moist inquisitive nose that nature had so elegantly represented in his low-brow aroma-oriented brain out from under the square, wooden, homemade bench where he lay.

A real intruder doing what I was doing would have been noisily challenged with loud barking and snarling, but I was no intruder to the family dog. The dog's aroma was mixed with the gentle soothing smell of smoke from the burnt out peat left over from the day's fire. The living room fire was like an eternal flame. It never went out entirely. As for the doggy aroma, who ever in that ancient community of animals and humans cohabiting in close proximity heard of washing and shampooing a dog? What a laugh! We had no indoor plumbing. We had no running water. We washed our hair in buckets, on special occasions, on Saturday nights, or when a visit from certain unmentionable irritating bugs was suspected.

I didn't have to see well to find my way around, for my mental map was clear. There was a kitchen cupboard next to the far wall. It was made of unfinished wood that a local craftsman had carved and carpentered and that my father had painted over. The cupboard worked; it served as a repository for family kitchenware, it served as a larder, it served as a decorative piece, and it served as something solid and enduring for women to lean on from time to time, like an indoor gossip fence.

The room itself spoke boldly about local craftsmanship. Here was no store-bought fancy furniture. Pieces were designed and crafted by the village carpenter, they were painted by my father, but let it not be said that all of my father's contributions to the family furnishings were confined to sloshing paint on to wood measured, cut and crafted by another, for he himself had also created a few of the domestic furniture pieces, but not many, to be sure, because the making of furniture was not his given aptitude in life, not at all.

Concrete floor pressing firmly against my bare feet padding across the slab covered in places by patches of worn linoleum that felt to my slapping feet like the smooth cool applications of a masseur, something I couldn't possibly have imagined at the time in that primitive rural cottage, but, then again, who can tell about the memory of man, not to mention woman? And who are we to say that past, present and future are not all in one great non-intellectual beyond human mind aspect of the universe?

Anyway, in the remains of a peat fire in the open hearth a spent cinder fell into the interior of the fire with a muffled crack. In the day-time the fire in the kitchen-living room was warm and inviting; it was always a cheerful-looking fire, it drew us towards itself, but, like the rest of us, after a day of aggressive output, it went to sleep at night, so as to replenish itself and make sure it never ran short of the energy we wanted from it, which suggests that, again like the rest of us, it was eager to serve Authority.

Somewhere up in the chimney there lived an elfin old man, up to who knew what stunts and antics in the night, or so someone said, but I myself never saw the Old-Man-of-the-Chimney, and I was never convinced that he existed at all, or that much intelligent life existed up in that dark cavity, but then again, on second thoughts, I couldn't be absolutely sure. Who could be absolutely sure of anything? In a multi-dimensional relative universe; as seen by a child!

Another sound broke the silence. It was the squeak made by the door of the cupboard opening as I gently pulled it in a small arc on its hinges to expose its dark interior. In my hand I clutched an empty medicine bottle. There were palpable ridges in the glass of the bottle, ridges from an emblem that the manufacturer had engraved on the surface of the glass. My mother had slowly emptied the bottle, spoonful after spoonful, according to the Doctor's instructions, and, as the level of the tawny-red liquid dropped, as the glass became more and more transparent, and finally, as the bottle's place was taken by another, full of a similar but not quite identical liquid, my mother's hopes for recovery of her health diminished. I lowered the bottle on to the hard concrete floor. It hit the floor with a click-chink sound and I froze.

I was the only one awake in that house at that time in the morning and I wanted to keep it that way. The sleeping people were my mother, my Aunt Catherine, my grandmother, my older sister Cathie and my little brother, Ian. Where was my father? He was away and I missed him. I longed for his company. His absence always left a large hole inside me. Once, upon his return from a trip, I awoke him at 3:00 o'clock in the morning so that he could play with me. I longed to have the hole-in-my-heart filled, and I knew it could only be filled by him, no one else. Well, in the meantime no one stirred in the house except me. I was safe. The cupboard was open. Dark as it was in the room, it was even darker inside that cupboard.

My probing hand touched cool porcelain. Success! It was a covered dish, exactly what I wanted. I pulled it towards me and removed the lid which I laid gently on the floor next to the empty medicine bottle, but my interest was not in the lid, or in the dish, but in its contents, which were left-over items from our Sunday dinner. Sunday was the only day in the week on which war-time rationing allowed us meat. Meat was nutritious, meat was precious, meat was a commodity that men and women wanted, wanted so badly that many of them violated laws to get their hands on it, and so it was that leftovers were always saved for future use.

Uncorking the bottle, I grabbed tiny morsels of meat, and especially of fat, from inside the dish, and I crammed them into the empty medicine bottle. There were other bottles nestling in that cupboard, among the dishes, pots and pans: there were bottles of sauces, there were bottles of spices, there were bottles of liquids I couldn't identify, and so it was that some sauces of unknown origin followed the meat morsels into the medicine bottle, to be followed in turn by a dash of salt, a dash of pepper, a piece of soft potato, a few bread crumbs, a smear of margarine, and finally by a splash of water from a jug that sat on the table above.

I wasn't finished yet, for there was one more ingredient to go into the pharmaceutical concoction, and that final ingredient was a sturdy shiny four inch iron nail. It was the kind of nail that the Islanders referred to as a spike, a word they, as Gaelic speakers, pronounced *"speek."* To me the word suggested power. A *speek* could be driven into timber right up to its shiny head, it could bind two long planks together, and I had the requisite *speek* tucked into my underwear. Out it came!

I thrust the *speek* into the interior of the bottle, I then replaced the cork and shook the bottle briskly, and there, in the middle of my ready-made concoction, as an essential ingredient, the *speek* gleamed and shone like a noble lighthouse in a fog.

Quietly and accurately, I replaced the cover on the dish, I picked it up, I pushed it back into place inside the cupboard, I laid the filled bottle alongside it, and then I closed the door. I couldn't avoid an audible snap as the brass snick slipped into its rectangular brass cavity and wood kissed wood. Afterwards, the door rested peacefully in the dark, secure in its role as keeper of the strong medicine. My heart pounded inside my chest, but not because I was doing wrong. On the contrary, I had an aptitude for what I was doing. It felt right to me. I was an adept. A desire had arisen within me.

I had just prepared my first bottle of medicine. The prescription was ready to be dispensed. The only thing missing was informed consent, for the patient who was to be its recipient was at that time unaware of its existence. That patient was my mother and she was asleep in "the room." She was suffering from "Iron-Poor-Blood," and the doctor who had diagnosed the condition, and who was treating her for it, wasn't getting the right results with his approach. His iron tonic wasn't powerful enough. Mine was to be more powerful.

I wanted to cure my mother! I wanted to rescue her from the ministrations of her personal physician. I wanted to rescue her from herself. Little did I know on that fateful morning of my first venture into medical diagnosis, pharmacology and therapeutics of what might lie in store for a boy whose mission in life was to cure his mother. Who ever heard of anyone, doctor or clergy, curing his mother? Even Jesus stayed out of that malarkey, and did she not let him know? Which is not to say that 'mothers' cannot benefit from 'curing,' and indeed fathers, siblings, and others, it's just that, well, it's a rich beautiful comedy drama of many dimensions, part of the Great Play, what with mothers showing up just about anywhere, anytime, in any color, creed, age or gender, no matter where I went, even if I traveled to the ends of the earth.

All of which I learned in good time.

10: GOSSIP SESSION

Gossip sessions arose spontaneously, casually, frequently, in those Island days, as welcome diversions from the tedium of the chores and daily routine of village life.
An open door, a cough, a greeting, a mutual exchange, then:
"Oh, laddie! Look at you! A fine robust lad, to be sure; soon to be a handsome young man, and all the girls will be gaga over you. Of course...."
"Of course what?"
"Oh, nothing, all good boys remember their mothers, first and foremost, that's for sure..."
Two women settled down, comfortable, drinking tea, gossiping gaily, having a great time, and there I was, all ears.
"...And do you know what that woman said? She said, and listen here now, sure as the Lord knows us: 'Now that I've got my man, now that I've finally got what I want, I don't need to be going to these long-winded boring prayer meetings any more, listening to all that blaa blaa blarney.' Imagine that! Just imagine an Island woman talking like that, but then again, it's not like it used to be, that's for sure."
"Oh, imagine indeed! Who needs much imagination?
"As for me, my life seems to be one long sacrifice. I certainly don't have time for gallivanting around. Who has time to play? Do you know what that young substitute doctor from away said to me recently? 'Do you read a lot?' I said to him, 'What, me, read? I don't have time to read. If there were 27 hours in the

day....Who has time to read?' Imagine him asking me if I read a lot. Who in the Lord's name does he think I am?"

"Maybe he's confusing you with one of these 'Big Shots' just because you worked at one time as a maid in the Highland hotels on the mainland. He's just a lowlander, after all."

"Surely not! These 'Big Shots' have nothing to do all day except read and play cards and ride their horses and sip their sherry and hoist their drams. It's a wonder they can take aim with their fancy shotguns without shooting their own toes off. Do you know what one of these London guests did one day? He spent half a morning meandering and wandering up and down the river, fishing without a hook. Fishing without a hook! He didn't even notice he didn't have a hook on the end of his line. Of course, it's no wonder, considering the stirrup cups that are available for gentlefolk."

"It's a wonder he didn't catch the horned-one-of-the-cloven-hoof. He wouldn't need a hook."

"Oh, they know each other too well! He of the horns knows who to leave alone, that's for sure, and also, I might add, who to pursue."

"Oh, och aye. There was another one, I think he had some kind of military background or something. At least he loved to flaunt his medals around, as if casually, but I knew better. Anyway, for months he'd go without touching a single drop, then, one day, when you'd least expect it, off his wagon he'd be and all, and nothing would stop him. Nothing could, is what I say, myself, and, do you know he'd lock himself up in some hotel in Glasgow or whatever, key inside and all, with God knows how many bottles. What do you think went on in that room? He wasn't exactly reading the Good Book, praying to his Maker and begging forgiveness, is what I say, but, then again, and, on the other hand, he was indeed a fine man, none finer in all the land."

"Isn't that the truth? And as for human kindness, the same man had as warm a heart as you could find anywhere. A big hearted man, to be sure."

"Oh, she put up with a lot from him ...that woman, she certainly did, but, on the other hand, when he was sober, he made it up to her many times over."

"The best indeed, when he was sober, as you say: Who could be better? The very shirt off his back is what he'd give you; aye, the very shirt off his back, no less, and he wouldn't ask you to return it either, at least not for a while."

"To be sure, you're right there, but then again, the money was in his blood, just like the *uisge-beatha,* and not only that, but-and here I tell you a secret I got from his very maid herself-he had money invested in the stuff, in the *uisge-beathe,* and in the breweries of beer too. Imagine! Soaking it up like a bone-dry sponge, and at the same time, making a handsome profit out of it. Oh, he's not one for going on the dole."

"Oh, himself had nothing against making the profit, the same man, I'll say."

"Not at all at all, the same man, but then again, he was such a good-natured man, even if his motive was the profit."

"A good heart indeed."

"Aye, so he did, that is to say, of course, *if it wasn't for one thing.*"

"As for that man they called Flush, I don't believe you could find a smarter man this side of Edinburgh, no, not one, and maybe not even in Edinburgh at that."

"Oh, was it Edinburgh he came from?"

"Was he the one who fastened bits of food and seed to a slim fishing line? and then fed it to several seagulls, one on each end, so that the seagulls ended up tied to each other. What a madman! Well, maybe that wasn't him at all. Maybe that was someone else. Whatever. Actually, it doesn't sound like a true story. It couldn't happen. I wonder who makes up stories like that, for, to be sure, no one would hear it from me, or from yourself either...still, I can't help wondering if there's truth in it."

"He had horses, didn't he?"

"Indeed he did, and fine beasts at that, the best in the Island."

"I remember when my father had horses, good ones too."

"To be sure, horses go back a long way in the Island."

"Not long enough."

"What do you mean?"

"Don't you know the story of the first horses in the Island? Well, I don't know how true it is, but it might be, and I don't know if you'll believe me or not...Well, when some Islanders saw horses for the first time, they noticed that the horses didn't chew the cud like cows, and what do you know? They called a community meeting, no less, a meeting of the wise men-no women allowed into the black house, I might add-and what do you think their conclusion was? *The horses were possessed!* They wanted to chase the demons out of the beasts. Can you believe that?"

"Oh, and it's myself that believes it?"

"I've known some men to froth at the mouth, as if possessed, but never mind, that's another matter. So long as a man doesn't drink, that's the main thing, I always say. Every man has faults of one sort or another. They can't help it, but then, when they're lads, they're so handsome, and so daring, and, to be sure, I can't help but love them, that is to say, just as long as they stay off the drams."

"Well, at least, in this blessed land of the Lord, we have men of the cloth who illuminate the way, tried and true men at that, which is not to say that there haven't been exceptions. There was, so to speak, a certain minister who took a couple of drams at a wedding once, when he didn't know he'd be noticed, and his time was short, salt water beneath his backside, is what he got."

"Who would want the whisky to take a hold of a minister?"

"When it takes a hold on a man, that man is helpless, even the best of them."

"Indeed, what man can stand up to the stuff? Not any man I've heard of, or woman either, for that matter. There was this one who had the big business in Glasgow."

"Oh, don't I know. I'm sure his mother was proud, when the poor soul was alive."

"It's an awful thing, the drink."

"It's the devil's own brew."

"Far be it from me to suggest that men are anything like weak in the head, or have no real backbone, what with them getting all the education and all, and making the money, and having access to all the best that this world has to offer, while their mothers and wives slave day and night to make ends meet, and keep the light going and all."

"Of course not; don't I know? It's just that I was thinking about his wife…Oh, don't get me wrong, I know she's put up with a lot from him on account of his drinking and all, but then again, what I'm wondering is what about herself? If you know what I mean, between you and me."

"Well, he certainly gave her money when she was alive, if that's any consolation, but that won't have influence with the Lord at all at all, but, to be sure, she's gone now."

"I was only remembering how she ….Oh, well, it's all in the past now, and it can't be undone."

"Nothing in the past needs to be undone among those of us who truly love the Lord and follow His ways."

"The Lord Himself knows who loves Him."

"Talk about loving the Lord, remember Danny? Of course you do. There was no more holy man in the whole Island, but then one day, when he and some cronies were collecting a coffin,-a coffin designed for a man of importance, no less-they started on the drams, and of course Danny insisted on removing his cap, placing it ceremoniously over his heart, and saying grace before downing his, and they all laughed about it, but then as the day wore on, and the sun sank low over the horizon, one thing led to another, and when the time came to pick up the coffin, none of them could remember where they had left it. Well, it's a good thing the Lord wasn't in a bad mood that day, and, another thing, it's a good thing the poor dear departed wasn't in the coffin."

"Oh, isn't that the truth! In fact, it's a wonder it didn't cause a haunting, is what I say."

"As a matter of fact there was a haunting reported for some years afterwards, in the very place, but the ghost is gone now, probably got tired of doing the same job night after night, so moved to another location."

"Which reminds me, my dear, talking about departed and gone. Where is your good husband these days?"

"My husband is busy at work, making a living, although a modest one, and glad to have a job, and I also glad to see his paychecks in the Royal Mail."

"Well, I'll say he's always good for a yarn and a jolly laugh."

"Not much money in that."

"At least he doesn't drink his pay away, like some people we know."

"You're so right, my dear, he doesn't drink hardly at all, but then again, he's so cheerful and carefree all the time, and of course, he's gone so much."

"Of course, your good husband has no powerful calling in life, like a minister or a doctor."

"No, that's for sure, and neither does he have a salary; oh, no, just a weekly pay, that's all. Not like some people we know, who think so highly of themselves that they talk of their husbands not having a pay packet but a *salary; a salaary*, no less! Well, I never...tich! Imagine that!"

And, to be sure, imagine I did, sitting as I often was in my own version of the lotus position, sketching, listening, hearing, envisioning, and remembering, to be sure.

"Imagine, yes, and let me tell you something, and it's this, no less, one of these days, wee Donald will be a big shot, no less, and maybe living in one of these big cities, living the life of a toff on a fine salary, probably driving a shiny motor-car, and here we are, gossiping like a pair of old hay bags on a peat wagon, while his little ears are perking up like cabbage leaves and taking it all in."

And watching life in a blazing fire, knowing that, why, a few drops of whiskey, which itself was *uisge-beatha,* when tossed into the flames,-not that any working man could afford to do such a thing, and only a complete show-off from town would do it anyway, certainly not a fine lad from the village-would crackle and explode into a blue-white flash.

And out of the fire came visions.

11: IT'S A MAN'S JOB

A group of boys playing *Pee-Po-Pash*.

There was no great intellectual or physical mastery involved in the playing of *Pee-Po-Pash*, at least the way we played it, for we paid no attention to the physics involved. We visualized the process intuitively. The name of the game was the sound we imagined pebbles made as they skimmed across the surface of water. Of course, we had to throw the pebbles, and there was no shortage of water on the island. It was a way of dawdling, an opportunity to tell stories to each other, making up little rhymes, laughing, and of living in the moment.

One of the lads found an old truck tire that had been discarded and someone else had an idea. Why not take turns at curling up inside the tire, held vertical at the top of a steep slope by other boys who would then give the tire a shove causing it to roll and bounce merrily down the slope with the "volunteer" inside? At the bottom of the slope was the loch on which we played *Pee-Po-Pash*. "I'll go first," said the innovative budding stunt man, and, miraculously, he stayed inside all the way down the slope, by which time he was going too fast to stop, and so, after one final bounce, he and the tire plunged into the water. Fortunately, there was no shortage of willing hands to drag the soaking-wet lad out, but not before he was left to wallow for a while.

* * *

The word "volunteer" had a challenging ring to it, suggestive of manly courage, giving a tickle to my imagination, and, when the call for two came, taking my chance, I agreed to go along with a tousled-haired lad, and so my new companion and I abandoned our play and off we went, cheerfully gabbing about the coming adventure, excited at the prospect of seeing inside a stranger's house.

The house was a small, gray, forbidding-looking stone structure with a thatched roof and a rough and ready looking gable, out of which protruded the usual pale-yellow chimney pot. Smoke. Silence. In the broad shadow of the building lay an old abandoned plough that once had followed strong horses along the lengths of fields, but that by then was out of any semblance of useful life, with its metal blades all rusted and its wooden handles stuck up in the air, thin and worn, like a pair of arms held up in supplication.

Supplication as a cry from the heart, a wailing, helpless anguish at lies told, lives betrayed in the name of freedom. *Freedom for whom?* It wasn't for widows, no way, that was for sure, except, of course, for spiritual freedom, something no man could control, try as they might.

The door opened as we drew near and a small, gray woman dressed in black greeted us. Her face broke into a broad smile. She was one happy woman, old and shrunken as she was, and dressed in somber fashion like an Island widow from the old days. "Oh, and you'll be the two lads I was expecting, no doubt. It's so good of you to come and help me out. If I had a man around the house, I wouldn't be calling for you, not at all, but then you know how it is these days. First, before we go any further, tell me, 'co leis thu?'"

"Who do we belong to?" my companion repeated. "Oh, I belong to...." He named his father and I named mine. The gray woman raised her arms.

"You're a long way from home," she said to me.

"I know my way along the meadows," I said. Who do you belong to? A left-over idea from the old clan system, in which the liberation of the individual was meaningless, loyalty and obedience to Authority was expected, and all were children of the Chieftain, proud owner of all that could be owned.

The woman spoke again: "Well, I want you boys to do something for me. It's most important."

She was a pale-faced woman, entirely without makeup, her hair a beautiful gray, tightly bound behind her head, and covered with a light scarf. If she were to visit a beauty salon and a fashionable ladies' dress shop, to be sure, she would appear very different, but then she would also lose her dignity. It was the dignity of a simple but intelligent woman who knew her place in life, but who also knew better than most what was essential in life. Noble, it was. No hostility. Suddenly she clutched the top of her dress in front of her throat with her left fist, as if it was in danger of flying open, although there was next to no wind, and she said, "How awful! I am worried. You boys look so young."

"Oh, granny, we're not young. If you want to know who's young, go and see his little brother. That's young for you. We're old boys."

The widow removed a pair of rimless glasses from somewhere in her dress and she placed them firmly in place. She could see better with her glasses on. "You both come from good families, I'll say, yes, indeed," she said.

"We know how to do it," I said. "Do you have them ready?"

"I'll fetch them. I'll go and get them now, and it's myself that's so sorry it has to be this way, but what can a poor widow alone do?"

She swirled in a swish of long dress and vanished into the dim light of the interior. Disappointing! I had expected to see the inside of the house. It was to be part of the adventure. I liked seeing into other people's houses. She returned with two glasses full of milk. A drink for the boys: "Drink up first, lads, then we'll get down to it, no hurry." Fresh milk from the widow's cow, not pasteurized.

"Well, lads, now that you've had your drink, and enjoyed it

too, let's get down to the matter of the kittens. Wait here."

Soon the widow returned, and this time she was carrying a white enamel basin, which she held stiffly in her arms, as if she very much wanted nothing more to do with this unfortunate situation. Maybe she wanted to wash her hands of it. Her upper lip curled up on the left side. "Here they are. They're all here," she said.

"Put them down; put them down," my friend said, and the woman did exactly that, by taking the basin in both hands, and then dropping to her knees on the doorstep, and, as she did so, her scarf fell off her hair, revealing a head of gleaming silver that swept backwards in a graceful curve until it fastened in a knot. She looked vulnerable, with her head exposed, and the scarf out of place, and her hands occupied with a basin full of squealing kittens. Inside the porcelain basin, five black and white kittens squirmed and crawled and pushed with their tiny noses, they opened their toothless mouths, searching instinctively for teats that were nowhere near, they gazed at us with filmed-over eyes.

"Well, there are five of them, far too many, I'm sure; don't you agree?" said the woman. "I just don't know what to do, and, as you boys know, there's only one way. How awful!"

"Oh, yes, far too many. We know."

"Have you boys done this kind of thing before?"

"Yes, yes, we know exactly what to do."

"Well, I'm sure you do and all, no doubt about it."

"We know a lot."

The woman stood up, leaving the basin on the step, but the kittens kept climbing over each other, clambering over the side of the basin and mewing, so she grabbed the basin again and held it against her side, pushing the kittens back inside repeatedly with her free hand. She spoke: "Boys, please hold this basin for me while I go and get the sack."

"Yes, the sack. We'll need a sack. We'll wait here for you."

The woman made one more trip inside, and returned with a sack; she opened it and she took a good look inside as if searching for something elusive, but I could see from my own view that the sack was empty, for the simple reason that daylight was visible through the fabric, apart from a complex system of shadows caused by some symbolic or heraldic painting imprinted on it. She gave the sack a good shake, she held it up to the light from the cloudless summer sky, she seemed satisfied, then she said, "Please pick them up."

We did so, and soon, the breast-seeking suckling kittens were inside the coarse light brown sack with its emblem of capitalism stamped on its fabric. We held the squirming wriggling sack between us.

"We don't have any string," I said. "We can't do without string."

"Oh, don't worry about string at all. I just happen to have some right here in my pocket. I have a small ball of excellent string. There's nothing like good string to hold a sack's mouth tightly closed, so here, let me cut you a generous length for you to use, but be careful now, you two lads, and make sure the knot's good and tight. I'd tie it myself if I was going with you, but of course it's a man's job you're going on, and certainly not work for an old widow."

The woman whipped a tiny pocket-knife out of a pocket in her dress and she cut a generous length of string from the ball. She gave the string to me, I pocketed it, and I said. "We tie good knots. We catch fish. We also catch rabbits alive without hurting them."

"Rabbits! How?"

"We trap them by the openings to their burrows, is what we do, and we get them out alive and well. We have pet rabbits."

"Well, well, what smart lads you are! Now, just remember one thing, it's very important that you put a heavy rock inside. You must first take the kittens out and then put the rock inside. Make sure the kittens go back into the sack on top of the rock, not the other way around. After that's done, you tie the opening of the sack tightly with this string. Listen carefully to what I say now. It has to be very tight."

"Without a doubt, and doubtless; yes, we know all about

it."

"Good. Now be off with both of you, and don't forget what I said."

We carried the squirming sack between us, I with one hand on its neck, my companion with his grip next to my little fist, and so, heavily laden, we trotted down the incline of the glen, we ambled across the green meadow where bright yellow dandelions pushed their leaves upwards, and where the good clean salty air blew. We made good time, and soon we were out of sight of the village. It was then we met Candy. Candy was an older girl and she wanted us to know it when she was around. We already knew that she had read in a newspaper that girls developed more rapidly than boys, which proved the superiority of girls over boys.

"What do you two think you're up to?"

"We're off to do man's work, is what we're up to," my friend said, with a swagger and a puffing out of his chest.

"Man's work, indeed," said Candy. "Well, I think you have a long way to go in that department, and if you think I don't know what you have in that sack, you'll be mistaken. I know."

"We know what we're doing, Candy."

"You may know what you're doing to some extent, but you don't know much of anything, is what I say, and I really mean it, like it or not."

We halted in our tracks, looking at Candy: "What do you mean?"

"I mean this," said Candy, "and nothing else. Do you know the difference?"

Inside the sack, the kittens squirmed and squiggled, they climbed over each other, breathing stale air while we breathed good clean oxygen-laden fresh air, in which birds flew, green grass grew and flowers bloomed, in which clean creek water splashed over pebbles and rocks. "What difference? What are you talking about?"

Candy gave a knowing sideways look, she brushed several hairs out of her eyes, and she stood up on her toes. "It's just this.

I have one question for you lads. Do you boys know how to tell the difference between boy kittens and girl kittens?"

Silence for three seconds, then we made a move as if to look at each other in amazement, but we didn't complete the motion, and so, in unison, and with straight faces, we said: "Oh, yes, of course we know the difference. We can tell the difference between boy-kittens and girl-kittens."

"Well, well, boys, I don't think you do. All you know is boy stuff. Maybe one day I'll let you in on a big secret, but not today, because you're far too young. You need to grow up some."

With that she strolled off, swinging her hips and whirling her dress, with us gazing after her, and then we left with our live cargo, only this time there was bounce in our steps and light in our eyes and from time to time we gave each other knowing laughing glances. We were in a hurry to get to a secret place, and once we were there, we looked at each other face to face and we laughed. We dropped the sack, we rolled on the ground, we laughed until the tears ran down our cheeks, and we beat our bellies with our fists.

"Can you tell the difference?"

"Can you tell boy dick?"

"Can you tell girl?"

"We know *mougili* too, and we know how to do it."

"Ha; ha! She really thinks we're little. Who does she think we are?"

"When Mac was doing it at night under the old bridge, the whole island could hear his balls banging against each other like mighty church bells gonging."

"Did you hear?"

"No, I was asleep, but I heard some grownups talking about it, hanging out by the peat stacks."

"Grownups think we don't understand."

"The buggers think we're too young."

"What's a bugger?"

"A bugger is someone like someone from the mainland."

"Grownups are full of *gigsh- and- kooksh.*"

"It's myself that says it and all."

"Do you want to be a grownup one day?"

"Oh, yes, I do."

"Myself too, I want to be a grownup when I get old."

"Hey, let's go, and hold that sack, lad, grab it now. Hang on."

Strolling in tall grass among the daisies and the dandelions, striding down the slope, laughing, hooting and leaping, slapping each other, lugging the sack decorated with a symbol of prosperity, with its live ill-fated cargo between us, we made good time. Sheep bleated, seagulls cruised above, a pee-wee cried, and all the time the sea breeze blew through our hair, against our faces, around our bare knees; it blew away beyond us, far away, back to the village it went, then it blew around the village cottages and out across the plum-red moor, all the way to the far coast of the island and then across the open sea, to end up we knew not where. Somewhere far above us where we couldn't see it, perched on a cushion of air, a lark warbled its little heart out.

"I've been thinking about it, lad, I want *mougili* when I grow up. What about you? Do you want *mougili?*"

"Aye, without a doubt, I want *mougili.*"

"Well, I'm waiting and when I get the chance, I'll take lots of *mougili*, lots and lots, maybe several times a day, actually, five times a day, or maybe six times. *Mougili* makes people happy. That's what grownups say. I listen. I hear."

By this time the green flower-speckled grass was coming to an end and the ground beneath us was becoming a rocky dry slope that ended in a massive black rock that swept out into the sea that tossed and turned uneasily. We ambled close to the edge of the rock, right down to where it ended. Below us the waves rose and fell. We were next to salt water, it was deep, and out of the sack came the five kittens. We placed a couple of large rocks in the sack, we dropped the kittens on top of the rock, we closed the sack, we tied the neck of the sack tightly, as tightly as we could, around the opening with string that the gray silvery-haired woman had given us, and we knotted the string several times. Only then were we ready. The sea heaved slowly and steadily. Shades of blue; patches of light. Dark brown mounds of eerie-looking seaweed waved to and fro below the surface of the water.

Between us we gripped the squirming sack, and, one on each side, we swung it to and fro like a bulky brown pendulum until the bag had as much momentum as we could put into it, then we let go. The sack flew into the sea and sank like the proverbial stone. Down it went, down beneath the shimmering glittering gleaming surface of the sea, down into the middle of the dark-waving seaweed, until it vanished. We waited. What was that? A wriggling thing broke the surface. It was one solitary kitten struggling to stay alive, full of fight and swimming for its little life, then another kitten surfaced, and another and another.

"Do you hear a baby crying?"

"What baby?"

"I don't know. I hear a baby crying."

"Yes, so do I."

Why wouldn't the kittens sink? Surely they knew it was hopeless. Why wouldn't they just vanish and drown like they were supposed to? Well, they didn't, and instead of sinking, they rose and fell, rose and fell, they rose up in the lap of a moving wall of blue-green water that carried them towards us; the wave deposited them with a long trailing splash right in front of us, then the wave burped and receded. The sea seemed to darken in a menacing kind of way as if a heavy cloud was passing over between us and the sun, but when I looked up there was no cloud to be seen, the sky was clear, the seagulls were still wheeling and crying.

Kittens with sightless eyes; kittens flying through the air; kittens back in the brine; kittens rolling, tumbling, swimming; kittens with four little legs spread out. Babies crying; babies wailing. My mouth drying up. Finally, slowly, belly by belly, kittens sinking, sinking, staying below, below the surface of the sea where they belonged. Yes, exactly where they belonged. What took them so long?

We left the sack behind us, spread-eagled, floating, its Capitalist slogan facing the sky, visible to any passing bird.

12: AUTHORITY

The front door opened without warning, a gust of wet wind rushed into the house, the corner of a newspaper discarded on the floor of the kitchen-living room-dining room flapped sharply, but the draft wasn't finished yet, for it whirled all around the room at least once, as if seeking for an escape, then up the dark cavity of the chimney it went, leaving the fire shivering in its wake.

"Who's there?" my father asked.

Six pairs of eyes looked up from the dinner table. No answer. This was no friendly neighbor come to shoot the breeze and exchange stories on a stormy night. A friendly neighbor would have opened the door with a shout that would identify her, followed by a comment about the weather and an enquiry about the well-being of all who were within.

A boot whacked on concrete. Someone had entered the house. Scrunch-klop. Somebody had pushed the door shut firmly from the inside. The visitor was a man, he was accustomed to asking for what he wanted, he was wearing heavy footgear of better quality than the kind that graced the feet of villagers, who wore boots that had steel tacks in their soles, boots that slammed sharply against concrete, whereas the dull sounds made by the intruder's boots suggested good solid durable expensive leather soles.

"Anybody in? It's Lane here." Oh, so it was the Constable. What on earth would he want?

A black shadow, followed by a lanky, red-faced man in dark police uniform filled the inner doorway briefly. The officer of the law stooped as he passed beneath the lintel, he stepped inside the dining room-living room-kitchen; he didn't touch or remove his checkered hat, and he eyed us with the authoritarian appraisal of a policeman. He eyed the room itself; he eyed each and every one of us, and he did it from under the visor of his black and white hat. Authority had arrived. Authority had come in the shape of a man of rules, a man of regulations, a man who knew boundaries, a man who knew what was within the law, what was against the law, what was right and what was wrong, but, to be sure, it wasn't his place to tell anyone what to do, or what not to do, only to uphold the law, and he knew how to do that.

My father, on the other hand, was something of a casual half-artist half-philosopher commenting with humor on the passing show of the world as he saw it, but the moment the Constable appeared in the living-room, my father put down the potato he had in his hand and he stood up abruptly, pushing his chair away from him backwards, for, inside the cottage, humble as it was, my father was the authority, not the Constable, and at that moment my father's authority was being threatened.

We Islanders feared authority, we hated authority, we loved authority, some of us even respected authority, but as for openly questioning authority, well... We lived in mostly law-abiding ways, we were overtly obedient, but then again, there were those of us who wouldn't or couldn't adjust and who resisted authority in ways that learned psychiatrists might classify as neurotic. As if blind obedience was not a worse form of neurosis! Anyway, in the presence of authority, villagers circled the wagons, and with good reason, historically speaking.

"Don't get up, please don't. All I want is a little information. That's all. Routine; routine," said the Constable, drawing himself up to his full height, which was enormous, as viewed by little me.

The Constable didn't look routine, what with his buttoned-up uniform, his aura of knowing something we didn't know, and with his confident stride. Routine, my foot! He was up to something. He wore a dark uniform. He wore symbols. Shadows flickered across the laden table. Shapes darkened the walls.

My father did not sit down again, as the Constable had suggested, and in two strides he was in the center of the room, facing the officer, but my father was not a tall man like the Constable, he wore no hat, and so, naturally, the Constable towered over him.

On the wall, visible to me beyond the two men, was a sketch I had drawn and colored. It was a picture of a man with a scythe harvesting the barley. *A man with a scythe!* My mother had hung it on the wall next to the lamp for all to see, by way of reward for me. She liked the picture. She was proud of my artistic ability. Well, on this occasion, in its rush around the room, the draft had hit the Tilley lamp perched on a nail in the wall above the table, whereupon the light dimmed, and the picture of the man with the scythe blurred, receding, slowly returning.

Black night wind moaned outside, and nature rustled mysteriously, as if the clouds, the grass and the sea were all alive and talking to us, hinting at long-forgotten secrets; secrets that we feared, that we had suppressed and distorted, secrets of betrayal, fantasies of violence. Hadn't the trees disappeared? Once, there had been a forest around where we lived, but no trees spoke to us, nor we to them, for the forest had vanished, its burial ground was the moor, its corpse the peat that we burned in our fireplaces, its smoke vanishing into the breeze. And not only smoke but people also disappeared in those days.

The black blinds fluttered, the thin brown linoleum on the floor shook ever so slightly, but the floor underneath, a hard uneven concrete slab, was solid and immovable.

The Constable stood on the linoleum-covered part, in the middle, surveying my father from beneath his black and white hat, with the silver buttons on his dark blue coat glowing and glittering in the mellow golden light from the oil lamp and his face partly in shadow, partly in light. Slabs of peat burned brightly in the fireplace, energy from what was long ago.

My father's face was angular, with prominent shadow-casting cheekbones, a straight nose, a firm jaw, and a pair of penetrating blue eyes. An English artist who had sketched a picture of him had given his image a mixture of sadness, humor and perplexity, as if the artist knew that the man behind the eyes suspected that nothing was what it seemed to be on the surface, that his subject knew there was something going on in life other than the obvious, something he had no control over, something unfolding relentlessly that it was his lot to live through.

My father never suggested to me that he saw in life an underlying unfolding drama that overruled the conscious desires of men and women. He never spoke of anything resembling a belief in destiny. There was so much we didn't talk about; a great chasm yawned, a longing, love unspoken.

Two men faced each other in the middle of the floor, with my father's wild windblown hair level with the Constable's lower jaw, his dungarees sagging baggily around his bottom, and black laces trailing behind his hard unpolished weather-worn working man's boots. His hands hung by his sides, his fingers spread out slightly extended, on his torso he wore a tight-fitting black sailor's polo, all of which, together with the changing expression on his face from relaxed to sharp native intelligence, gave him an air of competence. How strong he looked!, standing next to Authority, just like a good, caring father should.

The Constable pulled a small red notebook from his inside coat pocket with his right hand, and, as he and my father spoke quietly to each other, he began to write standing up. He had enormous hands and a small pencil. He wrote efficiently, or so it seemed to me, while from time to time holding the paper away from his eyes, as if he were slightly short-sighted and in need of spectacles. Once, he tried to erase something he had written, but the eraser on the end of his pencil was depleted, so he picked up a small piece of bread from the table and used the dry bread as an eraser.

My mouth dried up. A tightness in my middle. Was I in trouble? Guilt! Shame! Unworthy me, what had I done? Yes, there had been something and it hadn't been so long ago either. Was I not a member of the village gang? And had not gang members flung with accuracy a series of smooth pebbles straight to their targets? And these targets happened to be the porcelain cups anchoring the singing wires to the telephone poles. Well, I was about to be exposed, I was sure of that. My father and the Constable both had serious expressions on their faces. I couldn't hear what they were saying, but the word "regulation" seemed to be part of it, also the word "identification." I fancied that the Constable glanced in my direction a couple of times, but I suppressed any outward sign of emotion, then my sharp little ears began to detect phrases like "tracing" and "not so easy" and "rumor." Good! They weren't talking about me after all.

Suddenly the Constable, as if satisfied, put the pencil back into his coat pocket, closed his notebook and also replaced it inside his coat, but clearly there was something else on his mind. The dinner table was well lit from the nearby lamp and also well laden with cod-fish, fresh out of the Atlantic Ocean, sliced and boiled, along with boiled potatoes, boiled cabbage, fresh turnips, freshly baked scones, and butter recently churned in an urn. Not our usual fare. It was a special occasion. But it was not the occasion that interested the Constable. It was the victuals. He was glancing at the victuals, and his nose was twitching in a peculiar way, like the nose of a terrier tracking a fresh scent in the morning dew, only the Constable's nose wasn't down like a terrier's, it was up, and he wasn't trotting, he was hesitating; he glanced at my mother; he removed his hat.

Authority was human.

The laden table must have looked inviting to a man just in from the cold even although the table was rough and uneven, likely to rock to the weight of whoever leaned on it, but the Constable didn't lean on the table, he didn't show any interest in the finer points of locally-made furniture, or in the sketch of the man with the scythe pinned to the wall above the table.

"Here, have some," my mother said, pointing to the pile of

steaming hot potatoes on a large soup plate that was decorated with light-blue Chinese figures, strange esoteric figures that were worn with age. The potatoes were light-pink, smooth-skinned, freshly boiled over a peat fire that burned warmly in an open hearth on the other side of the room. The aroma of peat, of my father's St. Bruno's Flake, mingled with that of Black Twist pipe tobacco, of fresh fish just boiled, and of potatoes, pervaded the room. The flame of the fire, the warmth, was good, the food was good.

A long blue-coated arm reached across the table, strong bony fingers gripped a potato, withdrew it and deposited the morsel in its owner's mouth. The Constable's nose and chin were wet from the rain, and his cheeks were flushed from pedaling a bicycle along rough rural roads. He was a lean, raw-boned man who had a good working knowledge of the people and of their ways, he knew the value they placed on hospitality, and he was hungry. His Adam's Apple bobbed up and down below a prominent, powerful looking jaw, a prizefighter's jaw, it appeared to be, but Constable Lane was no prizefighter, not at all at all, for the large jaw was not accompanied by fighting eyes, and after all, it was the eyes that we looked to for evidence of passionate desire and belief in oneself. Despite his outward appearance, despite the uniform he wore, Constable Lane was a gentle thoughtful man on the inside.

As for the hat, the Constable wore it when he was on duty, which was anytime he said he was, and sometimes when he was off duty, but he wasn't much of a social mixer anyway, and whether these states of on or off duty had any connection to local affairs was anybody's guess. Certain aspects of rural Island life were still loose, despite the war that raged in the air, on land, and on sea around the world, and despite the on-going never-ending state of national and international crisis.

The Constable left after the second potato, stooping his way through the inner door. Scrunch-klop! Another gust of wet night wind swept across the floor, it caught the edge of the discarded newspaper, which flapped as if saluting the officer's departure. My father sat down at his place at the head of the table. Silence. He had a thoughtful expression on his face, and he didn't resume eating right away, although before the Constable's visit he had been, or so it seemed, feeding a voracious appetite.

My mother's eyes were neutral, not exactly a natural neutral, more like a controlled neutral designed to reveal just barely enough to get her point non-verbally across to her husband. She cleared her throat. More silence, then: "He wouldn't have...."

"If he took that damn collision mat off his head, someone might show him a thing or two."

"It wouldn't be you."

"My father's right...."

"You shaddup! Who asked you?"

"Yes, who asked you?"

The brown linoleum patch in the center of the floor, thin, old and stiff, seemed to shift its weight slightly with a subtle barely audible sound, as if clearing its throat also, and sighing, by way of letting me know it understood. The ceiling shrank. My stomach curled up into a tight, hard knot.

The reaper with the scythe retreated into a remote dreamy misty image before my eyes.

13: IT WAS HIS HEART, YOU SAY?

A black car slowing down in front of our house: the Minister's car, the Minister parking his black car, the Minister climbing out of his vehicle, looking at our front door, the Minister shutting the car door behind him, approaching the house; fear on my mother's face. Something was amiss. Ominous! A visit from the man in black, white-collared, Homburg on head; from the man of God, with his a measured step, his somber appearance. What news, what tidings, did he have on his serious intelligent mind?

Where was my father?

She met him at the door: "Good morning, Minister."

"Good morning, Jane, and how are you and your family today?"

"May I take your hat, please, Minister?"

"Oh, no, it's not necessary at all."

"Will you please sit down, Minister?"

How spick and span the Minister looked! What pale refined features he had. His elegantly-tailored suit, his snow-white clerical collar and his polished black shoes looked out of place in that primitive cottage wit h its rough furniture, its open fireplace and its general untidiness. The whole house was a mess. In particular, the room we used as our daily living quarters was a total shambles. An old worn boot, gray-clouded with dried mud, lay in the middle of the floor, a black cast-iron pot, the remains of its most recent broth still unwashed from its inside, perched on its stubby legs in front of the fireplace. To the side of the fireplace, an unpainted wooden stool rested upside down, helpless-looking, its three legs thrust up in the air, one leg partially dislocated from its socket. Assorted rags, pieces of the Daily Record and bread crumbs were scattered around the floor.

Culean, the black and white collie, shook himself awake from his snooze among the boots under the bench, rose nonchalantly and wagged his tail, which sent a cloud of invisible particles from a pair of oozing glands, one on each side of his rectum, towards the visitor's nose. A fine welcome indeed! Good thing we two-legged creatures didn't greet each other in that way. We couldn't if we wanted to. We two-legged mammals didn't have a sufficiently sophisticated aroma discriminative ability to enjoy such an approach to hospitality. Anyway, what did Culean care? Culean didn't care about social status, stylish hats, shiny shoes, sin, guilt, redemption, salvation, Calvinism, Catholicism, Judaism, Judgment Day, good news or bad news.

Culean lived the life he was designed to live, he made no effort to be some other dog, he didn't long for a different caretaker, he didn't want to be psychoanalyzed, get religion, or even a fancier den!

The Minister let his bottom down gently on the edge of the wooden bench that rested stolidly with its back to the window, and that served as roof for Culean's private domain, as if he was half afraid that one of the twenty one hens that clucked outside the door might have deposited her eggs there among the rags. Once his bottom was securely in place, the Minister removed his Homburg hat from his head and held it loosely in his hands between his knees. He smelled of paper, of books, of the Good Book, of tea-cups, of fine aged wood, of fresh soap and Cologne, essentially of the dry indoors, and not at all of mud, manure, damp dungarees, heather, sweat, tobacco and the wet, windy outdoors.

He was looking at my mother in a remote kind of way, as if gazing right through her, as if seeing something beyond her, and all the time twirling his hat around, as if casually, but then again, not exactly casually either. After a few seconds he cleared his throat, he moved his bottom even closer to the edge of the bench than it already was, he opened his mouth just a little, but he didn't utter a sound. He waited. He wanted my mother to begin the conversation.

"Yes, Minister, please, what is it? Please tell me. Hurry."

She sat down in a chair facing the minister, her knees held tightly together, her head held slightly to one side, her mouth pursed, her hands clasped in her lap, wearing on her face an expression of sour distaste, as if she was having acid reflux.

"Well, Jane, I'm afraid I have some bad news I must convey to you this day," the Minister intoned in the rich resonant baritone voice of the highly respected preacher he was.

"Yes, yes, Minister. What is it? Who is it? Speak; please tell me."

"I have just come from your brother's house."

"Oh, I knew it. I knew it."

"It's your brother, the Doctor. I'm afraid he's gone. He passed away this morning. It was all very sudden and unexpected. It was his heart."

The wailing went on for a long time. I hated it. I loathed it. I detested it. My ears sang. I twisted and turned inside. My middle tightened into a gripping knot. My mouth dried up. I writhed in my seat. Why was I being subjected to this banshee wailing from hell? Why wouldn't she shut up? Why was she doing this to me? Why was she torturing me? What had I done wrong? Where was I to blame? I was to blame, wasn't I? Guilty! I had to be responsible somehow.

As for the Minister, he looked very much like a man who wanted to be somewhere else. He wriggled his body, he blinked his eyes. Tears! From time to time he gave a wipe to his rimless glasses with a clean white handkerchief that he retrieved from and replaced into the upper pocket of his neat black jacket. What a spotless handkerchief of fine linen he had! How black his jacket was! Occasionally he smiled. He allowed the keening, with its howling and wailing, its breast-beating and gnashing of teeth to go on for what seemed to me to be an eternity, and what for him was presumably just long enough, and then he did what ministers usually did in such situations, what ministers were socially sanctioned to do; indeed, what ministers were expected to do. He fell on his knees and said: "I will now utter a prayer to the Lord."

Culean was looking nonchalantly at him from a distance of three feet with his tail half-elevated, as if unsure of why this clean, well-dressed stranger, who didn't smell at all like the people he was accustomed to, was adopting a doggy posture right next to his own household den.

But the Minister's posture had purpose in it, for the act of falling on his knees in prayer brought out the professional in him, it put him in control of the situation, it also brought peace and quiet to the room, and after it was over he stood straight up. Enough! I was glad it was over.

"It was his heart, you say?"

"Yes, Jane, it was indeed his heart. A sudden heart attack."

"What exactly happened?"

"His heart failed this morning. It was all very unexpected. Nevertheless, he must have had a weak heart for some time."

"Minister, I think he knew he wouldn't live long. The last time he visited us here, he hinted at the end of life approaching, as if he knew that there was something wrong. Also, a man told me that he saw him park his car by the side of the road, get out and walk around the car before climbing back inside, as if he was trying to work off some inner pain he was feeling."

"I'll telephone the family to let them know you'll be attending the funeral. Of course you can stay in the Doctor's house, and now for a word about yourself: If you need any personal help, please let me know, and I'll be happy to minister to you. Yes, indeed, now, don't forget."

I had always felt special because I had an uncle who was a doctor. There was something about him that I identified with. I wanted to be like him one day. An unusual man, a man who left school at the age of fourteen to become a fisherman, a man who knew even then that he would be a doctor of medicine one day. And villagers laughed at him for his strange ambition, but it was what he truly wanted, he accomplished what he wanted in life, he fulfilled his purpose, lived his destiny.

It was, of course, a time of major readjustment for millions of people. World War Two had come to an end, everybody was supposed to be happy, and many tried, each in his or her own way. Was this not the time we had waited for all these years? Oh, how we had longed for an end to all the strife, the killing, the mayhem, the mental visualization of violence, the waiting and wondering who would come back and who would never be seen again. Women's voices over the radio promised a free world, peace, prosperity, and happiness, although no songs came into our house over the air-waves. What! no radio? Who could afford a radio? what with many mouths to fill.

In Scotland, the anticipated peace-time prosperity failed to materialize, the nation was impoverished, its people worn out, exhausted, and we made do with less. With the military bases on the Island closed, the village seemed quiet and still, as if something was missing. What could it be? Something beyond the physical was lacking in our lives. Something had been killed, murdered in a towering rage. Perhaps the young men and women returning from the military also felt it. Many of them sought their fortunes elsewhere, by emigrating to Australia, New Zealand, Canada or the United States; some took advantage of an opportunity to acquire higher education in Scotland's universities. They had learned a few things. What did they learn? And how did they apply it? Good question!

America had arrived on the world scene. And a food parcel arrived from my father's brother in America. Turkey! I had never tasted turkey before. I had never even seen as much as a picture of a turkey. Now we had turkey from rich, fabulous America, the land across the sea where everybody was wealthy, where everybody was happy, where the sun always shone, and everybody loved each other.

The turkey was delicious.

14: A PASSIONATE PURSUIT

Another day; another message, this time by telegraph. A telegram from my father. He was sick, hospitalized.
Confined to the Western General Hospital in Glasgow, a city that to me seemed mysterious, far away and enormous, and the only way my father could communicate with us, following the emergency telegram, was by letter. In his first letter, he wrote that the doctors had made a diagnosis of Rheumatic Fever.

I admired my father and I wanted to be like him. I tried walking the way he walked. I saw him as savvy and smart, as a traveled man of the world, and I wanted to be like that some day, but imitating him had its limitations. I couldn't really be him, and my father's absence meant that my mother was dependent on favors from other men when she needed a "man around the house." It was a situation I was aware of and sensitive to. Most other fathers seemed to spend more time at home than he did. I wished he would. Why the hell didn't he? I admired him for his travels. Still, why wasn't he there for me when I needed a father to support me, when bullies got to me? Well, finally he was sick, debilitated, disabled, old before his time.

My mother explained to me: "Rheumatic Fever can weaken the heart."

"My uncle had a weak heart, didn't he?"

"Yes, but don't worry. Remember my own case. I was sick once, and I put all my trust in the Lord. I knew that the doctors weren't helping me, but I had faith that the Lord would bring about exactly what was in His design, and indeed, He brought about my recovery, by inspiring the doctor to finally make a diagnosis of low thyroid condition; a treatable disease. I recovered. It was the way He designed it."

My father stayed in the Western General Hospital a long time. Western General! Western General! We lived with that name for many months, then one day: "Good news from Glasgow! Your father's coming home. We'll give him our best care. Remember his heart."

"I know what I'll do," I said. "I'll catch a trout every day for him. There's nothing better for the heart than a fresh trout."

"Oh, you can't possibly do that. Nobody catches a trout every day. That's too much to expect. You don't even have fishing equipment. You have no experience."

"I'll make the fishing equipment. I'll catch the trout. You wait and see. When's my father coming home?"

"Next week."

Shiny fishing hooks were readily available for pennies in the local store. A small bamboo pole, wide at one end and narrow at the other end, was soon mine, and I connected the narrow end of that pole by string, and a short piece of a cat-gut material that, for some reason, I called "weed," to one of the hooks. Weed! I was in business. I was an able fisherman.

Out in the glen, walking alongside the creek, searching for a suitable location, it made sense to me to try one of the dark glassy pools. Dark mirror-surfaced water. The reflection of the bamboo pole stretched out over the water, its line falling out of its tip, my own reflection behind it. How beautiful the pole looked against a background of light blue sky! The sky clouded over. Rain was on the way, more than a passing shower. I could have sheltered under the ancient rock that was on one side of the glen, but I didn't do that. I continued fishing. Thousands of raindrops sputtered against the surface of the pool. Gone was reflection. Ten minutes later, I had a fish, a lovely speckled brown trout that would fill a pan. So what if I was wet. I was elated. Probably I could have caught more, but I didn't try.

This was no sophisticated fly fishing; neither was it fancy sport-fishing as relaxation from the trials and tribulations of city life, or from the onerous task of governing others; it was a passionate pursuit.

I got to know where the trout were likely to be and at what time of day, and, not only that, but my mind went beyond fishing; I did something else. While I was occupied with the business of catching a trout a day I was also exploring the glen in all its magnificence. On one side was a rocky hill, where pale ancient rocks of gneiss, a part of which made a perfect chair in its formation, protruded from a layer of soft earth that was partially covered with heather. The heather itself was spotted with blue and pink wild flowers. In places the glen was deep enough to create an echo I loved to hear, and so it was that I uttered an occasional gleeful laugh, a whistle, a shout. Why not? I had the glen all to myself. No landowner on his estate could have been any happier than I was. What did they know of the simple joy of being alive? What did they know of fishing for heart? They owned the best fishing waters in Scotland, and they protected these with gun-toting gamekeepers. What did these slogan-chanting Tories know of liberation? with their God; king; country! Frightened? Of course they were. They were terrified of freedom. They had to be. There's no other explanation for their conduct. Boot on the neck Authority.

Long-gone glaciers had carved the glen out of the earth, and it was along the winding bottom of the glen that the creek meandered as a series of mysterious-looking black-bottomed pools that reflected, on either side, the creek's overhanging earthy banks in glassy mirrored surfaces connected to each other by narrow channels. Between the earthy banks, the pools reflected the distant sky, deep as eternity.

In the narrow connecting channels, the light tawny-colored water was shallow and transparent, the bottom was of pebbled sand, greenish weeds, and smooth rounded rocks, over which the water trickled, flowed and swirled. That water spoke to me, and so did the glen. Out of the silence came awesome tinkling winkling falling rising sounds. It was a contemplative prayerful time for me, and I elicited God's help in ensuring that my father's heart would be strengthened. I felt the presence of God in the glen.

I prayed to God to deliver to me one trout, just one. I did that every day. I wanted one trout that would help my father get well again and every afternoon I returned home carrying one beautiful speckled brown trout, fresh out of the waters of the creek.

I had faith.

"Beautiful," my father would say, "I've never had such good food in all my life. My heart's getting stronger every day."

"You're a fine physician, too," my mother would say, with a smile.

Whenever she smiled in praise of me, her face became peaceful and serene, like the face of one possessed of timeless wisdom and insight. At moments like these, she radiated beauty.

These were happy days for me. I was in my element. I was in harmony. I knew exactly how it was that large lovely trout attached their lower jaws to the hooks I baited for them each day, but I wasn't telling anyone. I kept it all to myself. I didn't believe I was the one doing it. I believed that God delivered the daily trout. After all, each day I prayed for just one trout, and that was exactly what I got. I remembered what my mother had said about faith in God. And also, did not Mr. Maclelland, the Sunday school teacher, tell us to pray to the Lord?, and I believed Mr. Maclelland, not because he was the Sunday school teacher, but because his simple honesty showed.

"Put your trust in the Lord," he said, "and make your needs known to Him, and He will never let you down. He already knows your needs. He has placed you in your station and situation in life. The Lord gives you whatever talents you have in life. Remember that. Use your talents wisely, respect the Lord's work that you do in your lives."

Out on the moor there was silence, a deep profound silence that even the dark high flying birds of prey, their wings spread out serenely, shared, not that I ever went to sleep with one of these above me. They pursued nourishment; so did I. I had a simple belief in God. He would listen to me. He would hear me. He would answer my prayers, so long as I prayed for what I really needed. In the glen, I learned to pray alone, undisturbed by the expectations of others, uncorrupted by unreasonable desires. I knew that God was in the lives of people. I heard Him in the creek, I felt Him in the wind, I saw Him in the clouds that sailed across the sky, I smelled Him in the rich aroma of the heather, I saw Him in each beautiful well-fed speckled brown trout that came home with me each day.

    I often walked to where the creek emptied gently in a brown swirl into the Atlantic Ocean. I also walked the other way, away from the sea, following the creek out on to the moor, because that was where most of the trout were. One day I walked the full length of the creek, all the way to its origin under a lonely flat section of moor beyond the glen. So the creek's roots were underground! All that water, with its melody, its beauty, its cleanliness, and its life-giving properties, was coming out of some dark mysterious underground system of caverns. No one had ever told me about this. I had made a discovery. My heart danced expectantly. What else was down there? I could only imagine. No way could I explore the depths of the earth; no, but I could walk.

    And walk I did, further, beyond the glen and on to open moor that spread and undulated purple and brown and dark-spotted in all directions, as far as the eye could see. Suddenly, upon cresting a hill, I smelled the sea. What? It was indeed the coast on the other side of the island. A broad sweeping slope fell in front of me, all the way down to the tops of the cliffs that dropped sheer to where the ocean rose and fell rhythmically in its bed. I found a way down the steep cliffs and on to the sea-level rocks at the bottom, upon which the waves crashed, after which they receded in white water, before returning again in masses of speckled green, blue and purple.

    I imagined myself rolling among the waves, rising and falling in rhythm, stretching my limbs, laughing, keeping company with the Atlantic seals, a paradise on earth; then strolling along the pristine sands, floating weightlessly across the moors, and always naked, never dressed.

One day I brought my mother an unusual gift. It was a broach made of sparkling silver, with stones in it. I had found it in dust at the bottom of an "underground house," a large cavity dug deep down, about 12 feet in diameter, with a circular wall of stones carefully cut and placed one on top of the other so as to form a vault, closed at the top in an apex, and the whole covered by turf. Entrance was by a narrow descending tunnel.

And some young woman had lost her broach, and probably gave up more than her broach, in that perfect lover's nook, which at one time had been a hideout for local distillers of whiskey. The established authorities of the day, as those of today, frowned upon free trading, except when it benefited them directly, which meant that the authorities declared whiskey distilling illicit, and therefore the villagers of that time did what they wanted to do in dark secret places.

I loved dark secret places.

I loved swimming alone, and I did it often. I didn't own a swimming suit, I didn't want one. Why would I? What purpose would it serve?

I was aware that I was mixing with, and a part of, the same water that rolled thousands of miles to Canada, to the United States, to South America, to the Arctic and that, indeed, by currents and channels, evaporations, rainfalls, and assorted circuitous ways, percolated into every nook and cranny in the world. Mine was a sensuous non-verbal awareness, occasionally to the point of actually hearing faint musical sounds that vanished as soon as I began to focus upon them.

It was a time when the beaches were clean. My generation saw the last of the pristine beaches, full of cockles, mussels and edible sea-weed, which meant that, in my wanderings, I never went hungry or got bored. Every cliff, every little cave, every low tide, was a fresh adventure.

Into the surf I went one day, naked and happy, then across the bay and back, again and again, for hours, in the clean cool water, after which I climbed out of the surf, dried my body by shaking the water drops off, and by swinging my arms. Then I sat in the sun behind a tall black rock. Quiet it was, with the soft sea breeze, the aroma of ocean and the sound of the nearby rollers. I rested. This was life at its best: living, aware, being.

I stood up after a luxurious rest by the rock, savoring the lovely brisk feeling I always got after a swim in the sea, with my skin tingling all over, my eyes wide open, alert and quiet-hearted at one and the same time. My toes sank in warm sand, my left hand rested upon an old black rock, I took a step on to a stretch of beach, then another, and then I took off running.

Laughing all the way to the other end of that quarter mile of clean white sand, to the rocks at the far end, my heart beating steadily in harmony with a rhythm that wasn't mine to control, breathing air that was fresh, and at the far end of the beach, I rested.

Back the way I had come, sand beneath my feet, sea to my left, sky above, fluffy white clouds floating by, floating, my heart in the heavens, the whole universe within me, and joy of such magnitude that I imagined could never possibly be experienced anywhere on earth.

15: SEPARATION ANXIETY

The air smelled of rope, rain-water, fish scales and herring guts, overhead the seagulls cried and wheeled, but they were hangers-on, for the main seagull party was over for the day, the fishermen had coiled up their rubber hoses for the weekend, the merchants had closed their shops, working men strode towards the pubs, their hearts light in anticipation of an evening of revelry. One in particular had already sampled the mood elevating offerings of a pub, judging by the merry ditty he chanted, none too privately.
It was in the days when it was still possible to enjoy oneself in public without being arrested.

I was fifteen years old, strolling along the wharf, hands in my pockets, happy to be alone, happy to be me, not feeling in any way lonely, for indeed, I wasn't alone, deep within me, where it mattered.

A low, setting sun blazed behind the hill beyond the town, flinging a brilliance of yellow, red, white and pink into the sky above, between the rooftops, into the solitude.

And along the wharf a man approached. We would meet. He wore a hat cocked slightly to the right side of his head, and a tan raincoat, and he walked with the easy confident strides of a man who knew where he was going, and how to get there, and, as we drew near to each other, he spoke: "Well, hello, Donald. How are you?"

"Hello, it's good to see you," I said, smiling.

He was a sailor, a friend of my father's, and here he was, a grown man, addressing me amiably, man to man. Grownup to grownup. Great! My heart danced merrily. Good-bye boyhood! Hello, Manhood! here I come.

"It's Saturday night. Don't you have a girl-friend to go to the motion-pictures with?"

"Of course, I have a girl-friend. Well, no I don't right now."

"You're not shy, are you? I used to be shy when I was your age, but I got over that soon enough after I went to sea. Oh, yes, I soon lost my fear of girls."

"Who, me? Oh, no, I'm not shy. I'm not afraid of girls."

It was a lie and I knew it. I *was* afraid of girls.

"You're not exactly a chip off the old block. When your father was your age, he'd be up to high jinks, and, for sure, he wouldn't be alone on a Saturday night. He's never alone, that one. When he sits on his bunk, in the fo'c's'le, on board our ship, we all gather around him. He tells good yarns, I'll say."

"That's him, right enough."

"But not you. You're not like your father."

"No, I'm not a comedian. I don't tell funny stories. It's not in my nature. I can't do it, but I like good company."

"He's always got people around him."

"I'm different in that regard too."

"Years ago, we all liked having your father with us on long lonely voyages. He kept our spirits up when we needed a boost, and, to be sure, we needed that often enough. A ship without him was never the same."

"Well, he and I are different."

I had actually tried telling some of my father's stories but they didn't work for me, and nobody laughed when I told them, so I had given up on that. It wasn't me. I wasn't designed for it, not a comedian, but the attempt taught me something I never forgot about being.

"Well, I left your father in England. I'll be seeing him again, as soon as I return to the ship."

Delighted to meet my father's shipmate and fellow traveler, hovering on the brink of manhood, longing to be an adult, afraid of the jungle of manhood, not ready to be a fully-fledged sexual head-of-a-family adult man, of course, but a man tentatively, as in a trial run, wanting to test the barrier that grown men wove around themselves, willing to adapt, eager to know the requirements for admission to the club of male adulthood, but wanting a guide; yes, a guide to manhood.

Wanting personal news of my father, not the kind of news that came in letters delivered by mail carriers in dark navy uniforms wearing peaked caps with emblems of the Crown fastened above the visors, wanting man-to-man news, wanting my father to pay attention to me, longing for his love, wanting on another level to break through social barriers, yes, to leave him far behind. Could our love for each other survive it?

The sun was sinking, the sky darkening, the street lamps lit up, and several fishing boats tied by thick ropes to mighty cast-iron stays sunk into the concrete, rocked gently to the rhythm of the oily brine of the bay, to the rhythm of the sea, to the push of the breeze, to the pull of the moon.

"Any news?"

"Your father's smart. I couldn't have done without him. No, sir, I couldn't have managed."

"Oh, what happened?"

"I had some trouble with the authorities. Nothing serious, at least I didn't think so, but it could have become serious, innocent neglect on my part, but still, these people are very particular."

The sailor's eyes were deep with the kind of depth that a few people acquired after many years of living, the kind of depth seldom if ever seen in young people, the kind of depth that suggested wisdom that had little to do with knowledge acquired in colleges, not that there was anything wrong with college education as far as it went, and there was much to be said for it, but, on the other hand, college education had the same weakness as high school education, in that it neglected exploration of authentic human identity, it encouraged dependency in the midst

of debate, in short, it reinforced the neuroses of childhood.
"How?"
"What? What do you mean?"
"How did my father help you?"
"First of all, when did you last write your Old Man?"
"Above five weeks ago."
"Hmmm."
"How did he help you?"
"He guided me all the way. He wrote letters for me. All I did was sign them. I'm grateful to him."

The sailor's face had weathered over the years, it had been exposed to the elements, it had been salted by spray from many seas, it had been toasted by tropical sunshine, it had been blown by warm winds, it had been blasted by icy gales, and, to be sure, the man behind the face had weathered long lonely watches.

In the cabin of the *Helen Rose,* tied to the wharf next to us, a crewman pulled the string next to the wire cage that covered the electric bulb, which itself was a long cucumber-shaped glass thing screwed into a socket in the ceiling of the cabin, and a light blinked into life, and the cabin's interior, mostly of non-reflective brown-painted wood, lit up wanly. The crewman had a porcelain cup in his left hand, probably brimming over with hot strong tea, on his head he wore a gray working man's cap; on his torso he wore a dark navy woolen polo-necked sweater.

The light from the cabin of the *Helen Rose* lit up the right side of the sailor's face, emphasizing his sun tan. In the pupil of his right eye there appeared the reflection of a sad-looking, dark green shed that managed to stay erect on the wharf, just barely.

I nodded, proud of my father, happy to hear of his competence.

A multi-colored rippled reflection arose in an oily puddle on the concrete of the wharf. The puddle smelled of rubber and petroleum. A spent stub floated in it, leaking tobacco. The sailor offered me a Players Navy Cut cigarette; I accepted. He extracted an all-weather brass lighter from his coat pocket, flicked it into life, and extended his right hand holding the yellow flame. The flame warmed my face momentarily and delivered to me a whiff of petrol fumes and oil as I puffed fire into the Players.

The sailor's nose was small and straight. Wavy lines wove their way across his forehead. Dark hair crowned his scalp: it protruded from under his hat. He opened his raincoat, exposing a powerful-looking body, heavy but not corpulent, dressed in a blue serge suit. He smelled of tobacco, fresh soap and freshly pressed wool.

I felt myself grow in stature, glowing inside.

My father was intelligent, although not formally educated beyond whatever grade he was in when he left school at the age of fourteen. He spoke articulately, he wrote well in his letters, he read ably, he remembered what he read, and he had a grasp of what was going on in the world. Had he been where we were that evening, he would have been dressed in a tan-colored raincoat with the collar turned up, he'd be wearing a soft-brimmed hat, tilted slightly to the right and he'd be smoking either a tailor-made cigarette, a hand-rolled cigarette, or his beloved black pipe.

I stood up straight and tall, I was at peace, I smiled inwardly, I was inside the world of the grown men, I had arrived. Then:

"Why don't you write to your father?"

"What?"

"Yes, why don't you write to him?"

"But I do. I just told you I wrote him a few weeks ago. What are you talking about?"

"He tells me you don't write him very often, certainly not often enough. He would love to hear from you. He misses you."

"He misses me?"

"Yes, he misses you a lot and he would love to hear from you."

"That's what he said?"

"It was exactly what he said, and not once, but often. That's why I'm telling you."

What on earth was this man talking about? All the time I

had believed it was the other way around. Was it not my father who failed to write to me on time? Or, could it be that I had it wrong all the time? I wanted to hear from him more often. Oh, how I looked forward to letters from him! I loved reading his letters. So what was going on? Why this? Why didn't he tell me what he wanted? He never once suggested to me that he would love to hear from me more frequently. My father was a man of wit, a man of personal warmth, he was of a gentle nature, an artistic man, but he was a square peg without a niche in which to fit in the world he wandered in. He seemed different from other fathers I encountered. Nevertheless, to me, he was exactly right; well, almost exactly right, for there was one thing. I wanted, or imagined I wanted, yes, I passionately wanted to know him, to really know him.

Or maybe I got exactly what I wanted while believing I wanted the opposite, arranging my life in such a way that he would move away from me, and maybe he also pushed me away from him. Role changing. Thoughts such as these actually flashed through my mind, but I said nothing of that to the sailor.

Maybe my father thought I was acting like a big shot, too uppity to speak to him, that I was avoiding him because I was moving up in the world, with ambitions of being a doctor of medicine, no less, while he was just a sailor-crofter-laborer. I knew how he felt about young men who acted superior. He had counseled me to never act superior in the presence of working men and women, for they wouldn't like it, and I didn't like that particular piece of advice, not at all at all. I felt angry. So, I was acting superior to him! Was that it? Yes, it was, or at least that's what he was telling me, in a roundabout way. I didn't tell him I felt wounded. I didn't tell my father I was angry.

Right there and then, in the presence of my father's sailor mate, I felt embarrassed, I felt perplexed, as if I was letting the side down. Angry! Maybe I was acting superior after all. Well, I'd do something about that and right quick. I would write my father more often, maybe once every two weeks or even weekly. I'd make up for lost time, and, from then on my father and I would be close, just like a perfect family, but I kept quiet about my thoughts, and, after an uncomfortable silence, my father's shipmate said:

"Well, I must be going now. I have errands to run."

"Yes, I also have to go."

"Goodbye, Donald."

"Goodbye."

The sailor and I parted company. We went our separate ways, but something in me didn't feel right. Was there something wrong with me? Something in me was missing. As a result of my missing ingredient, I had failed in my attempt to negotiate admission into the world of men. I was a failure. I wasn't a real man after all. I wrote my next letter to my father the following day, and afterwards I wrote several letters in rapid succession, but I never mentioned my meeting with the sailor. Neither did he mention that he had learned of it, if he did.

After a few months, reacting to the response, I fell back into my customary pattern of writing, feeling what was the use? if I wrote often, I'd lose, if I wrote infrequently, I'd lose. We continued writing each other every few weeks.

16: SPIRITUAL THIRST

As a live-in student in the school I attended, I went to church every Sunday. We all did. Then, without giving it any serious thought, I missed a couple of Sundays, then another.

One the teachers spoke to me: "Donald, we missed you a couple of times in church. Where were you?"

"Oh, it's nothing important, I'll be back. I just had a few things to do."

"You're not having problems with church, are you?"

"Who, me? Problems! Of course not, none whatsoever, I assure you."

"Well, then, I hope you come back. I know it's your personal decision, but we do miss you, and maybe you could use some encouragement. Remember you're still young in the ways of the world."

"Yes, Sir, I understand exactly what you're saying."

Up until then I had fully intended, or at least I believed I had intended, to go back to church, even although I had missed a few sessions, but the moment the concerned teacher confronted me, as I saw it, something clicked inside me, and I knew I would not be going back. A phase of my life was over. I had walked out of one closet, into another one, I had closed a door, another door was opening, and a couple of weeks later I approached the teacher:

"I've started attending another church."

"Oh, and what church is that?" he asked.

I named a local church and, as I lied, I nodded, trying to look serious, trying to look involved, looking the teacher straight in the eye, keeping a poker face, and it worked, as I imagined it to be.

"Well, be sure and remember your spiritual needs."

"Oh, definitely, I agree that my spiritual needs come first. Yes, Sir, I'll pay attention to my spiritual needs."

The concerned teacher didn't approve of students drinking distilled spirits, or quaffing foaming brews, or even sucking on cigarettes, he didn't approve of places with sawdust on the floor, barrels of beer behind a bar, tobacco smoke, dimly-lit pubs. Pubs like the Far Island Bar. Neither did my mother approve of anything that wasn't prescribed by the followers of Calvin, even although John Knox, who had introduced Calvinism into Scotland, loved wine and was working his way through a barrel of good wine when he died. Of course, city water wasn't so good in these days, and that probably had something to do with Knox's appreciation of wine.

I imagined it was a phony make-believe world anyway, so let everybody go their own way in it, I'd go mine, and, to be sure, there was nothing wrong with being angry at the world as a prelude to self-examination, perhaps also to letting go of ego attachments.

An idea suddenly occurred to me. Why not try alcohol? It would be an exciting experiment. It would require me to live a double life, but so what. That in itself would be something worth doing, to liven up the routine of ordinary school life. I was in a new closet, was I not? So I might as well act it out. Not only that, but there was mystery attached to alcohol, the beverage had magical properties, it transformed mundane existence into exciting adventures. I toyed with the idea for several days; then, one dark winter's evening, when I was passing the shadowy back door of the Far Island Bar, as if on cue, a man opened the door from within, I made a right angle turn and entered. Immediately I was in the midst of a din of talking, laughing, booze-quaffing men rubbing elbows in a smoky barroom where rows of bottles sparkled and shone, just as The Doctor's medicine bottles had sparkled so many years before.

The bartender approached. He was a middle-aged man with an expressive face, and right then he was expressing disbelief, or so it seemed to me. Careful. Watch out. Was he going to throw me out? Ready for rejection, I produced my poker face.

"Are you sure you're eighteen?" the bartender asked me.

"Of course, I am. I'm eighteen and an eighth."

"You're a few weeks on the safe side."

"Let the lad have his liquid refreshments. It's good for the constipation. Doctor recommended. Keeps the bowels rolling," someone bellowed.

"It keeps *you* farting, as everyone can tell," someone else yelled.

"You can smell him a mile away."

"I was young once."

"Look at you now! What a mess. Bones and bowels, not to mention beer belly."

"Hey, Barkeep, move that booze along. There's far too much jaw-flapping going on in this place. What's the delay? A man can die of thirst around here."

"Don't worry. We bury our dead!"

"I just want to be sure the customers are old enough to reach the counter top."

I was where I belonged, and it felt good.

17: PAGODA

Swamper dragged himself around camp day after day with his feet wide apart, upon a broad base, lurching in an almost upright position, like a man on a swaying platform in a gusty wind, defying gravity barely enough to permit him to shuffle from place to place.
No laces in his shoes, missing some teeth, jaw weak and loose, cheeks sunken, slacks greasy in places from the residues of old spills, belt twisted and missing one loop, Swamper performed, a man doing his job. His job was to make tea, which he brewed in large urns with removable lids, also to clean out the bunkhouses, and to pick up useless junk around camp.

I was relaxing on my bunk early one Sunday morning, reading and smoking, when Swamper approached and cast his bleary red-stained eyes upon me. It being Sunday, there was no regular work, but those who wanted to work could. Double time!

He inhaled on the loosely rolled cigarette he held in his lips, he coughed and he said, "Oh, what a day! What a day! What a day!," then he halted next to my bunk and spoke to me, "Hello mate, I see you're not doing no work. Some people have all the luck."

"I'll be working in a few minutes. I don't make any money lying around, smoking and reading."

"Remember the Sabbath day, to keep it holy. Your mother told you so. Money don't do it. Don't you forget your mother, Young Fellow."

I smiled at him, indulgently, as if he were a harmless imbecile; I said, "I want to forget my mother."

"Can't never forget your mother."

"It's what I'd like to do."

Camp was in the remote mountains of the Scottish Highlands, and bunkhouses were old army Nissen huts that the military had discarded as being of no further use to them, or maybe the construction company had bought them as army surplus. We, if I can include myself in the construction team, although my input was insignificant, were building a hydro-electric dam that would stop and hold the rapidly moving river water, thereby creating a great lake that in turn would serve as a source of controlled power to move the generators. I was a student on summer break. The work was hard, the hours long, but the pay was relatively good, with nothing to spend it on, which served my two-fold purpose well, that purpose being, firstly, to save money for my education, and secondly, to gain experience.

I wanted to be a man among men, a real man at last, a grown-up. I wanted to be independent, I wanted to move away from my parents, I wanted to sever my long-lasting relationship with them. I was tired of playing minion to professors, I was tired of being somebody's son, I was tired of looking up to others, I was tired of waiting for the pieces of life to fall into place. I was tired of feeling like a misfit.

Many of the local men where I grew up worked construction, and I tried to identify myself as a man by doing what they did, if only briefly, and, to be sure, the men worked hard, with an efficiency born from experience, muscles moving elegantly, harmoniously, using their native intelligence.

Swamper's shirt might have been bright red at one time, but by this time it was a rusty brown color, with open buttons exposing dark hair on his chest, but even more than the shirt, it was the blazer that drew attention to itself. It was bright yellow in places, there were great dark cloud-shaped splotches where yellow had become one with dust and mud, all the buttons were missing except for one on the left sleeve, and that solitary button was engraved with an insignia of two golf clubs crossing each other.

Golf!

Swamper shook his head at me, he was about to say something, and I expected more about mother, but just at that moment, the man known as Leaper, the man from the mountains, or maybe he was from an east coast city, strode into the bunkhouse, shaking dust off his boots, looking light and lean as a leopard, carrying in his right hand a mean-looking wooden pick-handle that swung easily in his grip, just as if it was physiologically meant to be there. He looked straight at me:

"If that bloody bugger from hell says anything to you, let him have it with this right between the eyes." He thrust the pick handle straight at me: "Here, take it. You'll need it in this place, and remember what I said now. Don't let him off with anything. Let him have it good if he bothers you."

Swamper moved away from us, recognizing an enemy in Leaper, he shuffled off slowly as far as the doorway where he stopped and proceeded to lean on his broom and stare down the road, and it wasn't hard to guess what he was focusing on. *The Pub*. *The Pub* was a quarter of a mile away, a large whitewashed building, with several sedately smoking chimneys, a roof of heavy greenish shingles, a sprawl of secondary buildings at the rear, and set a hundred yards away from the road. On that peaceful Sunday morning, *The Pub* and everything around it seemed to be precisely in place, as if arranged for a Best of Scotland calendar photograph.

I took the deadly weapon from Leaper, something I instinctively did without thinking about it, and I laid it against the inner wall of the bunkhouse, with no intention of using it on Swamper or anyone else, neither taking the suggestion literally, for rough language did not usually translate into physical violence-I knew that much-but, momentarily at a loss for words, I finally said, "I'm not so sure about the tea. I saw the way he brews it."

"What way is that?"

"He takes off the lid, then he mixes the tea with the handle of the broom he sweeps the floor with, and all the time muttering to himself: "Your mother cared for you when you was little, didn't she? Well, she ain't here no more, is she? She wiped your arsh and put nappies on you, didn't she? I do hopes you appreciates all she done for you. And she made tea for you too, like I makes tea, so there, we're equal, just like even-Steven, ain't we?"

"Did he put any cigarette butts in the tea?"

"I don't know about that. I didn't see. I'm sure some ashes fell in."

"Bastard! Drunken no good son of a bitch bastard! To hell with him! A lousy excuse for a man. One day he'll get exactly what's coming to him. And I look forward to that day. Serves him right too, the dirty stinking rotten stumblebum, can't even hold his booze. He's full of shit, no doubt about that, I'll say."

Leaper cursed the way he walked, swiftly, sharply, efficiently, with an air of competence. He was a tall, lean, athletic man with hairy arms, a quick retort, a shock of dark hair and a way of letting people know in more ways than one that he was in charge of himself and that no one else should ever assume otherwise. Smart, in a streetwise kind of way, a man in the right place, at the right time, he strode out the door of the bunkhouse, but not before letting fly with one final curse aimed at Swamper.

Swamper looked mournfully at me and muttered: "Poor Swamper, poor old Swamper....Now don't you go listening to that man, Leaper, will you? But don't get me wrong now, I don't mean nothing against him either, like...now, you be sure and don't go telling him nothing I said like...I mean, I don't have no enemies myself. I don't hate nobody; no enemies. Now that's a nice lad, Young Fellow."

"I heard, but I don't listen, so don't you worry, Swamper."

"Young Fellow, why are you looking at me in that way?"

"What way is that?"

"You're looking at me weird-like."

"Oh, it's nothing; nothing at all. I was just thinking; that's all."

"Thinking don't do no harm, it's what you thinks."

"How do you know what I was thinking?"

My thoughts had been of pity and of amused contempt, a message he must have received, sensitive soul that he was, accustomed to it, and perhaps preferring it to no attention at all.

"If I was a young man, I'd quit," he said. "Yes, that's exactly what I'd do, quit, and right now, is what I'd do. I'd be a man and jack. Hell, I'd jack right now, today....A real man would jack right-away, and no bones about it either; that's what a real man would do, but I ain't no real man. No, I ain't nobody."

"Swamper, you're as good as the rest of us."

"Exactly what my mother always said! Didn't she now? My mother would like you, Young Fellow; yes, she would too, bless her old heart, but my Old Man was something else. Oh, yes he was at that. Never seen one like him, I tell you. Screaming at me; yelling at me; cursing me day and night. Fear is all I've ever known from him. 'You shoulda been strangled at birth, you ugly little bastard. You got no right to live, Shitface. I hope you die soon. You hear me?' He kept bellowing at me like this, and I mean day and night, and I never done him no harm...Not at all, no harm did I ever do him. Strangled at birth! Can you believe that, Young Fellow?"

"Well, Swamper, I believe it if you say it's true. Maybe your father had something wrong with him. Did he drink a lot?"

"I drink some myself, but I ain't no drunk, I can quit any time I want. I'm not one that has to have it day and night, if you know what I mean. As a matter of fact I did quit four years ago, for seven weeks and two days at a stretch, and I didn't have to have it then, so don't that prove it; right? and another thing about me is, I'm harmless, as anybody who knows me can tell you. I'm don't harm nobody. Just ask anyone."

"Swamper, you're a nice man, but then again, yesterday...."

"Yesterday was a day for the mahogany, I tell you. Saturday: wet, and I was all alone...then I met up with a bad crowd. Who wouldn't down a few, meeting up with these guys? They're something, these fellows, but nice blokes at that. So what if I downed a few? Maybe I did have a couple of beers."

"I know what you mean."

"Even the barman says to us: 'When are you buggers going to quit sloshing it down. Time's up, you know.'"

"At least you remember that much."

"I'll tell you what, Young Fellow, look in that corner, over there, behind that pile of rubber boots....See, there?"

"What is it?"

"Nothing is what it is. Nothing at all. I only wish there was one there. Ha;ha, I mean a craggan, a craggan full of plonk...and if you like I'll let you in on something, Young Fellow, and it's this, I tell you. When I was under the bridge with my half-gallon craggan and my loaf of bread, I was never happier in my whole life....No botheration at all at all. Ah, yes, I tell you, these were the days."

Just then a shadow passed across the brightly sunlit doorway, and suddenly Pagoda was standing there. Pagoda was a quiet casual-looking man wearing a tweed cloth hat, floppy overalls and soft brown leather boots. He was the assistant foreman of carpenters, a man from the lowlands, and intelligent at that, a man with a quiet, effective, grownup manner that suggested inner strength and wisdom. He beckoned to me with his head and he said, "Come with me this morning. You've been assigned to carpenters. I need your help. We have a job to do inside the dam."

I leapt off my narrow cast-iron bed, tossed my cigarette butt into the squat sturdy black cast-iron stove in the middle of the room, and I was ready for action: "OK, do you want me to carry anything for you?"

"You can carry some of my tools. Here."

I accepted the small load.

Pagoda then pulled out of his waistcoat a worn-looking steel pocket watch attached to a long steel chain, he flicked the catch, the cover of the watch flew open, he glanced at the dial, then he snapped the cover back into place before replacing the watch in his pocket, and off the two of us went, with Pagoda setting the pace, which was a serene but authoritative stroll. I felt comfortable in his presence, by his side, but had I not been with Pagoda, I would have moved more swiftly, more urgently. To get from the bunkhouse to our destination that morning, we had to cross the narrow, winding black-top road that ran the length of the glen, perched as it was half-way up the side of the mountain.

This was no great highway, traffic was usually sparse, but on that particular day, as we were about to amble across the road, around the curve came a bright blue and white American car, long as a yacht, with its broad over-developed rear end spreading out behind it, and, as the behemoth drew up to a stop next to us, the driver's side window rolled down. Someone wanted to talk to us. A friendly American. How nice! "What's that you're building down there?" the man behind the wheel asked, pointing to the dam. His left hand, with which he pointed, was soft and fleshy, and his ring finger sported a gold ring with a large diamond stuck in its middle. He wore cuffs fastened with gold cufflinks; on his wrist he wore a gold watch. A corpulent man wearing sunglasses; a pale-faced expensively-dressed woman; both staring at us without the hint of a smile. Where the hell did this woman think she was going? To the Waldorf Astoria?

"We're building a hydro-electric dam. This glen will fill up with water from the river. Soon, that river will have to work for its living."

"Well, it don't look like much of a dam to me. In fact, it don't look like nothing to me. Where I come from we build them big, bigger than anything you've ever seen. We build real dams. That's what we do, where I come from."

The car widow rolled up smoothly, the vehicle accelerated and we were left there, gazing at a receding cloud of dust that rose slowly into the air and hung there suspended for a time after the car had rounded the next corner and swept down the far slope, leaving, or so it seemed to me, in the dust cloud, an image of corpulence.

Pagoda and I continued in silence across the construction

site, around the large groaning rumbling machines, over discarded rubble and around muddy puddles until we got to the dam. From our position at the bottom of the dam, men on the wall, and especially on top, looked like small midgets, and for the first time, I wondered if I could handle heights. I was soon to find out. Up a series of long wooden ladders tied to metal spikes hammered into the dam face we went. On top, the dam felt dangerously narrow, the wind pushy, the ground far away, and I knew I had some accommodating to do, but on that unusually casual morning, luck was with me, for Pagoda had a job in the interior, so down we went again until we were thirty feet from the bottom.

Pagoda led the way to a solid concrete ledge, along which we walked for a few yards. We then entered a tunnel that led into the interior of the dam. One hundred feet inside, with concrete all around, millions of tons above our heads, and pure silence, unbroken except for the muffled sound of our own footsteps and an occasional klink-like echo in the distance, I was in an unfamiliar world in which all around me seemed dreamy. A series of bare electric light bulbs, strung together with wire attached to the roof of the tunnel, lit up the gray dam wall in a bleak uncertain way, as if the electricity was unsure of itself, unwilling to be aggressive in such a place, and, indeed, there was something about it that demanded respect, like the atmosphere one feels in an ancient empty church built by long-gone craftsmen.

Finally, after much walking, we found what we were looking for, which were some timber supports, and we set to work.

"So," said Pagoda to me, "I hear you're going to the University. Is that true?"

"Yes, it's true. I've got my application in and I believe I'll be accepted."

"I never went to a university myself, but I respect learning; indeed, I love learning. I read, I observe, I get to know people, I learn about life. I work at construction sites for six months a year, and I spend every winter in Portugal and France, relaxing and enjoying my time in this world. What do you think of that?"

"I've never met anyone who lives like that."
"Well, you have now."
"How do you manage?"
"I've seen much violence and I'm a changed man as a result. I saw you step on a little beetle this morning. You deprived that helpless harmless creature of life. I'm not saying you were wrong, I'm not saying you were right, and maybe you did what you had to do, but I can tell you there are Buddhists and other people in the Far East whose wisdom goes back a long way, who believe that all of life-I mean every molecule of life-is sacred."
"I'm not a Buddhist. I'm not from the East," I said quickly; too quickly.
"A good answer! A fine answer indeed."
There was a silence, during which I sensed that there was something wrong with what I had said, but I wasn't sure what, or how to improve upon it. I didn't even know enough to figure it out. What I said was: "But, if you don't mind my asking a personal question, don't you want to save money for the future? After all, you might need it later."
"I'll get to that in a minute, but first, let me ask: What if your own soul was in the beetle you crushed? What if you knew it to be so? I don't mean some specific separate soul of yours. I mean some shared soul of the universe. And, what if you knew that all your actions came back to you inexorably in one way or another? What if you knew that coming around was unavoidable?"
"What are you talking about?"
"What if you knew?"
Pagoda was a small man, about five seven, lightly built, who looked at the world in a thoughtful kind of way through a pair of heavily-lidded eyes that had bulging fluid-filled bags beneath them. Some people-and this was something I learned later-referred to his smile as a superior smile, like the smile of a man who believed he knew something that others were incapable of grasping, or who was in on some cosmic secret, but Pagoda's smile to me was gentle and compassionate.

A carpenter's apron, crammed with tools, hung over the front of his pelvis, as if it were his true pride and joy, exhibited for all the world to see, but the most distinguishing characteristic of Pagoda-the one that gave him the nickname by which he was known in camp-was the shape of his silhouette from behind, when he stood in a doorway, which resembled no less than an oriental pagoda leaning ever so slightly to one side, and with a hat on top, not to mention a pair of sloping shoulders.

"I've never heard of anything so ridiculous in my life. Who ever heard of believing that he shares his soul with a beetle?"

"Some have ears to hear."

"I have ears, but...."

"But what?"

"I don't know what it is I'm supposed to hear; I don't know what I'm supposed to listen to."

"Be patient."

"Is that it?"

"Do I look like a man who is worried about the future?"

"You don't seem to want like the rest of us."

"Am I insecure about the future?"

"No, you don't seem to be," I said. "In fact, you look like a man of peace, like a man at peace with the world. You quarrel with no one, you do things your way, you never get angry, yet no one gives you a hard time. No one challenges you."

"We're all in this life for a reason, every living thing, and here I include the animals, fish, birds, trees and flowers. A few of us know why we are alive in our given bodies, but most of us don't. Some of us find out before we die. Most don't."

"A reason? What about Swamper? What possible reason could he serve? What use? He's something, more of a liability, I'd say, muttering and mumbling half-coherently, drinking, looking lost all the time."

"What did you see this morning?"

"Oh, just him, gazing longingly down the road at *The Pub*, muttering, 'What a day; what a day; what a day.' He wanted a drink first thing in the morning. Imagine that!"

"Imagine your mouth dry as dust, tongue sticking to the its roof, eyes hurting, throat like sandpaper, hands trembling, thinking jumbled. Imagine floaters sweeping in and out of your vision, maybe even evil voices jabbering in your ears. Imagine knowing that a drink would relieve all of that immediately, aye, and maybe even offer some tranquility to boot, or possibly an uplifting of the spirits. What would you do?"

"I wouldn't get myself into that shape in the first place."

"You don't know."

"Yes, I do. I'm absolutely certain of it."

"How do you know?"

"I just know."

"Did Swamper ask you for money?"

"No, he didn't ask me for anything."

"So he didn't want anything from you."

"That's right."

"Well, then, he didn't do you any harm, did he?"

"No, he didn't. In fact, he's nice to me. He calls me 'Young Fellow.'"

"But you don't approve of his way of life, do you?"

"No, I sure don't."

"What else?"

"Well, he said he was pissed off because *The Pub* has quit serving booze on Sundays, which the innkeeper used to do until recently. He was looking at *The Pub* so longingly I'll never forget the look in his eyes. 'It's themselves that's to blame,' he kept saying over and over. 'It's themselves that's to blame.'"

"You like that, don't you?"

"I don't follow you."

"It helps you feel superior, doesn't it?"

"I'm not trying to act superior. It's just that I'm not in any way like Swamper."

"It's scary, isn't it?"

"What is?"

"You could become what you despise in others."

"Why on earth would I do that? I don't get it."

"What you despise in others is in you. If it weren't, you'd be neutral. You project yourself on to others."

"It doesn't make sense to me."

"Anything else about Swamper?"

"He's always talking about drinking, like it's on his mind all the time. He was telling me about his friend Mike…Mike, the one who caused the riot one Sunday morning. It was after that riot that the innkeeper refused to serve them on Sunday mornings. 'He drangalot, you know,' Swamper said about Mike. 'He drangalot, always did, my friend Mike.'"

Pagoda put the chisel he had been using into his tool bag, he looked quietly at me with these eyes that were half-covered by their lids, and I found myself gazing directly into the center of his eyes, between the lids, tempted to drop my own eyes, but feeling transfixed by Pagoda's gaze. He spoke to me: "There but for the grace of God go you. Can't you see what Swamper does? We must be open to teachers who walk among us. Closed minds don't learn. Closed minds follow the world's bosses. Look at it this way, you're a young man, just becoming an adult, and you don't know what's in store for you. What if you are destined to be like Swamper one day? What if one day people mock you and humiliate you because you demonstrate to them their own dark secret side that they don't want to look at, especially in public? What if you must give such a demonstration one day?"

"What? Me! Certainly not; not at all. Not me; no way."

"You don't know. I'm repeating myself."

"What are you talking about?"

"I'm telling you that you don't know your future, or your destiny."

A tightness in my solar plexus; a light-headedness; short sharp breaths, I felt attracted to this man, I wanted to escape his clutches, I kept looking at him, irritated, frightened, silent, speechless.

"I'm talking about this, Donald. All of us live out our destinies. We plan on living in certain ways, but destiny always wins. It's a requirement of life. I've read some psychiatry, and, as I understand it, psychiatrists believe that the unconscious drives us, but I believe it is destiny that drives us, and of course destiny may very well work through our unconscious, so you can call it that if you want, but you'd be missing a very important understanding of life. Actually, the unconscious is not a place, certainly not, neither is it a physiological process, it's just a figure of speech, and an idea that offers far too many excuses to the moral cowards of this world. But, as for you, you don't know what your future will bring you. You don't, but whatever it is, rest assured it will be what it will be. Humble and wise are those who don't fight their destinies."

"I don't understand everything you say, and I've never studied Buddhism, or anything from the East, so I can't debate it, but the way I see it, I make my own luck, I direct my own destiny, and the more I know, the more skilled I am, the more I prepare myself, the better luck I have, and the better my destiny. Yes, that's the way I see it. I know what I want. I want to be a doctor of medicine. Here I am working on a construction site, but only for a short while. I'm here to make money. And you're telling me that, for all I know, I might end up like Swamper. Why would I want to be a drunkard? Of all things! It doesn't make sense. I don't agree with what you say."

"Donald, I know nothing. My mental image of myself gets in the way of my knowing."

"What are you talking about?"

"Have you ever heard of Dharma?"

"No, I haven't. Is it more Buddhism?"

"Look it up. I know you have a dictionary."

I had never expected to meet a man like Pagoda anywhere, far less on a remote construction site in the mountains, where rough and ready was the norm, where the language was coarse, where able-bodied men worked hard for many hours each day in all weather, where introspection was minimal, and where, on Saturday nights, certain men, away from home and with no women to subdue them, drank until closing time. Even the devoutly religious people I knew did not talk in the least bit like

Pagoda, nor did any of the men I knew who had spent time in the Far East.

Pagoda was one of a kind.

"But we need our mental images of ourselves. We need it!" I said. "Without a sense of ourselves, where would we be? How can your mental notion of yourself get in your way of knowing?"

Pagoda was absorbed in the task of carefully measuring a right angle in the timber structure that appeared to be holding up the weight of the dam, but of course it was doing nothing of the sort, it being only a prop, like a stage prop, designed to serve a temporary purpose for the engineers, after which it would be discarded. He removed a small stained black notebook from his vest pocket, opened it, and when he was finished measuring he wrote something down. Then quietly, sedately, still with that smile, he placed the notebook back in his pocket. Just at that moment the lights dimmed momentarily, and I startled, but my companion took no notice of the brief power gap, even although we were deep inside a remote dimly-lit cavity in the belly of a gigantic man-made monster, alone with no communication with the outside world.

Pagoda began gently stroking a smooth curving length of timber that was directly in front of us, just as he might have stroked a beloved pet dog, or the arm of a warm seductive woman.

I did not look up the meaning of dharma that day or the next, or for many years to come.

18: THE SHACK

The outer entrance to *The Shack,* where the men pissed their beer away, smelled of urine. All the way along the damp mud-floor stone-walled roofless corridor leading to the door.
The cast iron padlock, large, black and cold to the touch, answered to my key readily enough. It was the "Key to Enlightenment" I held in my hand! A private joke, of course, that gave me a chuckle as I thought of what I was doing that night in an obscure remote corner of a tightly buttoned-down, technically dry Calvinistic community. The lock yielded to the key, allowing a chain to drop, the planks to creak open, spilling distant starlight into the total darkness within.

I entered, pausing just inside the doorway to savor the aroma.

Inside the plank door and to my left was a pile of cut dried peat, for use as fuel, left there on the black dirt floor to dry, and beyond the peat pile there was a thin partition of wood with a loosely hung door that no one ever bothered to close securely. It was the door to the inner sanctum of *The Shack,* and a dark silent sanctum it was that Friday night, smelling of ashes, of stale smoke and of man.

I got down to work.

Soon, the inner door squaaked on its hinges and the first patron of the evening strolled in. He wore a worn fedora hat tipped jauntily to the right side of his head, a wide smile on his broad face, and his authoritative presence showed as he stood in the middle of the floor, slapping his hammy hands together, blowing briskly on them, holding them above the stove. As if an unlit stove would warm a man up!

"Here, mate," I said. "This is what you want."

Still standing in front of the stove, getting imaginary warmth, the man tossed back the double whiskey I had handed him. A shudder and a smack of the lips, a slight turn of the head, face down. He handed the empty glass back to me, bottom up, dripping its last clinging drop on to the black dirt floor. After he downed his second double whiskey, he looked around, took a pace backwards and slowly he eased his bottom on to the wooden bench behind him. A sigh of satisfaction. Ah! Feeling better already.

Blood alcohol level climbed, booze penetrated the fatty surfaces of brain cells, slipped into their interiors, applied the brakes on tiny chemical messengers shuttling between brain cells like a microscopic taxi service, releasing the pleasure molecules, the feeling chemicals, and, soon, the tight stress lines on the man's face were visible no more. A miracle! Relaxed, the patron lit a hand-rolled smoke and inhaled. A red disc glowed in the dim light.

"Well, my friend, how about putting a mug on? A mug to follow?" I asked.

"Aye, a mug now that I'm getting warm, but for real warmth on a night like this, there's only one way. It's a great night for snuggling up under a couple of blankets with a human hot water bottle, if you know what I mean. It sure is. Aye, lad. On a night like this, there's nothing else like it. I feel it in my bones."

"A night for the heather!, to be sure, but no hot water bottle for me."

"Well, then, Donald, how about a wee dram? Have one on me, lad."

"I don't mind if I do, my friend."

"What are you studying these days?"

I gave a brief account of what I was doing to further the more formal socially sanctioned aspects of my education-as opposed to real education-and the man laughed heartily. He knew. Intelligent, he was, yes; not formally indoctrinated in some institute of 'education.'

I was home on holiday from the big city, where I was in the early phase of studying to be a doctor of medicine, but that night the city was far away, and I was caretaker and bartender in *The Shack*. My role in *The Shack* was an avocation, a labor of love, it was a role that came naturally to me, and I made sure that, rain or shine, *The Shack* was open and ready for service by eight o'clock in the evening whenever I was in the village. Hours later I would douse the fire and close the door when the last man left, which would be in the wee hours of the morning on Fridays.

The Shack was a one-room structure with walls of dry stones sitting on top of each other in two vertical layers about ten inches apart, with black dirt packed in between the stones. No concrete. Some modest attempt at stone masonry was evident, but not much. Utilitarianism, not elegance, was what the volunteer builders went for in this place where they themselves were owners, patrons, negotiators, and whatever else might be required. No plumb lines were used during construction; no windows, and, crude as these walls were, they did what they were supposed to do, they provided shelter from the elements, they held up the roof, itself a rough and ready timber and thatch job held down with rope fastened to heavy stones resting on the outside tops of the walls. Poking out of this unruly thatch, slightly off-center, out of place as the only factory-built item visible from the outside, was a yellow clay chimney pot.

The chimney pot was a comfortable fit, like an old felt hat upon the head of a much traveled man, and yes, *The Shack* radiated a sense of maturity, even although it was by no means ancient as buildings went. Not at all. What was ancient about *The Shack* was nothing physical, but rather the function it performed in the community, which was timeless, like the secret reading of prohibited 'subversive' literature in an authoritarian regime, a foreign culture, it would have to be, to be sure, not our Oh so liberated Western cultures.

Symbolic of the deepest human longing for liberation from society's man made egocentric state of captivity; for mukti, for moksha, unspoken, maybe for something beyond words.

The Shack was a club, one without a license, without legal sanction, without a public sign to identify it, with no attempt at elegance, situated at the end of a dirt road pitted with pot-holes, on the edge of a misty, rolling, heather-covered moor. And its ambience was superb. A regal, robust, vibrant atmosphere pervaded the place. Inside it, one might expect to find men who lived by their own rules.

What kind of rules? Had this been a Saturday, closing time would have been at exactly 11:55 p.m. No violation of the Sabbath! It was about the only inviolable rule. But this was not Saturday; it was Friday. Well, there was one other 'rule,' if one were to insist, and that was the honor code regarding money, and, indeed, somehow the money balanced out exactly the way it was supposed to. It was hard to tell who was in charge of supplies, if anyone was, and indeed no one had that responsibility assigned to him. A wooden box. No lock. Congeniality.

Not that there wasn't opposition to *The Shack*. There had to be, otherwise it wouldn't have had much of a mission. After all, we were living in a dualistic culture, and, the wages of sin, some said, was death, and, to be sure, sin and booze were never far removed from each other. Some spoke of brew: stuff, illegal stuff, stuff that drove the youth away from what was good, constructive, towards what was destructive, evil; stuff, devil's brew, seductive stuff, and the young in a downward moral spiral, all because of *Stuff*.

That Bearded Old Man in the Sky again!, invisible, always present, always observant, that Being of rules, keeper of the balance sheets, deliverer of dire punishment to violators of His rules.

Eternal damnation wasn't something we spoke of, at least not in our family, but still, lurking somewhere inside us, there was that fear, barely conscious, sometimes forgotten, but never vanishing permanently. I didn't like it one bit, and I voted with my feet. I quit attending church while I was still in high school, walked away from the whole idea.

Laughing at the opposition to *The Shack,* pushing any hint of fear out of my awareness, not knowing that, by doing so, I was giving fear of God-and not the kind of fear that some consider evidence of faith-strength and power over my life and my fate, naively unaware of the tenacity of internalized values.

Living a double life.

The Shack was not the kind of club you would take your girlfriend or wife to for an evening of entertainment, but then no woman would ever want to go there anyway. No way! Quite apart from the obvious fact that women's bladder functions, and their sense of propriety, would not readily accommodate to the kind of open-air relief that men practiced, who could blame them for staying away? Ah, yes, the ambience.

A Tilley pressure paraffin lamp perched on the wall, slung from a slim, curving brass handle hammered into the wood for that purpose, provided light. Yes, there was a lining of wood on the insides of the walls. The brass pot of the lamp seemed to tighten as I pumped compressed air into it; for a moment the mantle hissed, then it swelled into a white glowing globe that gave off circles of red and yellow.

Next the stove: The men had acquired a cast-iron pot-bellied stove that sported a tall pipe leading up to and through a hole in the roof to the yellow chimney pot up top, but this dubious concession to modernity made next to no difference to the smokehouse effect within. The place might as well have been a smokehouse for kippers.

Ashes from the previous night's session had to be swept up, and, to that end, an old, long-handled broom and a short-handled shovel came in handy, so that the pile of ashes outside grew by several shovels full. Some of the ash, left in the bottom of the stove, helped nurture the fresh fire of dry peat and rolled-up newspaper, fueled by a dash of paraffin, lit by a tossed match, and soon a warm blaze roared bravely, sending hundreds of yellow sparks through the chimney pot into the heavens above.

Communion.

I cleaned the glasses, if that term could be applied to a process of dipping them a couple of times in a bucket of water from an old barrel that was half full of a bug-infested flow from a neighboring roof, followed by a careful wipe with a grimy rag that lay around the beer barrel, until they shone and sparkled like the crystal in a grand hotel. Ah, the glasses! Shot glasses for the whiskey, pint glasses for the beer, all laid out in a row on planks next to the tap. Then compressed air, pushed by a foot pedal, shot into the beer barrel, giving a satisfying hiss until the tap delivered a comfortable brew of foam-tipped dark liquid that warmed the hearts of working men of an evening.

On rare occasions, when I was a boy, I had had brief glimpses of the inside of that inner sanctum, with its dark doorway, its rough, open fire burning and smoking in the middle of the floor, its dancing shadows under a flickering lamp perched high on the wall. No stove in those days. Peat and tobacco smoke percolated everywhere, and aromatic it was, in a most esoteric way; stale day-old smoke combining with the rich smells of fresh peat-smoke, beer, whiskey, tobacco and sweat.

These early-life visits were infrequent, the visits of boys, brief eye-openers into the secret world of grown men. Not that the men minded when I told them wild stories about sexual adventures with girls. All lies, of course. What else? The men slapped their thighs. They roared belly-shaking laughter. A brief episode in my life. Rare visits that petered out, remote but not forgotten.

In December, when I was sixteen years old, I walked back into the smoke, the smell, the talk, the laughter, the camaraderie, and soon, someone gave me a key, a possession I prized, and the night after I got the key I came early, opened up, cleaned the place and made it ready for a good night's revelry. I had been accepted. I was in. Yes, finally, I had identity. I was in from the cold, snuggling as into a warm cozy aromatic woolly blanket next to a comfy blaze.

The Shack was a place of shadows, a place of mystery, a place of mysticism, a place where magic potions were mixed, a haven offering warmth not found in village life or in city life either, a temple offering magic journeys, spiritual journeys not of this world. Ah, the beauty!

The patrons were part-time crofters, part-time weavers of Harris Tweed, ex-sailors or active sailors, men who traveled around the world in the great ships of the Royal Navy and Merchant Navy, often in hostile surroundings and in harm's way. They were well qualified to serve on ocean-going ships, and they did so whenever they felt like it, coming and going several times a year, but when at home, in their cozy custom designed cove, content as clams, they celebrated life, they let their hair down, they rested, they reconstituted, they claimed the right to do so.

Brave men, brave and humble in the life roles assigned to them by fate, karma or destiny, subject as they were, despite their native intelligence, to the whims of windbag rhetorician rulers of nations, medal laden controllers of masses.

And so the lads arrived, one by one, dressed in bib-top dungarees, sweaters, denim jackets and caps worn at work all day; dungarees and caps showing mileage; light-blue denim, fading, looking exactly right in that primitive place of entertainment; men drinking, smoking, laughing at old stories told and retold, finding comfort in each other's company, rubbing elbows, touching souls. And in the dungarees there were bulges, some round, some rectangular, outlines of tins of tobacco, from which, one by one, as the spirit moved them, men extracted tobacco that they dropped into paper wrapper cylinders that they rolled smoothly, licked, inserted between their lips. Matches sprang to life against rough denim, against tough thumb nails, followed by deep satisfying drags. Pints of beer and shots of whiskey moved around the room from man to man. Empties made return trips for refills. The warm glow within me was in harmony with the warmth of the finally blazing fire.

Enter a tall lanky smiling man with a battered soft hat on his head. A brightly colored fishing fly stuck into the hat, a five-o'clock shadow on his chin, a pair of Knickerbockers on his legs. It was The Driver. A thousand welcomes, Driver! The Driver, sitting in the warm, covered cabin of his truck, had lumbered along the single narrow winding road, groaning up hills, squealing into glens, lurching into the wind, but, like the agreeable reliable man of his word that he was, arriving in good time with *The Stuff*. He was like a congenial half-apologetic distinguished philosophical man of gentle birth who had fallen upon hard times, like a titled man from the south, a man of artistic tastes, a man who found himself compelled to make do as best as he could in a world that failed to appreciate his dignified aristocratic status, a world that permitted a refined gentleman no option but to commercialize his talent.

No sooner did The Driver show up than I sprang into action, a couple of men joined me, all three of us slipped silently out the door, and minutes later we returned carrying a forty-five gallon barrel of beer. A second barrel followed, then a dozen bottles of Scotch whiskey.

The Driver never took part in gossip. No way. Always amiable, always pleasant, polite, never off color, seemingly pliable but never vulnerable, always in control of his words-no angry words ever out of his mouth-, and, as for his conduct, beyond reproach, a perfect gentleman.

But The Driver was no abstainer, and, after the supplies had been safely stashed away, he accepted a generous glass of whiskey and there he stood, in front of the stove, by then glowing warmly in a friendly way, and he smiling like a happy Cheshire cat ensconced indoors and comfy, out of the cold and the rain, but, of course, it was no Cheshire cat that was holding the glass elegantly aloft in his right hand, his pipe in his left hand at chin level, sipping the whiskey as if it was fine Japanese green tea and he a connoisseur of the same, a wee story to deliver, a tale to hear.

The glass held high contained liquid gold, a magical potion that, against the mellow glow from the lamp, flowed and swirled and left behind, clinging to the inside of the glass, a series of drops and lean flowing streams. The liquor sang and sparkled with an inner fire. No wonder they called it *uisge-beatha!*, the 'water of life.' Yes, indeed, it had life in it. Beautiful! Would it not be a grand idea to distill the *uisge-beatha* for myself? A clean cold brook erupted like a natural fountain out of a green hillside next to a remote beach. It would be easy to hide the still in any of the numerous crevices in the neighboring terrain. I knew the place like the back of my hand. It was one of the places where I loved to wander alone: walking, climbing, resting in the shelter of the slope, contemplating, feeling complete in the beauty of life, far removed from the life I led in the city, in a duality culture, its citizens drawn towards values based on splintered perception, interpersonal competition, the pursuit of what was transient, and away from life based on what was permanent.

It wasn't the first time I had had the idea of distilling the *uisge beathe*. Indeed, it was a fantasy I toyed with from time to time over the years, and it felt real to me, as an avocation, something to enjoy in more ways than one, but not in an entrepreneurial kind of way, not as a way of making a living, it being too noble a calling to be reduced to labor market level.

The Shack, despite its being a social blessing, had its limitations. What if a man became desperate when *The Shack* was closed, such as for example on a Sunday? or early on Monday morning? Too bad! Or maybe not, according to certain people, but then again the way they said it, and the ones who said it, and the manner of reporting, and much more, would have to be taken into consideration when weighing the evidence, as many intuitively did. What kind of Islander would be a violator of the Sabbath?, or such a rotten scum as to stock up on whiskey on week nights so as to sell it at a premium on off days? Such gossip was clearly not to be taken seriously. Why, apart from myself, there wasn't one of the men who didn't darken the church doors fairly regularly, and serious about it too.

Friday nights were usually busy, and this Friday night was no exception, and, so it was that some men socialized and some did not have much to say, or so it seemed. One contented looking patron who had spent most of the evening smiling broadly at no one in particular suddenly changed his bland expression to a scowl. "He told me I had ears like red cabbages," he said. "What do you make of that? I may have red hands, but that's from hard work in cold surroundings, but I don't have big red ears." A pint glass, its dark liquid contents swirling to and fro, was in his right hand; his left hand was a fist that rested on his knee. He raised his voice: "To hell with him. He should be rounded up. He should be straight jacketed. Tarpaulin him. There's a farm for people like him."

"Who the hell are you talking about?"

"Why ask? He thought he had a great plan for winning the pools, and I invested a few bob in it myself, but of course he won nothing, and his plan went to the far winds, then one night when I happened to mention it to him casually like, and me being very polite, as I usually am, and minding my manners, the bloody bugger dropped a couple of red hot cinders, full of ashes and muck out of the stove, into my pint."

"Sure and it must have made a frothing foaming brew, just like fresh warm milk from a fat well-fed cow. Morning milk. Mother's milk. You ought to know about that"

"Who are you calling a big fat cow?"

"Easy does it. What about a game of 'Catch-a-Ten?'"

"There was this man called Bones...."

"Too many cinders spoil the broth, or is it the beer?"

"Who said something about mother's milk?"

The story of *The Shack* began when a few men got together and started to meet regularly to socialize, converse and share community concerns. To that end they chose an old building to serve as a clubhouse. On rare occasions they would purchase a keg of beer, enough to deliver a modest libation. It was a good idea, and yes, its time had come, but then, as the years rolled by, and hard liquor arrived on the scene, the booze began to flow more freely, the hours stretched out to their farthest limit, and duality reared its head.

"We mustn't stay too late tonight, boys, on account of the tragedy and all...."

"What are you talking about, man?"
"Oh, nothing at all; just remembering, is all."
"What tragedy?"
"Well, there might just be one. Who can tell?"
"I'm just here for a quiet pint."
"Still, when you come to think of it...."
"What's the harm? is what I say. What would she say?"
"It's herself who would take a dram whenever she had a chance."
"Exactly what I'm thinking myself."
"What do you think she would say?, I mean if she were right here where we're at ourselves. She would tell us to go ahead and celebrate, is what she herself would say, and don't I know for sure?"
"'Have one on me, boys,' is what she would say."
"No doubt about it, she's a grand lassie, none better in all the land."
"Oh, to be sure, the best in the world."
"None more hospitable, especially to lads away from home, as we so often are. Like a mother away from home."

And I was a dry straw thatch soaking up the soft floating mist blowing in from the sea in summer time, and there was more to the mist than moisture.

In that place, I felt in harmony. A few well-meaning people advised me, accompanied by serious admonitions and dire predictions, to stay away from *The Shack*, but my parents, to their credit, were not among these advisors, and, in any case, I laughed heartily at advice whenever the giver of the advice was out of sight and out of hearing. Who ever heard of good advice? Hadn't the principal of the high-school lectured us at irregular intervals during my time there?, ranting and raving about gentlemanly conduct, about moderation in all things, about the desirability of conducting ourselves with decorum? And was he not right in all that he said? Well, let him do what he wanted with his advice-keep it for himself if it was that good.

In *The Shack,* the company was relaxed, conversation was

easy, there were no clocks, no collars, no ties, no eagle eyes, no Established Authority, and the men sitting in a circle spoke of ships they sailed in, ships with exotic names cruising into exotic ports where exciting men and women did exciting things; they spoke of far-away lands, lands that I too would visit one day, lands that beckoned me with their warmth, their colors, their complex aromas, their melodious music.

A man, who had been quiet for some time, as if in contemplation, suddenly straightened up out of his slouch, stabbed the air in front of him with a black pipe that trailed blue smoke behind it, and he spoke up: "If there's any law that's worse than the law of Hong Kong, I'd like to know about it."

"What'd you do? Were you fighting with the Chinese?"

"Did you order Chinese food and refuse to pay for it?"

"Were you fighting with the Maoris?"

"Shut up, you idiot, the Maoris are in New Zealand."

"Don't I know it, lad. I've been to a few Maori parties myself."

"Listen, lads, I don't know whether you'll believe me or not, but there I was, minding my own business, simply coming off of a one, taking a stroll, enjoying the fresh night air, if you know what I mean, when all of a sudden a swarm of cops surrounded me. They jumped all over me, and as everybody knows, I'm not exactly a wimp. How many men do you know who can toss a full beer barrel over his head as easily as I can? I tell you, I have more hair on my chest than the Queen of Sheba in the days of her glory had on her fanny. Well, for a moment I made as if to brawl it out, all six feet four inches of me, but then I changed my mind and went along with them, so in I went, into their damn wagon, just like a wee lamb, which, as you know, is not like me at all at all, especially when someone is giving me orders I don't like. And what did I find inside that wagon? A bunch of the finest most honest-looking citizens I've ever laid eyes on, that's what. 'What did you do?' I asked them. 'Nothing,' they all chorused. Well, not exactly a chorus in perfect harmony, like a Gaelic choir, but close enough."

"'Neither did I,' I said. 'I haven't done anything.'

"And what do you think the cops were doing all the time? Laughing; laughing at us!"

19: IF IT WASN'T FOR ONE THING

The muffled din of men's voices, a dusty floor, dim lights over the bar, rows of multi-colored bottles, reflections in the ornate mirror, visions into mystery beyond dilemma, music to my ears, and beauty, a mysterious universe, ready to be explored, no limits at all: Would I like to cavort and romp and frolic and indulge in holy visions of ultimate beauty, transcending mundane dimension, imagination roaming freely, all in one room? Magic! Well, some other time. On second thoughts, why not?
I walked upstairs to the lounge on the second floor. A pint of beer and a shot of whiskey would do just fine, and Ishbel-not a real identity-was there serving, cleaning, mothering.

"One more round, Ishbel. Same again, please," a man next to me said, ordering for his table.

Ishbel, the barmaid, had the bored look of a woman who had seen it all, had heard enough, and who would listen, or at least mechanically go through the motions of listening, but not take anything she heard in that place seriously. She shone empties casually, she held the glasses up to the light to check on how bright and clear they were, she laid the glasses down on a shelf underneath the bar, out of sight of the patrons, but she interrupted her routine to take the order, and, as she refilled the glasses, she wore a mini-smile, more like a relaxation of her facial muscles than a genuine smile, reminiscent of titled nobility in a Rolls, and, to be sure, her face had yet to harden. The expression in her eyes was neutral. The men knew Ishbel, or at least they behaved as if they did; they approached her in a familiar way, they referred to her by name, and they seemed to derive a special pleasure from uttering her name, and from hearing her repeat their names.

I know her personally, you know."

A shot and a pint each....The man at the bar made two trips to the table with his order. He sat down in his chair, he lit another cigarette.

"Aye," said his drinking buddy, an over-coated man, in a voice that carried in that almost empty room. "You're the best friend I have, and I don't mind telling the world, not a bit of it, no, not for a single solitary moment."

"We two go back a long way, sure enough."

"It's a great thing, friendship. I've been around, here and there, and I can tell you and I'm the one who knows it and all, and I ask you: What can be better than friendship? Nothing; is what I say myself. Nothing! and I tell you, indeed, without a doubt, one of my best friends in the old days was an Englishman. Think of that."

"Indeed what?"

"Aye, although I'm not one for boasting or anything like that, but when I say I've been around, I really mean it, as I'm sure you'll appreciate yourself, and I'll tell you something else.... Now, I wouldn't tell this to another soul, not one, so it's just between me and you,...Right? It's like this...it's like this: I'm really one hell of a smart highly intelligent man of parts, but I keep all that to myself, as you yourself know."

The expression on his face might have been world-weary if it belonged in another context, not in a place such as this, but as it was his facial muscles were relaxed, his jaw loose, his eyelids heavy, his movements slow and deliberate, and his speech measured, and so world-weariness might be questionable, which is not to deny him his world-weariness, for what it's worth.

"I know I'm the one that's saying it, and you know yourself I don't like to boast, but I'm brilliant, is what I am. Brilliant!"

The man with his back to me seemed to have a different opinion, judging by the way he sank in his chair and by the low but urgent tone of voice he used, as if he was suggesting to his friend that it might be wise to keep it quiet, to stop drawing attention to himself, but the self-styled genius wasn't hearing, or maybe he chose to ignore…"I'll tell you something else, I could do anything. Aye, my friend, anything; that is to say, of course, *if it wasn't for one thing!*"

Friend stretched his right hand out to the pint glass and he moved it a little sideways on the wet table top, leaving a wide untidy trail of beer, and then he moved his change so as to rescue it from the dark brew. Too late! A bank note, with Her Majesty's portrait on it, was already soaking wet, smudged and crumpled. "Without a doubt you're way ahead of me, that's for sure, but why don't you tell me about it tomorrow, not tonight. OK?"

"It's myself that says it, but who knows what I'd be doing and all, maybe a brain surgeon or a ship's captain, that is, if I set my mind on it."

If it wasn't for one thing.

Maybe dark bitter beer as chasers for whiskey in a pub on a wind-blown low-sky half-rainy night, when gazed into, might act as a mirror that would reflect from the depths of a man's mind some secret fantasy that would inspire him to become what he never could aspire to in dull routine workadays, but of course the gift of membership in the Noble and Exalted Society of Boozy Dreamers was not for everybody, not at all at all, only for a select few, to be sure, aye, so let it be.

I didn't crave alcohol, and neither, I suspected, did most of the patrons. What I craved was intimacy. I wanted inner warmth. Something was missing from me the way I was, or so it felt like. Had I lost intimacy? Had I lost the capacity for love? I knew I was warm and affectionate inside, but my outside was remote; it had to be, but, regardless, I had come into this life in order to find love, again, something I intuitively knew, and another thing, my powers of intuition worked well for me, realizations from deep within, snuggling myself warmly, satisfying sensations, shutting out the world, alone, contemplating, visualizing, reaching out, doing.

Maybe I was perfect the way I was. Maybe trying to fit into a rigid authoritarian controlled system we called society presented a situation, or maybe something was missing from the world's cultures; aye, indeed, no maybe about it, there was plenty missing, freedom for one thing, mutual cross-cultural respect, unconditional love for another, but we didn't talk about such matters.

Or, maybe the world's societies were exactly the way they were supposed to be, I was exactly the way I was supposed to be, there was no fault, no one to blame, neither another nor myself, and my sense of alienation came from my ignorance of who I was at the core, why I was in this life, and the superstitious beliefs I had about manipulating my destiny, and about attaching blame to others or circumstances for what I didn't like.

Meantime, no longer alienated, the spirit gliding with me in its arms, communing with me, releasing me from the demands that I imagined others placed upon me, from what I imagined others wanted from me, and maybe, just for a little while, I would be one with the whole universe. Why not? My mood escalated into a lofty sphere, my heart lightened up, I smiled inwardly. Life was good; aye, to be sure, life was.

Tables, rickety ones to be sure, there were, and seats with shiny slippery covers, which was more than could be said for the public bar downstairs, where men for the most part, and occasionally some women, drank and talked and rubbed against each other, and smoked and laughed and babbled, and told stories, short ones, and not well told, but good because they worked, good because they weren't commercialized, good because they were spontaneous, good because no one claimed personal credit for any of them, and they worked.

And two men sitting at a table in the lounge, imbibing, smoking, sharing and airing fantasies as intimate as pillow talk; two men bonding on a whiskey night, out of the cold, in the warmth, out of the dark, in the mellow light, forgetting impossible dilemmas; two men on the drinking side of a duality in which the other side raved against booze, and needed booze just as much as those who drank it, just as surely as dry needed wet, as surely as up needed down, as surely as north needed south, as surely as vice needed virtue, as surely as saints needed sinners. We lived a life of twos. Who among us had ever heard of patiently allowing the oneness of life to arise within us? Who had ever heard of transcending the double nature of our human mental processes? How were we to know that our debates were divisive?

Certainly not I, and, if those who comprised that august body known as Established Authority had in their travels heard of transcending ego to experience a state of oneness with the rest of life, they failed to appreciate it, as far as I could tell, based on what I heard and read about them. And, in our lives, whiskey worked to maintain the status quo, in that it offered occasional brief periods of relief to those of us who labored to serve Established Authority, to those of us who voted for laws that favored The Establishment, to the obedient and to the disobedient, the disobedient being also obedient, come to think of it. Maybe that's the way it had to be. Maybe that's the way we all wanted life to be. Maybe we were blind, all of us.

The Overcoat, the one facing me, was or appeared to be deep in his own thoughts or fantasies, he paid me no attention, nor did he seem to care whether or not I was aware of him. He was also collared and tied. He had a mess of unruly hair and a face that had soaked in sunshine not available in Scotland, and he had cut himself shaving, or so it seemed, in two places, and I knew that, if that were indeed so, his hand must have been unsteady, unusual for a sailor, and the Islanders were among the world's best sailors.

The man with his back to me was the older of the two men. He was dressed in a brown suit, wearing a pair of polished new shoes, on his head a soft felt hat, but he wore no overcoat, and he had the hands of a crofter, strong and brown. He also spoke in the soft gentle accent of an Islander who lived permanently on the Island, as opposed to one who lived abroad and who visited the Island occasionally from some faraway land, to which he had emigrated, searching-for what?

Ishbel shone glasses, standing behind the bar, next to the large square ashtray that held a burning cigarette, but Ishbel was not of the dreamers, although, to be sure, she was quiet capable of enjoying a party when she felt like it, which wasn't too often, or so it was rumored among those who gossiped about such things. However, in her role as barmaid, which itself was no mean performance, she was superb. There wasn't a single story she didn't smile at, if not indeed laugh at, but by the end of the evening, she simply wanted to go home, rest her legs and relax, bless her heart.

And the ceiling lights, viewed hazily through the empty glasses that Ishbel held up periodically for inspection, just like a good mother, beamed a dreamy series of circles, streaks and splashes of yellow, green and gold, a work of art, that, without Ishbel, and to other than members of the Noble and Exalted Society of Boozy Dreamers, would not have been.

...if it wasn't for one thing....

20: MARJORIE

Saturday night and cigarette smoke hovered in the air the length and breadth of the room, just above head level, a gray semi-transparent fluff that rolled and writhed and wriggled like fog in a late-night movie graveyard scene. But this was no movie, the night was still young, and students stood all over the floor in the dim light, bodies jostling each other, their voices a hubbub.
I didn't think of myself as a tightly controlled man, I didn't think of myself as a man in need of relaxation by means of a chemical substance, I didn't think of myself as striving to please others, I didn't think of myself as fearing "Authority," fearing that if I failed to please "Authority," someone in authority would retaliate mercilessly against me. What exactly would "they" do to me? Humiliate me? Take away whatever I had? Render me powerless? Whatever it was, I had to protect myself. I imagined everybody thought the way I did, but, paradoxically, I imagined that other men had something I didn't have, and that, consequently, they felt complete, confident and in control.

Well, it was time for me to change. I would take action. I wanted to get what other men had. I wanted to be what other men were. Yes, indeed.

What better way of becoming a real man than through a woman? Yes, a woman would make a man out of me. A woman would fill the void within; maybe even take the place of booze, then again, maybe not. Well, there were young women upstairs on the dance floor. I felt something warm in my middle. I straightened up my shoulders. Upstairs I went.

Ambling across the floor of the ballroom, I found myself face to face with a young woman, and a few moments later we were dancing together. Her name was Marjorie. We danced together several times that night, I felt comfortable in her company, and that in itself was significant, seeing that, in the company of most young women I felt threatened, imagining that they wanted something from me that I couldn't deliver or I didn't have. And so it was that I avoided most young women, or abandoned them, before they had a chance to betray me. But that night was different.

"It's not been a great day," I said to Marjorie.

"Why? What went wrong?" she asked.

"My motorbike went on fire," I said, laughing.

"What?"

"I just bought it a few days ago. It's a big one, a Royal Enfield 500cc. The throttle jammed wide open, and the exhaust pipe fell off. Flames were shooting out of the engine where the exhaust pipe had been attached. The flames were next to the petrol supply line and getting close to the petrol tank. The tank was full. This scene went on for several minutes. I tried switching the engine off, no luck. Finally, I remembered that there was a valve somewhere in the fuel supply line and I managed to close it. The petrol tank was actually hot by this time. Another couple of minutes and it might have exploded. If it had...."

Marjorie looked at me with a gentle but skeptical expression on her face, an expression that suggested that she didn't want to tell me I was full of it, although she knew I really was, and that she was prepared to listen to me, but not take my story at face value. It was a complex expression she had on her face. As for me, I was laughing. Why? What did I have to laugh about? Not much, by my account, but then again my laughter was in part a substitute for crying, as laughter sometimes is when we suppress what we don't like to confront, but then the 'unconscious' communicates mutually in non-verbal ways, which was one reason that Marjorie was giving me the once-over visually not so lightly.

"What about this motorbike?" she asked.

"Oh, it isn't new; it's a used bike."

"Sounds like somebody sold you a dud."

"It wasn't in good shape. I didn't know."

"It's broken, isn't it? Something's missing from it."

"Missing or wrong inside…and of course, the exhaust pipe is all burned up now, after its trial by fire."

"Can it be fixed?"

"Of course it can be fixed, but it'll cost me, and I do want it to work smoothly the way it's supposed to work. I saved up money I earned during summer break on a dam-building site in the Highlands."

"Heartbreaking! Are you sure you weren't cheated?"

"I'm not heartbroken."

"At least you must be angry. I would be, if it was me. What about your investment? You bought a broken machine."

"I'm not angry, Marjorie. I'll work on it. I know what I'm doing. I wasn't taken in. Maybe I was deceived, maybe not, maybe I deceived myself. Anyway, all I need is a good mechanic."

"Yes, I'm sure a good mechanic can work wonders."

"I like talking to you, Marjorie."

"Where do you live, Donald?"

I told her where I lived, in a rented room not far away. I said, "I walked here tonight. I didn't come by motorbike! Can I take you home?"

"Well, I don't know. I came with two girl-friends, and we'll be going home together."

"So, why don't you check with them? Maybe they'll go home without you."

A few minutes later she was back. "Yes, you can ride home with me, walk me home," she said. It meant a bus ride from the city center to the suburbs. We got off the bus at a bus stop close to her home, she then turned to me and said, "The last bus to the city leaves in a few minutes. You had better stay here and take it, so I'll say 'Good night' to you, Donald."

"Good night. Maybe I'll see you next week."

I was feeling better already. I was about to become an adult male, an authentic grownup, a take-charge hirsute type; I would be fearless, I would be strong, I would be decisive, a real man among men. Wasn't that what we were supposed to be? Like the heroes we saw on Saturday nights in the local cinema.

The following Monday found me at a garage, where an mechanic, clearly identifiable by his thick brogue, said to me: "I hope you're grateful to your parents for all they're doing for you. No doubt they're paying for all this. Do you ever stop to think of that? Do you remember all the sacrifices your parents made for you? Do you? Have you forgotten how much you owe them?"

Was this some guilt ridden shame driven Southern Irish Catholic? Taken by surprise, and right on the button, I couldn't think of an answer, so I paid and left riding my beautiful as-new machine feeling ashamed of myself for practically taking the bread out of the mouths of my parents in order to buy a motorbike for my pleasure, self-centered, narcissistic, exploitative, no good, un-Christian, devious creature that I was. The bike was supposed to have empowered me. It was to have delighted me. Well, it had let me down, just like....I became angry. Angry! And what about this damn preacher-moralist-mechanic? What the hell did he know of my parents? What did he know of me? To hell with him! To hell with him and his sermon! My bike was good, a viable part of me, no less.

Soon, I was proficient in maneuvering and maintaining the machine, I fell in love with it, I drove it night and day, I drove it through sleet, rain and sunshine, I drove it through cities, down valleys, up hills and across plains. It was indeed a durable machine, and it practically became a part of me over time. Marjorie often rode behind me, closing her eyes when cornering, with her arms around my middle, fearless.

As a rider, goggles protecting my eyes, gray khaki overalls shielding me from cold and wet, right hand gripping the throttle, I felt some of the sense of freedom, of connectivity, of oneness, of joy, that I used to feel when I was alone and naked on a beach on the Island, or fishing alone in the glen, but not all of it, for something in me seemed to have changed. I had lost something. I couldn't identify what I had lost. Something was missing, to be sure, that much I imagined intuitively, but I had no one to talk it over with, nor did it occur to me that I should.

I didn't know that self-examination honestly performed was a noble undertaking. Self-examination! What was that anyway? I had no real education. I didn't know that what passed for education was indoctrination into society's group think and introduction and training in some socially desirable skill, an apprenticeship in how to be useful to Authority-not in questioning basic premises-in ways that would be rewarded, so long as one toed the line. Well, at least I didn't know too much, and I kept my questions to myself.

On the coldest and wettest of days, the warmth of the engine between my legs was always comforting, its roar encouraging; always there was another slope to climb, another hill to crest, another valley to roll into, another plateau to streak my way across, and the two-lane highway stretched to the horizon, with the end of the road never in sight. I never wanted it to be. I felt restless, on the move, motivated by something within, like a man in pursuit of the secret of life.

Why not ride all the way to London? Edinburgh to London was a long way, but what the heck! The following Easter break I went off alone, heading south, and when I reached London I simply drove right into the great metropolis with its throbbing traffic, its complexity of streets, and its millions of people. What a place! Was this not where the British Museum was located? where the Houses of Parliament were located? where the largest hospitals in the country were? and where the Queen lived? London had the biggest of everything, including the biggest of all houses, if one could call Buckingham Palace a house. Before my visit was over, I too felt bigger, more educated, more adept, more world-wise.

The time came for me to return to Edinburgh, and off I went riding north, and I hadn't gone many miles before the sky darkened, the temperature dropped, and rain began to fall. This was not the soft-as-silk summer rain of the Island that I was accustomed to, it was a cold driving April rain that sent a chill right through my khaki overalls, it sent thousands of tiny icy spears of water into my face, it numbed my ears, it half-paralyzed my fingers, even although I wore gloves. The goggles at least helped protect my eyes. The rain, however, was part of a wide, slow-moving storm that I couldn't get out of, but I rode on. Towards noon, it got even colder, the wind blew more fiercely, and I seemed to be the only motorbike rider on the highway. By mid-afternoon, it was no longer rain that was driving into my face, it was sleet.

Visibility was poor, the road was icy, I was icy within, but the engine delivered warmth where I wanted it, and its steady roar was comforting even if somewhat hypnotic. Occasionally, I had to slow down to negotiate one of the roundabouts that were situated at intervals on long stretches of road. Roundabouts were stone circles inside of which were flower beds, the purpose of which was to slow traffic and to allow for cross-traffic. Somewhere in the north of England I hit a roundabout, and it was exactly in the middle of its flower bed that I landed head first. Head first up to my chin! Happy landings! One moment of total darkness, then I was up and on my feet like a circus performer who had just orchestrated the whole thing. Several men came running towards me. Soft black earth that had saved me from injury was plastered all over my face. My beautiful motorbike lay on its side, its rear wheel spinning freely, not touching road surface.

Before you could say Away we go, I was once again seated in my favorite position, the engine kicked faithfully into its usual friendly roar, and off I went. I wanted to put miles between me and any nosy policeman who might have been in the vicinity. The last thing I wanted was a man in a dark uniform with shiny buttons and a peaked hat asking me questions, demanding to see my driving license, writing things down in a notebook, staring at me.

It was night when I got back to Edinburgh, and, instead of going to my cold empty downtown flat right away, I went to Marjorie's house, just to visit along the way, and there, bone-weary, black-faced, numb with cold, and ecstatically happy, I sat down to a generous glass of whiskey and a hot bath, followed by a hearty meal and a clean bed, in which I fell fast asleep in no time at all. Deep, dreamless sleep, sleep without ego, replenishing sleep, sleep in which, I later learned, I was at one in my deepest soul, my Atman, with my Creator for re-energizing.

21: FATEFUL ANNIVERSARY

Marjorie climbed into the rear entrance of a double-decker rust-colored City-of-Edinburgh bus, the pneumatic doors hissed shut behind her, and, for a moment her bright-red coat, her red shoes, and her hair falling darkly over her shoulders, flung a page of fashion into the street, then she vanished into the crowd of night riders.

I stood on the sidewalk, on the receiving end of a soft drizzle of rain, overwhelmed by a profound conviction that Marjorie and I belonged together. Yes, I was in love with Marjorie, and she with me, I knew that we were destined for each other, but I didn't know how to talk about love. As if to do so would make me vulnerable, open to exploitation, naked, alone, and, embarrassing, it was, as if there was something to be ashamed of, and maybe, at some level, there was, at least according to infantile fantasy, that ghost-like haunting fantasy that always seemed to hover around, injecting itself into the on-going drama and comedy of our lives, but there I was, savoring the aroma of Marjorie's hair, reminiscent of fresh fruit and greenery, of heather bloom.

The ponderous vehicle lumbered away from the sidewalk, splashing through the rain puddles, it slowly picked up speed as the engine responded to the gear shifts, then it receded into the flowing traffic; finally it vanished into the blur of city lights, a resonant groan fading away.

The following evening, Marjorie and I went out together.

It was the second anniversary of the night we first met. We both liked small warm cozy restaurants where we could relax and enjoy each other's company in an ambience we delighted in. That was what we wanted that night, and, to that end, we chose a place we knew on the High Street. The chef, standing by a blazing fire inside a rock and cast-iron oven in the middle of the room, prepared our meal for us. He placed melted butter in an omelet pan, along with sliced mushrooms, he swirled it together until the mixture was soft, he broke several eggs and he spilled that mixture into a bowl, where he beat it up. He then added two tablespoons of water, followed by a dash of milk. He took the buttered mushrooms out of the pan, put them aside, slid the beaten egg mixture into the same pan with one hand while holding it over the flames with the other hand, and, as the eggs cooked, he drew them into the middle, folding the mixture up one third. He laid the mushrooms delicately on top of the eggs and folded the remaining two thirds of the half-cooked preparation over. For a minute he left the delicacy alone, and then he flipped it on to a plate, almost ready to be served. A culinary delight.

The wine was Italian Chianti, poured out of a pot-bellied bottle wrapped in woven straw, the music was Vivaldi, our table was a small one, its cover decorated with a brightly colored flowery pattern that poured over the edges in folds that felt cool to the touch of my knees, presumably to Marjorie's.

The subtle aroma of delicious food expertly prepared permeated the room; the sound of muffled conversation was a pleasant background hum, the waitress wore a small, smart-looking apron. In her right hand she bore a long wooden match that hissed in a mild kind of way as it flamed. A candle stood in a holder in a cool-looking pewter bowl in the middle of the table. She lit it. Soon, wax flowed down the side of the candle, a candle crowned with a silent flame.

Marjorie smiled at me; I smiled at Marjorie; I reached under the table for her hand; I found it on her left knee, she opened her hand, we touched, we held hands, we tingled together, the candle-light lit up Marjorie's face from below, shadows danced around her eyes, and the minutes raced by all too quickly. Or else time stood still, or both. Finally, it was time to go home.

It was dark when we returned on board the last bus of the evening to the quiet residential suburb where Marjorie lived. I expected to walk back to my own flat in town after leaving Marjorie at her doorway, and, arm in arm, in the quiet darkness, we approached the house. What? A strange car was parked outside the garden gate. Who could it be so late in the evening? What could it mean? No visitors were expected. The car didn't look all that friendly. It had an ominous authoritarian look about it, dark. I glanced at Marjorie, but I had nothing to say, being less sensitized to alterations in her family circumstances than she was. We hastened our approach to the front door, and the moment we opened it, we sensed the presence of strangers in the house. There were two men in trench coats standing in the living room, hats held in their hands, next to Marjorie's mother, who was also standing. All three of them stared at us as we walked in. There was a moment of silence, then Marjorie's mother said, "Daddy's gone. He's passed away. Gone."

"What? Passed away! What happened?"

"He passed away on the street, Princes Street. He just collapsed," Marjorie's mother said.

One of the policemen spoke: "It was a heart attack, we believe."

The other policeman said, "His pipe was in his mouth. It must have been very sudden. He passed away immediately."

"We understand he had a history of heart disease," said the first officer.

"Yes, that's true. He was taking medication for angina pectoris, but we thought it was well controlled," I said. I could talk comfortably enough about a clinical disorder, I could talk about disease in an intellectual clinical way, but when it came to revealing my own emotions when confronting human mortality, I was no better at it than anyone else, despite my medical studies, or possibly because of them. Death was remote, no warmth, no aroma of fresh mown hay, of seaweed, of heather; mysterious it was, but somehow, it seemed to me, associated with the secret of life, fascinating.

The policemen were in civilian clothes, but, having delivered their message, there was little else they could say that would be meaningful. One of them was exactly my height. We looked directly into each other's eyes. His were bland, minimally expressive, controlled benign, and his hair was combed to the right, with a divide on the left side. He held his hat in his left hand. He was about thirty five years old. The other policeman, who was forty years old at least, said, "Well, we must be going. We're sorry about the sudden bad news. Let us know if there's anything else we can do for you." The two men walked out the door and departed, probably happy to get it over with, and we never saw them again. There was, of course, 'nothing else' they could do for us.

Marjorie had only recently finished college and started teaching. Her first assignment was not an easy one, the students were rowdy, but Marjorie was a good learner, her skills were improving steadily and she was becoming competent. Alfred, her father, and Janet, her mother, had just returned from a trip to Norway, which was in celebration of their twenty fifth wedding anniversary. The trip had gone well for them. Marjorie had received frequent post cards from her father. She and her father loved each other in a healthy way.

The three of us stood in the living room. Marjorie did not cry. Neither did her mother. Neither did I. We were stoics. Marjorie's mother asked me to stay overnight and I agreed to do that. We talked about generalities. Relatives were notified. Friends called to express their support and some came by to visit. They were kind, they expressed condolences, they spoke in low voices, they held their eyes downcast, for, after all, they were almost at a funeral, and they themselves were still alive.

The Old Man with the Scythe was among us, unseen, unheard, silent, invisible, uninvited, a threatening presence, and, of course, He would know, yes, He would know what it was about love that embarrassed us, what we were ashamed of, that frightened us, or maybe he was nothing but a fantasy, and he knew nothing, for no one actually believed in such imaginary bogeys any more, if they ever did, or even spoke seriously about them, and certainly I didn't, but then again, fantasies had consequences...jokes also, cartoons, and yes, stories told by mothers to children.

Marjorie's favorite aunt arrived on the day of the funeral with two tranquilizers that she had obtained from her own doctor, one for Marjorie and one for Marjorie's mother. Marjorie swallowed her medicine, whatever it was, and maybe she felt more tranquil as a result, for her aunt, a good-natured woman, was being kind, sharing her sedative feel-good medicine.

But there was a family acquaintance whose dog had died on the same day that Marjorie's father passed away. What a coincidence! Or maybe it wasn't a coincidence at all. The dog had grown fond of milk as she aged, and also had taken up chasing cats in the neighborhood. The dog had been beautiful, a thoroughbred, with papers to prove it, fit to stroll among the gentry at dog shows, in her younger years. Maybe Marjorie's father would feed saucers of milk to Maggie the dog in heaven, while watching out for stray cats!

"What? Who said that? Feeding saucers of milk to Maggie the dog in heaven! How absurd!" I said to Marjorie.

"He's just an acquaintance. He lives far away from us. We haven't seen him in years."

Enough of that!

A profound sense of loss at the sudden death, and some disbelief, as if maybe the policemen would return with better news, but they didn't and they wouldn't and of course death was final, irrevocable, but also mysterious; in a way unthinkable. How hard it was for me to contemplate my own death. I had never openly expressed my affection and respect for Marjorie's father while he was alive. I had grown up in a culture where young people, at least in my family, did not talk openly about their feelings with senior men and women, and even although I was in my twenties, I was still a student in a strange city, I felt junior in status, and not only that, but everyone in the city, at least the ones I met, worked hard at producing, progressing and mastering their personal worlds, and at controlling the events of their lives. It was a way of life that ensured that there was little time left over for, or inclination for, contemplation of life itself, or of birth, or of the purpose of life, or of death, and when death struck like a trap-door slamming shut in the night, taking Marjorie's father away from us permanently, we felt betrayed.

Angry? Who wouldn't be? An interesting question.

I was preparing myself for a career as a physician, hoping to serve the sick, the wounded and the lame, I had high ideals, I was young and vigorous, so what possible reason had I to fear death? None that I knew of. After all, The Old Man with the Scythe would not be visiting me for a long time, I believed, so why bother to think about it? or about meeting the Other Old Man, the one with the beard? Both mental images of the one, idolatry. What did I know of Self? or of reality beyond space and time? or of Atman? or of Brahman? What did I know of birth? I had no idea that, if I wanted to know something about death, I would be well advised to learn something about birth, I would be well advised to ask myself seriously, until I found an answer: *Who am I?*

When Alfred left the office that evening to return home, he didn't know he was closing the door behind him for the last time, and, as he walked along the street and lit his pipe, he didn't know he was lighting it for the last time, he didn't know he was about to take his last couple of puffs of tobacco smoke, and Marjorie and I, in another part of the city, ate, drank and made merry, totally oblivious of the tragedy striking deeply into her family a few miles from where we were feasting.

It was the Lord, of course, and none other, who took life away, but then again, it was the Lord who gave life in the first place. Well, if life belonged to Him, if He gave and took as He wished, He was welcome to do whatever the bloody hell He wanted to do with our lives, capricious, tyrannical, cruel authoritarian creature that He was, Ultimate Authority Itself! Oh, better not have such thoughts, in case....Better not allow ourselves to be angry with Him, or else...Who knew what the Old Man might do? Who knew how He might judge? Control such fantasies. Suppress. Don't even mention it. Look serious; pious. Hold anger inside. Suppress, keep a tight lid, the Lord works in mysterious ways, the departed are in a much better place-if so, why so reluctant to depart this place? but anger under lid doesn't evaporate, it escapes in subtle ways, cries out for medication, so, have a drink, crack a few jokes, laugh, get religion, get melancholic, that's better, at least for a while.

As for death, I hadn't had a single intelligent conversation with anyone on that subject, or on the subject of birth, in the course of my life, except in simple or in clinical terms. All I had were my own fantasies. None of the older people I knew seemed to want to discuss birth or death in any thoughtful, philosophical way. We didn't ask ourselves questions like: "Who am I?" Or "Why am I in this life?"

The day of the funeral came. It was to be a cremation. The time came for everyone to get ready. Marjorie stood alone in the middle of her room, I stood in the living room, I walked in and we looked at each other, we stayed in each other's arms for a long time.

The funeral service seemed to me like any other funeral service. I didn't like it. I hated it, I felt estranged during the proceedings, but everything seemed to go according to plan, and, after the service was over, the mourners went to Marjorie's house for refreshments. The neighbors had prepared tea and sandwiches. Marjorie's mother suggested to us that we go out for a while, so as to take a break. We declined the offer initially, until it was repeated more aggressively. Please do. Go! Go and relax for a few hours. It will do you both good. We left, we took the bus downtown, we strolled around the streets for a couple of hours, and then we visited our favorite pub. Some of our friends were there. It was a quiet visit. No laughter; no loud talk; no jokes. We didn't stay long.

A few days went by:

"I was not included in any of the plans for the funeral. I was not mentioned in the obituary that was published in the Edinburgh newspaper. I was left alone. I was out in the cold. I wasn't even mentioned as a daughter."

"Why? What's going on?"

"I feel hurt, humiliated and abandoned. I'm angry. My father and I were close, but we sometimes had arguments, sometimes they got intense, even if they were over trivial events, but we always made up quickly, and we never bore each other any animosity, nor did we harbor hostility to each other."

"And?"

"Mum hated our arguments. I don't know why. They were harmless. She's the one who made a big thing of them."

"Your mother wanted me to sit beside the two of you at the funeral," I said. "It was important to her. I didn't want to intrude upon the family, and I was reluctant to sit beside you, but she was emphatic about it and I appreciate her doing that. To me it means that she accepts me as a member of the family."

"It's true. She does accept you. Also I loved my father. We were close. I was closer to my father than to any other person. I still feel his presence around me. I don't believe my mother feels his presence as I do. She seems more stunned by the death of my father than I am. The sense of presence to me is not weird, it's like something good, I know he's here, and it's comfortable, as if it's the way it should be."

"I've heard of that happening; I've read accounts of people having such experiences, but I don't know how it works. You're the first one I personally know who's had the experience. Maybe certain loved ones who depart from our lives do have a spiritual presence around us for a while."

"I loved my father and he loved me, so if there's something to the idea of a spiritual presence, and I believe there is, it's happening in my life. My awareness of my father's presence is not my imagination. It's much stronger than that. It's almost physical, but not quite. Of course, I don't actually see anything, I don't hear anything, I know him."

"It's to tell us that all is well and good in his existence, to reassure us, so let's remember it in that way."

"We'll remember it that way."

The Sunday following the funeral, in church, the minister read the following statement from the pulpit, saying that it would be inserted into the records of the church:

"On Monday evening, October 6th, on his way home from work, Alfred died suddenly.

"Born in Cockpen, at an early age he came to Edinburgh, where he received his education and training....He took a prominent part in Sunday School work and the Christian instruction of youth.

"Some years ago he joined this congregation and shortly afterwards he was ordained an Elder, bringing with him a width of outlook, which in these days of ecumenical emphasis, is so vitally necessary. Modest by nature, genial by disposition, he had an unique capacity for making friends. A superb elder who kept in close and constant touch with his district and exercised pastoral care over them, his life was under-girded with a strong sense of the reality of God, and the centrality of Christ.

"Alfred was a good man. He did justly, he loved mercy, he walked humbly with his God. In gratitude for his devoted service, this congregation would extend its sympathy to his wife and daughter in their grief."

22: KNIGHT IN SHINING ARMOR

It was Monday morning and I was one of five junior medical students recently assigned to the Professor's department. The Professor spoke: "I give you each five patients to work up. I give you a few days to examine them. Get to know them. Be prepared to discuss them clinically; intelligently."

A week! I'll get this done easily in less than a week. I'll start working them up today, I'll get all my work done quickly; I'll breeze through this assignment, no problem. And so it was that by Tuesday afternoon I had completely interviewed, diagnosed, and written up four of the five patients assigned to me.

"I've got a knack for clinical diagnosis," I said to my flat mate. "I'm glad I got this assignment. "I'm doing great. It's a piece of cake."

"What's the hurry? You don't have to do it all in one long session."

"I don't think of it that way."

"How do you think of it?"

"If it's got to be done, I'll do it right away. Work before pleasure is what I always say."

"As your father always said?"

"Oh, no! My father is the opposite of me in that regard. He's casual about work."

"Wait until you get to Psychiatry."

"What about Psychiatry?"

"They'll see through your bullshit."

"What bullshit?"

"It's bullshit to labor like Hercules so the Professor will like you. Go ahead, go ahead and lick his shiny black shoes. Go ahead and grovel. Be a brown-nose."

"Thank you; you're so-o kind. Are we friends, or not? Well, screw you. I'll finish my work early, and anyway, you're wrong about me-wrong; wrong; wrong."

"Are you afraid he won't like you? Are you afraid he'll like others more than he likes you?"

"Me; afraid? No way, I'm not afraid of him, I can assure you. I don't kiss anyone's boots, and as for the professor, he's great. I'm looking forward to having him teach me. I'm lucky."

"You and your luck. I wish you more of it. You'll need it, with your methods."

"What do you mean?"

"You're bribing the Professor. You wouldn't think of buying a pair of shoes for him, would you?"

"I'm going back to the hospital tonight myself. I really like it there. Maybe I'll spend a few nights in the Casualty Department, as a volunteer."

"Well, while you're being so kind and considerate, caring for the sick; while you're so-o self-sacrificing, while you're worrying in case you've left some stone unturned, I'll be going out, I'll be enjoying myself. Maybe I'll have a couple of beers at Mick's.... Why not? And afterwards, there's a good movie on at the Playhouse."

"Maybe I just want to be the best physician I can be."

"I have a cousin in Glasgow who's a psychiatrist. He says people have hidden wants and fears that they're blind to. What is it you want? Are you blind to it?"

"Don't be ridiculous. I'm not blind."

All of the four patients spoke to me without reservation, and I had a good working relationship with them. I was a contributing member of the treatment team. Imagine that! Although I was only a student. I enjoyed listening to patients, they seemed to enjoy talking to me, and of course, I always introduced myself to them as a medical student. A medical student on the clinical level! I was beginning to feel like a real physician. I had real clinical responsibilities. Wasn't that something? And, to be sure, these patients in a significant way contributed to our education and to whatever progress we made in our profession. My patients told me intimate details of their lives, just as if I were a fully fledged physician.

Feeling great about my clinical progress, and confident in my ability to do this work, I left the fifth and last patient alone, expecting to work him up in the following couple of days, secure in the knowledge that I had plenty of time in which to do that. After all, I was sailing through the assignment, I understood the clinical syndromes well, I made accurate diagnoses right on target, and I suggested correct treatment methods. My career as a medical student was barreling along marvelously. My future career as a physician was assured. What more could a junior medical student want?

Wednesday morning came and all five of us students were in the ward ahead of time, waiting for the arrival of the Professor. A tense silence prevailed. Our conversation was muted. We straightened our ties. We cleared our throats. We glanced at our finger-nails; we glanced at the swing doors that separated the ward from the corridor that in turn went straight through the inside of the ancient building. Who knew how many feet had tramped the floor slabs of that corridor over the years? Some in shiny shoes, some in elegant footwear, some in muddy working-men's boots, some barely shod.

At eight o'clock sharp the Professor strode in the door, a touch of gray at the temples, well-rested, gripping the doubled up jet-black rubbery tubing of his stethoscope in his left hand-were these Sterling silver fittings on his stethoscope instead of the usual stainless steel fittings? Or even platinum?-and looking straight ahead. What a gentleman. He practically walked on air. I eyed an imaginary point above the Professor's belt buckle, over where his belly-button ought to be. He did have a belly-button, didn't he? Just like the rest of us? And if he ever took a drink, it would surely be fine cream sherry, or very old whiskey, aged in oak casks, poured from a fancy decanter into a glass of delicate Edinburgh crystal. Well, enough of that. A resident-physician, who was standing inside the ward, close to the door, reading a chart, brought his shoes together smartly, snapped shut the chart he was reading, grinned a quick smile and uttered a crisp, "Good morning, Sir." The Professor, by this time trailed by the head nurse in full professional regalia: starched hat, badges all over, stiff skirt, blue and white colors, gray no-make-up face, nodded to the resident as he marched past. The pair reached our little group. The Professor spoke:

"You may leave now, Nurse."

"Yes, Sir; certainly, Sir."

The head nurse's hard heels clicked audibly on the recently cleaned linoleum floor that smelled of wet mop as she marched briskly back towards the nursing station that was her territory, or at least she claimed it as her very own.

"Good morning, students. Come this way. Follow me."

A man who knew exactly what he wanted, a man who asked for what he wanted, a man accustomed to getting what he wanted, the Professor strode towards a bed occupied by a thin, bespectacled man who held his hands clasped together in a prayerful position on his lower chest outside the bedclothes: "Good morning. How are you today?"

"Good morning, Sir, I'm fine."

He didn't look so good, a thin-faced, pallid, vaguely yellowish man, worn-out, weary-looking, and as for that cough! Cough; cough; cough...aahheh; cough! The man in the bed looked older than his chronological age of sixty years. He reached for a tissue, a movement that required him to stretch over to his left side where the bedside table was, encouraging air to be sucked noisily through unhealthily thickened lung tissue, tissue that should have been a semi-transparent membrane effortlessly accepting molecules of oxygen from the air, and releasing carbon dioxide into the atmosphere.

The patient kept, next to his tissues beside the glass that

held his government-issue false teeth, a battered rectangular tin with a faded yellowish design on its lid, in which he kept a supply of loose tobacco that he rolled into the cigarettes he loved to smoke, and that helped him cough up gobs of phlegm each morning. Therapeutic, in a perverse kind of way, somewhat like the hair of the dog.

Not the kind of man who kept his cigarettes in a solid Sterling silver case decorated with an aristocratic-looking gold emblem, not the kind of man who opened his cigarette case ceremoniously, with a flourish, eliciting a sound like the door of a Rolls-Royce opening and closing, not the kind of man who would have a jeweler inscribed scrolled message inside his cigarette case. No, he wasn't, but he was the kind of man who knew his place.

He knew his place in a phony society that the working public willingly paid taxes to support, that they proudly identified with, that they fought to the death to defend, that they bled all over the world for, blind members of a society in which the blind led the blind, no serious questions asked-after all, why challenge a basic premise that ours was a noble cause that everybody already 'knew' to be true? Why ask questions? Few, if any, did. Why not ask why not?

On the ward, the smell of soap, laundered hospital towels, bed sheets and excrement recently removed, hung in the air as an ominous reminder of our universal ultimate helplessness. Was death far away? And beyond death lay what? How about that Bearded Old Man? the one who remembered every single sin we committed, both sins of commission and sins of omission, the one who passed final judgment, the one who knew exactly how undeserving we were, despite out posturing, the one who was judge, jury and executioner?

Meantime, the Professor, preening himself as he spoke, like a rich roly-poly Roman aristocrat who had just been bathed, stroked, massaged and oiled all over by a couple of eunuch slaves, and who was quietly waiting for the day's news from his messengers, was the center of attention. What? The Professor in a flowing white toga, bare feet in fine leather sandals, smelling of fresh oils, nonchalantly twirling the ends of a long 24-carat gold chain wrapped around his waist, strolling in the atrium of his mansion, birds chirping in the trees, a group of enraptured listeners sitting at his feet; the crème de la crème of the learned medical rhetoricians, elegantly waving a scroll!

He established his position standing at the head of the bed, to the left of the patient, his right arm stretched out along the black cast-iron tubular frame, a position that only a man in charge would take up, his left arm hanging down by his side, his left fist gripping the rubbery rolled-up stethoscope.

"Whose patient is this?"

"Mine, Sir," I said.

"Tell us all about him."

"I can't, Sir. I haven't got to him yet."

"And why not?"

My chest sank like a sack of cement, "I can't get to them all at once. I'm busy. I've a...a...all at once," as a series of short sharp expletive-like sounds like a dry hot ratchet running backwards; the wrong thing to say, in the wrong place, at the wrong time, in the wrong tone of voice; I knew it as soon as I spoke, and the tightness in my chest confirmed it; as did the shove...

Out of the Island bogs, out of the pubs, out of *The Shack*, from the beaches, from the moors, dilemma-laden, into a status-oriented, power-driven, authoritarian society, led by smooth, self-assured men groomed from an early age for leadership roles. Talk about culture shock! An awkward, socially inept, clumsy, unsophisticated youth from a remote island of peasants, and, worst of all, chock-full of self-righteous indignation, who, instead of pleasing the Professor by preparing most of my assignment ahead of time, drew attention to myself in a way unlikely to be forgotten, or forgiven, in that place.

I didn't tell the Professor that I had finished with four out of five patients, leaving only one to another day, that the very one I had left to do another day happened to be the one he had asked me about, and that, in fact, my performance far exceeded expectations, and probably that of the other students. I didn't want to tell him. No more Roman rhetorician. No more crème de la crème. Out the window with all that crap! To hell with him!

The face of the sick man in the bed was frozen. He continued holding his hands over his lower chest in a prayerful position. He was staring at his hands, in his place.

The Professor asked another student to interview my patient. He was a smiling well-dressed young man who spoke in a well-modulated voice, in a cultivated accent that suggested formal education in some expensive big city school, probably in the south, which meant that his parents had money, and, to be sure, he hadn't spent the days of his youth meandering between a simple cottage in a remote village on a windy island, the moors, the beaches and *The Shack*.

I stood there out in the cold, impotent. A grim outlook for me! The sick man answered the questions put to him quietly, without elaborating, without smiling. He knew something. He knew how risky it was to advance uninvited out of one's place, to dare taste the delicacies of a higher caste in an authoritarian culture.

"Where were you born?" asked the student who was doing the questioning.

"I'm a Highlander, but I've lived in Edinburgh for many years."

The subject of drinking alcohol came up, as it should have, in the course of a clinical interview. After all, "alcohol for those who are accustomed to it" was frequently an accepted part of the treatment regimen: "How much do you drink?"

"I don't drink beer or whiskey. I used to, but thirteen years ago, after drinking too much whiskey, I threw up blood, and I quit. I haven't had a drink since. As a Highlander, I grew up loving whiskey. I'm sure you know all about that. Oh, yes, I've done my share of quaffing." It was a weak attempt at levity. The Professor nodded. He frowned. He glared at me, or at least I imagined he did. Was he suggesting something? Were our people so different? At the time, our sub-culture was essentially pre-industrial and agrarian. Was it true that we were superstitious?, that our religion was dark and brooding? Of course, it was all so subjective, it was a splinter of perception, and of those who had their own agenda, and no one had a global view to make sense out of a complex unfolding life drama. Of course, on the Island, we spoke our own language, the Gaelic language, which happened to be older than English.

Who ever heard of humanity as one? Of human beings sharing some mysterious life presence with all there was? I had forgotten all about Pagoda, the quiet dam-building man who lived by his own rules and values, who looked at the world through heavily lidded eyes. How many years would it take? How much drama?

When I got back to the patient later that evening, he was polite and cooperative with me. He taught me much. I wanted to be a physician. I knew I would be a good doctor of medicine some day, but for the time being, I would have to be patient. I would bide my time. Yes, that's what I would do.

The man in the bed had been exposed to big city industrial pollution in factories in a climate where for many months of the year cold wet air swept across the city and damp acid fog hovered around buildings, including the tenement where he lived with his wife and family. He was unpretentious and straightforward. He didn't blame the factory owners or anyone else for the chronic debilitating essentially incurable diseases that were relentlessly destroying his internal tissues.

As for me, I would stay hurt a long time. I did not know that "hurt" had its own reward, the reward of being a "victim," with all that that implied. I did not know I was creating karma for myself. Of course, I could find some companions who "understood" me over beer. Such people were a dime a dozen. They had their own agendas. What did they know about living one's destiny according to what was permanent, versus chasing the alluring glittering transient?

The last day of the rotation came. We students were to

ceremonially receive certificates of satisfactory completion of the clinical rotation. Standing outside the Professor's office, dressed in our best suits, white shirts and ties, wearing freshly shined shoes, quiet as church mice. Into the office, one by one, and outside, we were all ears, on high alert, lounging nonchalantly as if we didn't have a care in the world, and, to be sure, our keen ears picked up the unmistakable cultured voice of the Professor: "I enjoyed having you on my unit. How did you like the rotation?"

"Sir, it couldn't have been better. I really learned a lot, much more than I had expected. I'm delighted."

"Do you have anything to add?"

"Nothing, Sir, except to say that you yourself are a great example of what a true physician should be, an example I shall never forget, an example I shall hold in high esteem no matter where I go, and, not only that, but you're also a prince of a man."

"You're going to be alright, young man. You'll make an excellent physician. You'll make your mark. Just keep up the good work."

Each student came out smiling, walking erectly, with his or her shoulders thrown back as if some miracle of personal growth had taken place in there, and maybe it had. But then, my turn came, and, knowing I wasn't going to get any chatter... An adrenaline rush, my eyes lit up, my face relaxed, I suppressed an impulse to laugh...I had hard heels on my shoes and I knew how to wheel around smartly.

Graduation would come, I was going to make it easily with plenty of margin to spare, I had confidence in myself professionally, I would leave behind me the drama I was growing weary off, yes, on one level growing weary of, but by no means finished with; it was time to start all over somewhere else, I would make a fresh start in life in a far-away land where no one knew me, where I would be accepted, where I would identify with the power-elite. I would be pleasant to those in authority. I would play the game, I would be smooth and oily and suave when talking to them, just like an old experienced adept, and all things would be new, I would be new, people would like me, and all would be well in the end.

Of course, had I told the Professor the whole story, my personal drama would have fizzled out like a match in a gale. But who wanted to be a match in a gale? Not me! No way. I wanted to be windswept, gale-tossed, half-drowned, tossed on the beach, sending out distress signals in the night, anxiously awaiting the rescue squad, and, if they failed to show in good time, it would be to hell with the rescue squad. They were no damn good anyway. My hour in the sun! After all, other people, especially those in authority, were causing my problems, weren't they? And my drama was a 'problem!' A passionate young man, I wanted attention. If people didn't pay attention to me, I'd make them. And so, attention I got, one way or another, come hell or high water. *A drama knight in shining armor!* I didn't know then what I came to know later, namely, that my drama was simply a series of life events, events in part created by my fighting against my destiny, events that, because I fought my destiny, I had to live through in my role in the Great Drama, events that would fizzle out once I knew; comedy.

I didn't know that all these actors in my drama were there to help me! How could they help me? By taking part in my life, by representing significant others in my life, by being in my experience, in the whole, by pricking my comfort zone, by "educating," me, not by intellectual lectures, but by allowing me to live in my drama again and again, until finally I got it. Once I got it, I came to myself, and later it was, to be sure.

The day came when, my heart dancing merrily, I walked briskly out of the medical department, and, once out, I paused on the second floor corridor, gazing out the window. Who was that down below? What were they doing? A man, possibly a senior physician, dressed in a fine pinstripe suit and a black hat, carrying a neatly rolled-up umbrella in his left hand, was walking, while a resident-physician, wearing a spotless white laboratory coat, marched behind him at three paces, keeping step, around the quadrangle.

The late morning summer sunshine cast sharp black shadows on the concrete slab between the old stone walls that were like structures out of some strange alien medieval world, the dark shadows looked cold, dust blew in eddies like tiny virulent demons under heavy stone arches.

Out on the street, it was a beautiful July morning, the sun was shining, there was a gentle breeze, there were sounds of life in abundance; women in summer dresses strolled along the sidewalks, men in shirt-sleeves without coats walked briskly, children ran playfully, trim rhododendrons graced the cast-iron rails of private gardens, fresh flowers bloomed in half-open windows, and all of us breathed clean fresh air.

Standing on that street, the gentle breeze in my hair, gazing into the plate glass window of a store, I saw my reflection, and I said 'Hello' to the fresh faced young man gazing back at me from the glass, a youthful citizen of the world, a man with a future, a man in his first day of a future life.

23: QUEEN BEE

I wrote my parents a letter. Great news! I would visit them for a couple of weeks prior to graduation, I'd bring Marjorie with me, we'd have a happy family reunion, and my mother would accompany us to Edinburgh for my graduation. What about my father? He was welcome to attend my graduation, but he had already told me he would not be coming. He had the house to look after. There were domestic responsibilities. I knew that. It wasn't a rejection. At least I didn't see it as a rejection. I felt comfortable with it. I said so, but then again, in that mysterious psychological process of no specific location that we call unconscious,-that we deny knowing-who knows?

My mother was a pre-feminist. What's that? The night after our arrival in the family home, after one glass of liquor, she lost some of her hammered-down controls: "Men accomplish the important things in life. Women don't have a chance. Boys get to do things, as for girls...I haven't accomplished anything in my life."

"You brought us into this world. You raised us three children. You encouraged me to get an education. You encouraged me to educate myself. If it weren't for all the help and encouragement you gave me, I would never have graduated from the University of Edinburgh. I wouldn't be where I am today."

"Hmmmph!"

"Is that all?"

"Men can do what they want in this world."

"What did you want for yourself when you were young?"

I really wanted to know, but it wasn't to be. She clammed up. I tried to keep her thoughts flowing, wanting to learn something about her life and her feelings, her ideas, her fantasies, her dreams, and what might have got in the way, but she looked down at her hands, which she clasped in her lap, with her eyelids half-closed, and she remained in that position long enough to let me know that my probing was not welcome. The conversation was over. I suspected that what might have got in the way of her ambition were family responsibilities, a sense of duty, a teeth-clenching, jaw-jutting, eyes-focused, no nonsense sense of *duty to another*, by God! as opposed to 'duty,' according to destiny, and, yes, I emphasize the opposites.

"Marjorie and I are going for a drive," I said the following day, after church.

It was the Sabbath. The community observed the Sabbath in a strict way, in a fundamentalist way, grim and sere, and, didn't I know that going for a pleasure drive on the Sabbath would be a violation of that prescription? Maybe Edinburgh had loosened me up. What about a little drama? Why not? We went.

On Monday morning there was an uncomfortable silence at the breakfast table. It was an ominous sign. I waited for the event: "When I read your letter telling me you were bringing a woman home with you, I had to sit down, I suffered a collapse; I asked your father to fetch me a glass of water. Your father went to the supply."

My chest tightened within, my breathing became shallow, my ears shut down, everything seemed remote, and suddenly I knew I'd never get away from Her, unless destiny intervened, and I didn't know how. I wanted to leave. I had to get out. I didn't know how. Patience. Soon, it would be time to depart anyway, but then a complication arose, in that a couple of days before we were due to depart the Island for Edinburgh by sea, the sailors went on strike. "There's a strike on," said the ticket agent the day of our scheduled departure, as if we didn't know.

"Is there any way of getting to the mainland tonight?" I asked.

"There's no way. There's no plane leaving tonight, and anyway, all seats by air are booked for at least a week, and probably beyond."

We turned around to leave and the ticket agent said, "We'll let you sleep on board tonight, seeing you have nowhere to go. A lot of people are doing that, but the ship is not sailing until the strike is settled."

"When will that be?"

"No one knows that."

That night we boarded the passenger ship, prepared to spend a quiet evening on deck prior to turning in for the night. At least we would have shelter for the night. The following day we would address our problems in traveling. The night was calm, the wind barely noticeable, the stars were clearly visible, and the vessel rocked gently up and down on her moorings, as if impatient with the disputes and disagreements of men and women, disputes that prevented her from doing what she wanted to do, what she was designed to do, what she was destined by nature to do. She was raring to go, or so it seemed to us. Or was she? Maybe it was we who were impatient, stuck as we were in a situation beyond our control, maybe it was we who projected our fantasies on to the beautiful ship, or then again, maybe at some level we were truly one. Indeed, the throaty throb of the engines below reminded me of my own mortality, my own inability to control even such mundane aspects of my life as travel to an important engagement. Below us, on the dock, a gathering of men and women grew, strikers and hangers-on, uttering murmurs, murmurs that escalated into angry noises, snarls, curses, gesticulations, threats, or at least what appeared to be. Was the anger directed at us who were on deck? What had we done? Nothing out of the ordinary. We were just travelers, non-participants in whatever labor dispute was the issue. A tight sensation arose inside me, in my middle, accompanied by shallow breathing, a feeling of curling up, a coiling within.

Marjorie and I went below, to cabins that we shared with some other people, for there were not enough private cabins to accommodate everyone, but there were enough makeshift bunks, and we knew that there were sailors who wanted to treat us humanely. We slept fitfully.

The following morning we were walking on the docks, feeling dejected and not hopeful that we could make it to Edinburgh in time for graduation. The same walk I had done in years past. A stranger approached. He wore a dark suit and a hat, his shoes were polished, and when he spoke it was with a Glasgow accent. He was obviously a businessman.

"Yes, we're travelers," I answered to his question.

"Where do you want to go?"

"We want to go to Edinburgh," I said.

"I'm arranging transportation in a fishing boat," he said. "Are you interested?"

"Of course. There are three of us. Can you take all three of us?"

"Yes, you're in luck. Are you with us?"

"How much is it?"

He mentioned a price that seemed high to me, and he knew by the change in my facial expression that I might have been short of money, so he said, "It's a bit pricey, but it's a way out of here. There's no other way."

"OK, we'll take it; we want to go."

"Don't tell anyone about this. Please have your money ready and meet me at the hotel in one hour. We found a skipper who'll do it for money. What we're doing may be illegal, and somebody's probably a scab, according to union men, but we're getting what we want and somebody's making hay while the sun shines."

We travelors were men and women of several nationalities and, by the time we crammed our luggage and ourselves below decks, so that no one could detect us, we were close to each other indeed. We couldn't have fallen down if we tried. We were about thirty passengers, jammed tightly into the crew's quarters, standing up, with those who could-and I wasn't one of them-gripping whatever parts of the ship's structure they could cling to.

So it was that, one morning in July, a motor fishing boat steamed out of the harbor, past the shelter of the bay, out into the sea that separated the Island from the mainland of Scotland, and towards freedom. As for that sea, she was a temperamental lady, one of Mother Nature's drama queens, prone to mood swings and more, and, yes, she commanded respect, something she got from those who knew her well. She was stormy at times, often she was restless, and at all times she was subject to attacks of buffeting wind. Long lasting howling winter gales were common. But this was not winter time. It was summer time and the sea was at peace.

Once out of sight of land, and out of sight of coast-guard spotters or nosy union men, one of the crew poked his head down below and shouted, "Alright, you can all come up. Nobody's going to see us now. You'll be much more comfortable on deck than packed like sardines down there in the dark."

"We're going to need some assistance here," someone shouted from below.

"We're ready and able," the fisherman said.

"The way this boat's rolling and diving, I'm not sure I can make it up to the deck. I'm a woman. I'm wearing a dress and high heels."

"We'll help from below," a man said. "Heave away; heave away!"

"Heave away? We're not hoisting cargo. This isn't a rust bucket of a coaster."

"It's not the Cunard line."

"Easy as she goes," said the crewman. "I'll come down myself and give you all a hand up and my mate, Danny, here will haul you from above. Everybody'll be nice and cozy in next to no time."

I helped my mother up the ladder, then Marjorie, with assistance from the fishermen. The pitching and rolling was significant for people who had no sea-legs, and who were unaccustomed to the swell, but nevertheless we all made it up to the deck safely. On deck we sat wherever we could find places, some of us on the hatches, some of us on long round wooden spars, some of us on rolled up fishing nets.

I took a place in front of the mast, standing on deck, enjoying the sea breeze, with the salt air in my face, watching the herring gulls swooping, listening to their cries. I couldn't have been more delighted. I loved the heaving green-blue sea swell, I marveled at the whirling whitecaps, I was at one with the elements in that pristine place, breathing the cleanest air in the world in the midst of the beautiful, vibrant colors and the aroma of life itself. My face relaxed into a serene and happy smile. Standing in front of the mast, I felt as if that giant external spine pointing gallantly at the passing clouds was my symbol of liberation, and, to be sure, there it was, swinging gently to and fro, backwards and forwards.

I spread my legs apart, knees flexible, steady as any sailor of old, feeling at one with that lovely vessel, with the power of the engine a steady throb behind me, enjoying the haunting cries of the gulls as they whirled overhead, hustling for food, for handouts, or just along for the ride. Why was it that flying gulls seemed to be enjoying themselves? Were they really laughing? An illusion. My fantasy. Maybe, or could it be that creatures with such small brains actually enjoyed life? Well, why not? For one thing, they didn't have organized religion to cope with, or organized psychiatry...A fantasy of living happily in the moment, in the Play of Life, a fantasy, no, no fantasy in my boyhood days, I actually lived it. Something precious I had lost. Anyway, getting back to the gulls, there was plenty of leftover food on board the boat that day, for the crew had provided us with sandwiches and tea, which some of us took, but then again, there were others, quite a few, who didn't eat because of the swell.

The boat acted out her designated role, in her element, like a live creature in the green-blue water, her bow rising and falling, rising and falling, in the salt air, the spray against her skin, in harmony, as I too was in harmony, as were the lovely herring seagulls, doing exactly what they were designed to do. This was living. Life couldn't be better.

Oh, to rise and fall in the waves, in silence, rhythmically, in harmony, in water saltier than my blood, easy to float in. What about a deep dive? It wasn't all that deep. Just how deep was it? Maybe five hundred feet. Deep enough. Dark and cold. Another world. Strange creatures that never saw light. Mystery down below, in the dark, easier to examine than the mystery of life, which was perhaps why so many made careers out of intellectualizing the outside, and so few sought Truth within. On the other hand, maybe the secret of life was down there, beyond oxygen, beyond algae, beyond Authority.

"Sit down. Sit down." It was a woman's voice. "Please sit down. Oh, do sit down."

I froze. My chest tightened. I didn't look around. *Sit down. Sit down Do sit down. Please sit down.*

Surely it couldn't be happening. It was. "Oh, do sit down. You're going to fall in. You'll drown."

I didn't move. I couldn't. A part of me was dying.

Again: "Do sit down; sit down. You're going to drown, I know it."

I felt a firm hand on my shoulder. It was a deckhand. He looked at me with a neutral expression on his face and he said matter-of-factly, "Captain wants you to sit down. Your mother's concerned." The crewman, a small tidy man, dressed in a polonecked sweater and jeans, spoke with authority. He had a clean-shaven face, quiet brown eyes and strong hands. I said nothing. The crewman and I made eye contact. The sky above me shrunk like a giant zipper snapping to.

I left my place in front of the mast, walked to the center of the boat and found a place where I could sit alone, as far away from my mother as possible, feeling as small as a smelt in a bucket. *Captain wants you to sit down*! My heart raced, my face felt swollen and red hot. *Your mother's concerned!* Well, I was already dead, so how could I drown? After all, the dead don't die. The faces of the rest of the passengers were expressionless. For them the trip was simply an inconvenience, something they wanted to be over and done with and the sooner the better, but for me....a reenactment of death, a dummy run, so to speak, or maybe-and more likely-an after demonstration, for, as I found out later, we do recreate, so to speak, our life dramas, and I had a girl-friend! A woman I loved, someone to take a place in my life, no less, and, to be sure, I imagined that my mother would not approve of any woman in my life, not a single solitary one, and my father would go along with Her.

Do we really believe children are to be released? I submit that we don't. And here I don't refer to my life. I refer to all children of all parents, rich or poor, world wide, not that I'm qualified to speak about everybody or every culture in the world. No one is. But I exercise my right to express myself, and I have professional experience to support my opinions. I failed to internalize my parents' images as people who had raised me to release me, maybe at the age of 25 I didn't 'want' to be released, maybe I didn't 'want' to go out into the world alone, maybe I 'wanted' to illustrate the insanity of life, the drama, the comedy, as opposed to the way we like to or claim to believe life is-my destiny.

But, there's more, and it is this: The whole thing was just one man's role in the Great Play, the VrajaLeela, for a while, as part of His Play, no more, no less, for me to know His love, for His joy, for me to know that all roles are equal, no soul is greater than another, the Great Play cannot work if we despise our designated roles, and, once we know, we smile, at least I do.

I wanted to be a physician, I knew I would make a competent one, wounded healer that I was, and I wouldn't be alone in that well known role in the medical profession, for, to be sure, I would have plenty of company, no doubt about that.

There were several women in that fishing boat on that day crossing the Scottish sea to the mainland, and one of them in particular-she might have been American, but I wasn't sure-was looking at me in a gentle kind of way, smiling. She got my attention. How different she was from the others! It was as if she not only knew, but she cared, and, as if translating her caring into action, morally courageously, she smiled at me personally, woman to man, not woman to boy, gazing directly and benignly into my eyes. Why? What was the gentlewoman thinking? Or, more to the point, what was she doing?

You will make exactly the right decision, precisely the right decision, for you, at the moment you make it, regardless of how, or in what circumstances, you make it, whether spontaneously, or after due consideration, whether your inner eye is closed, or whether your inner eye is open.

Yes, we made it to Edinburgh, and my graduation was without a hitch, apart from a certain rumbling ruminating grudge against Her, and, after it was all over, Marjorie and I ended up on the west coast of Canada, in British Columbia, and soon after settling down, we got married in a simple civil ceremony in the office of a justice of the peace, with a few friends for company, and no international communication at all at all.

I threw my energies into my work.

PART THREE
UNITED STATES OF AMERICA

24: LOYALTY

I was one of a group of five psychiatrists, from various parts of the country, visiting a large psychiatric hospital. We were members of a larger group that was attending a national professional conference. "Please come and pay us a visit. You'll enjoy touring our hospital. We'll make you welcome," a local physician, one of the conference attendees, had said.
"We'd like to. When?"
"Tomorrow morning. I'll arrange it."
Just like that, it had been arranged. That was why we were there. We didn't really know each other, and, as for me, I felt like a visiting dignitary. I was at a stage in my career when I believed in treatment methods as being specific, I believed that one or more psychiatrists in a given hospital might be knowledgeable in, and capable of practicing, certain methods of treatment that I myself didn't know about. I wanted to learn. I was eager.
"Do you have any questions?" the Administrator asked, after we had completed the tour.
"No, I don't have any questions. Thank you for showing us around," someone said, and someone else seconded that. I supported. Our remarks were greeted with a gracious "You're welcome." I tried to come up with at least one question, but found it hard to come up with fresh questions about old programs.
"Very well, then, please follow me," the Administrator said. "I'm taking you to the office of the Superintendent."
The Superintendent's office was in the main administrative

building, which was the tallest building, even without the conical spire that rested on top, a spire that gave the building a solid, theocratic appearance. Churchy; a cathedral-like edifice. A series of wide arcing stone steps led up to the main door, a large, dark red, heavy-looking solid oak barrier with ornate black painted metal hinges visible on the outside. Would the hinges creak when the door swung? Like an ancient castle door in Transylvania? I half expected an apparition, but no such luck. Instead, solid walls, walls fashioned out of enormous rocks, sculpted by stone masons who had long since passed away, for labor intensive work of this kind was no longer fashionable, nor could it be, because of the cost. Certainly no private building would be built like this. This building had "government" displayed all over it.

Once inside the building, we found ourselves in an austere looking hall with a high ceiling, yellow painted walls and a series of long bright lights shining down from above. The yellow paint showed some wear and tear, there were several rusty-looking stains and the beginnings of cracks in the paintwork. Our guide led us through a door off to the side of the hallway, into a reception area, on the far side of which was the office of the Superintendent. Himself! The reception area was well-furnished with solid-looking chairs, a coffee table and book cases along one of the walls. Gray filing cabinets lined another wall. A woman sat behind a gray desk. On top of the desk was a sign: "Miriam."

"Welcome," said Miriam, glancing at us with an easy smile. "Please sit down. Make yourselves comfortable."

She dropped her glance back to her typewriter and resumed her typing. We were dismissed until further notice. The woman's hair was a mixture of auburn and gray, she wore a pair of rimless eye-glasses, and a pale-green sweater:

"Dr. Smith is out of town today, so he can't meet with you personally, but he extends a warm welcome to all of you. We hope you're finding your visit informative."

She remained seated all the time she spoke, and as soon as

she saw that we were also seated, she seemed to lose interest in us. There were papers on her desk, as well as a typewriter, some pens and pencils and a telephone with several extension buttons. The woman wore next to no makeup and she looked serious. I looked at the rows of gray filing cabinets. Whose lives were represented in these? What methods of treatment? Whose hopes and dreams? Whose surrender to the inevitable? I had only recently graduated from long years of training, I was still young in the profession of psychiatry, just recently certified by the American Board of Psychiatry and Neurology, but I was working full time, I was full of energy, I was ambitious, I felt competent, and, as always, I wanted to know more.

Miriam was a smoker, judging from the pack of Marlboros that was visible on her desk, sticking half-way out of a leather case, lying alongside a slim red cigarette lighter. But where was the Superintendent? If he was away on business or on pleasure, who was in charge? Was Miriam the representative of authority in the whole institution? To be sure, she had about her an air of experience and competence. Power. She was the boss's woman; she was The Big Man's woman, WombMan herself, no less.

Apart from the initial glance she gave us as we entered the room, Miriam made no direct eye contact with us for what seemed a long time. Several minutes went by, then she again acknowledged our presence by glancing at each of us individually one after the other. She had clear intelligent eyes that glanced directly at us without being intrusive. A woman accustomed to greeting visitors. On her own territory. She may not have had the formal education, but she knew. We had nothing to say. Miriam was the first to break the silence. It was her privilege.

"Now that you've had a chance to relax, do you have any questions?" she asked.

None of us had.

"Well, then, the Superintendent wants you to do something. It's very simple. It'll only take a few minutes of your time. It's the policy of the Institution," she said matter-of-factly.

"What does he want us to do?" one of us asked.

"Please wait here," she said, and with that she got up from her chair and walked through the open door of the office of the Superintendent, which was directly behind where she sat. Her legs, viewed from behind, were well-proportioned, and she wore pumps, but she was too old and too maternal for us to see her as sexy, although sexy she might have been at one time, had she allowed herself to be. Matronly. Soon she returned carrying several sheets of paper in her hands. Forms. Miriam approached us and handed me the forms, because I happened to be the one sitting closest to her. "Please pass these around. There's one for each of you. Please fill up and sign these papers. Thank you, Doctors," she said.

I glanced at the papers she had given me. They were detailed forms for applicants who wanted to work in that state institution. I was surprised. I looked at Miriam.

"The Superintendent wants you to fill these forms up and sign them," Miriam said.

I passed the papers around, giving one to each of my companions and we began to read. What was this? We weren't looking for employment. I hoped the Superintendent hadn't misunderstood the purpose of our visit. If he had, he was in for a big let-down. Miriam repeated, "The Superintendent wants you to fill these forms up please," and then she resumed working at her desk; typing, arranging papers, looking efficient, confident and in charge, like a good superintendent's woman should.

"These are applications for work. What's this about?" one of us asked.

"We're not looking for jobs," I said.

"As you know, these are applications for employment in this hospital. The Superintendent wants each of you to please fill one of these up and sign. Please go ahead. There's nothing to be concerned about," Miriam said.

"I told you we're not looking for employment," I said.

"We know you're not seeking employment and all we want is for you to complete these simple forms."

"It doesn't make sense."

"We know it looks unusual, but please go ahead."

"Why?"

"It's just that it's the policy of the Institution and the Superintendent wants you to go ahead and sign. We know you're just visiting for a day."

One of us handed his form back to the Secretary, saying, "It doesn't apply to me," and then each of us handed our forms back to the Secretary and for a moment I felt relief, but the Secretary shuffled the papers, tapped them on her desk top and began to hand them back to us, this time on her own, one by one, and she said, "Just fill up the forms. Rest assured we keep everything confidential. It's just that we want you all to comply with hospital policy. You will not be asked to do anything else."

Did the Superintendent have to justify our simple visit to some higher authority? Surely not. If not, what did he want from us? He wanted something. He had to. Surely the secretary wouldn't be so insistent without instructions, even if she was mother to that whole authoritarian institution. What the hell did the Superintendent want? What would Authority want? Authority wanted what authority always wanted, still wants and will want.

One of us removed a pen from the socket in the clip-board and began to write, slowly at first, then with more confidence, and then the man next to him followed suit, and soon all of us were writing, clip-boards on our knees. When we were finished, we each handed the completed forms back to Miriam. She took all five sets of papers, walked with them into the Superintendent's office, returned and resumed her place at her desk. All her movements were smooth and effortless, as if she was meant by nature to be managing a desk in that Institution, a woman in the right place at the right time. And so was I too in the right place at the right time, registering an account that I would remember all these years.

"It's time for us to return to our hotel," one of us said. "We have other sessions to attend in the hotel. We don't want to miss out."

"Can we use the telephone? We want to call a taxi," I said.

"Please don't trouble yourselves. I'll call a taxi from here. I know whom to call," Miriam said, and she immediately pulled a card from a rolodex and began to dial. She requested two taxis to transport us to our destination, and, sure enough, they didn't waste any time getting to us. The taxi drivers opened the cab doors for us, closed them behind us, and we rode back to our hotel absorbed in silence.

25: MEDICINAL MALADY

It was the weekend, the northern states were buried under a frigid crust of January snow and ice, I was laid back in an easy chair in my living room drinking whiskey, and I was content. I had been drinking whiskey for several hours. I liked drinking whiskey. I liked the taste of it. I liked the effect it had on me; a releasing, counter-inhibiting, liberating effect; a warm, dreamy, cozy buzz. In whiskey I found myself, and I was happy to be me, but, in the midst of my delight, I wasn't paying attention to Marjorie. She must have gone out somewhere. Where was Marjorie? It was quiet around the house without her.

The door opened and in walked The Doctor: "You've been drinking," he said as he approached me. He seemed to tower over me, but that was my illusion. The Doctor meant business and I had had my mind on other matters, so I was taken by surprise, to say the least.

"No, I have not been drinking," I said.

"Yes, you have, and it's obvious. You're under the influence."

"Well, maybe a couple of beers. What's wrong with that?" I said, trying to look visibly shocked at the very suggestion that I might have "been drinking," Who, me? I was unaware that my efforts at exaggerated facial theatricals only made me look ridiculous.

"Yes, you have been drinking. Drinking! Well, I'm going to do something about it. You yourself know we don't negotiate on these matters."

"It's Saturday morning," I said. "I can have a weekend to myself. It's time I had some relaxation anyway. I've been working too hard recently."

"Marjorie is rightly concerned about you. She's with me on this."

He was doing his best to sound authoritarian, and succeeding as far as I was concerned, and, indeed, he sounded like an Irish construction boss giving orders in the mountains, except that, of course, no self-respecting Irish construction boss would have been concerned about someone having "a couple of beers," and, to be sure, the good doctor was no mountain man; he was no construction boss. He was well liked by his patients; middle-aged worn-out world-weary men and women liked him, as well as the sad, the scared, the perplexed. The hospital staff also admired him. I liked him myself. He was indeed an experienced physician and on that fateful Saturday morning, I was on the receiving end of his unwelcome ministrations. Unwelcome or not, however, something he said got my attention. I was caught by surprise. As a rule I didn't drink in the mornings. This time was an exception. How could I have forgotten? What the hell was I doing? I had never done anything like it before. Hoisted by my own petard! no less. Although I was in no mood for introspection that morning, I knew that my drinking habits were becoming a problem. I had to admit that The Doctor was right. Well, all the more reason to deny my need for it most vehemently. I had my status to sustain. I didn't want to give up whiskey. At that moment, the prospect of life without whiskey seemed impossible to me, as did the prospect of life with whiskey, the way I felt. On either side, the abyss.

"What do you mean you're doing something about it? What are you talking about? What's up," I said, as if I didn't know. I was ready to bargain, hoping to find a loop-hole to wriggle through, despite the fact that I knew that, if the situation were reversed, I'd be doing exactly what The Doctor was doing.

"What's up is you're out of line, that's what. Anybody steps out of line....You're going to a treatment center. You're going tomorrow. I've already called on your behalf and they have a bed ready for you. I have your air-line ticket. You need help. I'm here to help you."

"Like hell I'm going. I don't want your damn help. You can shove it. Why the hell don't you go and get help for yourself?"

"Either you go to the Treatment Center or you go before the Board of Directors of the hospital. Take your pick."

The Board of Directors! These were the people who signed final papers on all of us who were on staff. I was not employed by the hospital, but I was on staff, which meant I had privileges to do some of my work there. This was getting serious. Momentarily, I put myself in the place of any Board member, and I saw not much room for bargaining. Non-negotiable. And their decision would follow me wherever I went. Instead of a loop-hole I saw a noose. What the hell was going on? At that moment I knew where Marjorie had been all the time she was missing from the house that morning, when she should have been at home, attending to household chores like a good wife. She was out there, yakking to The Doctor about me, spreading rumors about me, telling him how awful I was, how much I drank, that I was a "Jekyll and Hyde;" she was out there ratting on me, betraying me, the bitch! Well, too late to negotiate now. I had lost control of my life, or I had handed that over to someone else, and "treatment" had been arranged without a word to me. Lied to and betrayed by a woman I trusted. After all I'd done for her. But I had to admit that I had rattled a cage or two, and screwed up royally in full view of the public, or close to it, by Old Lord Feusag in the Sky! Some attention! Some answer to my secret sense of abandonment. Some way to reassure myself that I was a viable live human being! I should have been more careful of what I was longing for.

Goodbye alienation! Hello Shining Knight!

In the old days, on the island of my birth, whiskey inspired the down-trodden, it salved their wounds when there were no physicians, it put laughter into their lives when they were down-hearted. Whiskey helped the dying transcend the cough and the pain of "The Old Man's Friend." Whiskey made their mortal passages out of their biological bodies easier, for "The Old Man's Friend" was of course terminal bronchopneumonia. Whiskey also put a song into the hearts of the poetically inclined.

Whiskey was friend and physician to men, women and children in times of loneliness, distress, sickness and despair, and there were such times all too often in the remote regions where my people lived; and whiskey dissolved the inhibitions they subjected themselves to, it dissolved man-made barriers that separated them from each other. It was indeed the gift of the Great Spirit, it was the spirit itself, it was the essence of life, and, to be sure, it was *"the-water-of-life."* Without whiskey, what was life? Desolation. Who would want to live without The Spirit?

We of the Island had an intense, passionate, relationship with the *uisge-beatha,* meaning "water-of-life," and what a value-laden word that was! We attributed magical properties to the liquor not entirely unlike the fantasies we cast upon our images of Established Authority. The "water-of-life" could inspire, it could demoralize; it could cure, it could exacerbate; it could be a god, it could be a demon, and, indeed, how one regarded the liquor depended upon one's character structure, one's experience with it, and one's desires, not to mention one's destiny, of course.

The islanders had known for centuries that whiskey had medicinal properties, and, what do you know? During World War Two, the British bureaucrats had agreed with the Islanders, by drafting a new law that limited the sale of Scotch whiskey, so that, during that war, whiskey could only be had by physician's prescription, legally that is. Whiskey as medicine! Finally, whiskey drinking as medicinal was official, and government approved, no less, but, of course, all that was long before some committee of doctors, mindful of their responsibility to society, not at all self-serving, desirous of saving adult men and women from themselves, classified whiskey drinking as a disease. From medicine to malady in one fell swoop!

What were the consequences of and fall-out from new war-time laws? Were they entirely different from what the lawmakers said they intended? Or, were they exactly what they intended, in that strange way that people have of arranging the circumstances in their lives so as to give them exactly what they want? One might surely imagine some interesting diagnostic acrobatics, not to mention ingenious remedies on the level of the therapeutic thunderbolts of Jove, in the noble, next to holy profession. Did not its members walk on hallowed ground? Oh, yes, and their pens had power!

Even the clergy needed whiskey. Without whiskey, what would they have to rail and thunder against? And thunder they did. But not the doctors, at least not in the old days, nor did they in the days of my youth, although, to be sure, I imagined the modern physicians as "educated" in a model of disease that included efforts at liberating oneself from the insanity of life as itself a disease. Sanity as insanity: self-cure as insanity!

Such were my thoughts as I sat alone, cold-sober and silent, on a Sunday afternoon, in the airplane that was transporting me to the Treatment Center, otherwise known as "Rehab." Maybe I should have been, or maybe I had been, alive in the old days of Island "moonshine," when men captured clean water cascading down a slope known to this day as "The-Slope-of-The-Still," in a lovely sheltered hollow facing the sea, and where there still existed a rectangular elevation of soft green moss. Inside that rectangle, when the rectangle was a building with four walls and a roof, men worked at their skills, and to be sure, it wasn't all hard labor: they told stories, they laughed, they slapped each other's backs, they shared their drams, they waxed poetic and they sang their songs, but all that was in the distant past, this was now, I was on my way to be "rehabilitated," the modern American way, no less, and, in the process, if I wanted to continue as a member of the noble profession, I would have to confess in front of a group. Yes, I would have to confess my shortcomings, my failures, my sins, *in front of a group*. What's the worst thing you have ever done? I knew that to be one of the key questions I'd be asked. Oh, to be sure and it's my failure to see the light, I'd say, and thank you, all you groupies, for saving me from myself; now I'm ready for the cure.

Ostracized from the noble next-to-God profession, versus ostracized from the Noble and Exalted Society of Boozy Dreamers!

Didn't the communists use groups, directed by representatives of authority, to control individuals? Rewards given for submitting to the authority of the group-meaning indoctrination by The Party-rewards withheld, punishments given, for refusing to go along with the group, And didn't religions? How about all groups?

On the other hand, joining an esoteric group meant entering into blood comradeship with an elite few, belonging, being in on secrets denied to the majority. It meant empowerment. A member of a secret society, no less.

Hey, maybe my professional record was far too crispy clean, anyway. Who the hell was I performing for? Who was expecting what from me? What did it mean to "let someone down?" I had enslaved myself primarily, not to whiskey, which was secondary, but to some Authority that I internalized into my fantasy life as being essential to my survival. Well, I was still alive. I was a human being, a man. I had something to say, and, to be sure, whiskey served as facilitator, liberator and anesthetic. It temporarily subdued the pain of unresolved dilemmas, of which the core one was whether, on the one hand, I was living for myself, with whatever consequences, or, on the other hand, whether I was living for another, with its consequences. *Whiskey saved my life! But, to be sure, there was a price to pay.*

Tell that to my betrayers, I thought to myself. Tell them I like a dram. Tell them I have a right to my own way of life. Tell my betrayers that my great-grandfathers loved to transform a little barley mash into the *"water-of-life."* Tell my betrayers that the liquor allowed Islander of old to pay feudal dues to the overlords-boot-on-the-face Authority-it gave Islanders something to barter with, and, of course, there would be some left over for personal use. Why not? It was a way that the men and women of these past generations had of demonstrating self-respect, of transforming their lives, if only briefly. Would my betrayers listen? Would they understand? Would they be compassionate? Myself, I could hear the clink of chains. Well, I would give the damn bullshit torture so-called treatment my best shot. Yes, I would make it work. I would jump through hoops to turn my life around, or at least I'd pretend to, I'd be a model of sobriety, honesty and virtue, a well adjusted man.

"Your dental hygiene is good," said the doctor who examined me upon admission to the Alcoholism Treatment Center. He seemed surprised that I had good dental hygiene, and good teeth. The nurse, a middle-aged woman with a professionally prepared hair-do and a stiff white uniform, stood off to the side, smiling. She seemed to be enjoying herself. What the hell was so funny about all this? She seemed to know something about me. Or else some personal fantasy manifested in that smile of hers.

Once the doctor was finished with me, the nurse told me to sit in the lounge and wait. I did. Half an hour later, a lanky bald-headed man strolled amiably in my direction and identified himself as my counselor. The introduction offered me hope. I liked him and I wanted to spend time with him. He identified himself as an alcoholic. Better yet! I was going to become a member of an elite group after all. "Do you have a problem with alcohol?" he asked. "Oh, I do," I answered. "I'm here to solve my problem." What was I saying? I didn't tell him, and he didn't suggest, that alcohol was a solution to my problem, that it worked rather well, thank you. My thoughts switched and I had a fleeting fantasy of being a member of a group with secrets, sacred rituals, undertaking midnight ceremonies in smoky dimly-lit cellars, having candle-lit handholding chanting sessions, memorizing a secret code, practicing a special handshake, maybe a special tug at the ear to identify ourselves to each other in public. An Insider at last! Accepted. Good bye alienation. And all these normal people-the ones adjusted to a mad world-wouldn't know what we were up to. Well, to hell with all of them!

"What do you drink?" my counselor asked
"Whiskey."
"How much do you drink?"
"As much as I want, on my days off, of course, and I must say, I like it, but I don't drink it when I'm on duty. Oh, no, not at all when I'm on duty. I drink on weekends."
"What other drugs do you use?"
"None, I've never used narcotics or sedative-hypnotics."

Our conversations became an ongoing process during the course of my stay in "Rehab."

"Do you have any unreasonable fears?" He was carrying a clip-board, on which he scribbled something. *If it's not in the record, it isn't...* The counselor had dark eyes and a pale slightly pock-marked face that was an asset, not a liability, to his appearance. He was a mature man, quiet and self-assured, and if he had anything for sale, it didn't show. Well, he had his job to do, and he was expected to perform well in that, which meant that, like it or not, he was selling himself to some extent. Did I have any unreasonable fears? What kind of a question was that? Me, have unreasonable fears! After all, I was a psychiatrist, wasn't I?

"No, I don't have any unreasonable fears," I said.

"Well, I do," he said with a smile, "but these days, I regard them as thoughts that fly around in my head from time to time, and I don't fight them any more, so they don't bother me the way they used to."

He laid the clip-board down beside him on the chair. He had stopped writing. I looked into his eyes. I said nothing. I wasn't used to this kind of approach from a professional. I had never heard a professional admit to a less than perfect internal life in the presence of a patient or client. I liked it. I liked his approach, he was a complex human being. "How angry are you at your wife for arranging for your admission?"

"Oh, I'm not angry at Marjorie at all. I would have done the same thing if I were in her shoes. It was what I wanted for myself, deep within me. I am the one who got drunk once too often. I was a part of it. On the other hand, my work has always been good, despite my drinking. I know Marjorie loves me. She wants the best for me. Why else would she do it?"

"Are you willing to take an honest look at yourself?"

"Oh, yes, indeed, it's exactly what I want. I want to be totally honest. I have nothing to hide."

"You know, I was in treatment once, and I thought I was being honest, but when my wife came with her version of the story of our lives, I learned a few things about myself that hadn't occurred to me when I was reminiscing on my own."

He spoke in a mild voice. Was I getting exactly what I wanted in life?

"Maybe I'm angry because I'm trying to live the way I want to live and trying to live the way I imagine someone else wants me to live, at one and the same time, like trying to be in two places at one time."

"Think about it."

The following morning another nurse gave us a lecture about staying drug free and hale and hearty. "I don't regard most of you people as clean," she said. "To me, the only really clean people are those who use no chemicals, and that includes tobacco products. Many of you smoke. You're not drug free if you smoke. And as for all that coffee! That's the way I see it...I just love cleanliness."

In the Treatment Center, we were encouraged to avoid confidential conversations among each other, everything had to be revealed in group, but surely the counseling staff would be an exception. Why not confide in my counselor? Well, I might indeed do just that, but then again, didn't my counselor represent Authority? Yes, he did, and in that place, he was Authority. But my counselor was competent, I liked him, he was intelligent, he had a capacity for empathy, and it wasn't the sanitized intellectualized version of empathy that often came out of conscious efforts at being empathetic.

I tried to avoid knowing too much. I wanted to be fresh and new. I knew that there was in each and every one of us the potential for life at its best. My counselor's life seemed to be in order, he was comfortable with his role in life, he liked what he was doing, he was good at it, he wasn't striving to be someone else, he wasn't doing what he didn't want to do. His state of simply being was written all over him.

"You'll find what you're looking for here," he said to me one day, "so, be aware of what you want."

"I want to change my way of life. I want to live a sober life," I said. "I want to do my work and be emotionally aware."

"Does that present a problem?"

"Most of the counselors, but not all of them," I said, "are 'recovered alcoholics,' whatever that means, and it may be bullshit, and they've been attending meetings for years, so naturally they're one up on us. One-upmanship! How come they're always one-up on us? No doubt they're living better lives than they used to live, but they seem phony. All of them are so grateful!, and all of them identify themselves as being spiritual beings internally. What are they talking about? Why don't I get it? I don't feel grateful, far from it. I feel angry. I'm pissed. Am I supposed to pretend to 'get' this damn program, whatever that is? Who the hell wants to live by a program anyway, like an old fashioned piece of clockwork?"

"Keep talking."

"My profession is not me. As it is, we physicians grow so accustomed to using our professional façade that we get stuck in it. We'll go to any length to preserve it, and it's phony."

"It's your life, after all. If you don't live your own life, its ghost will come back to haunt you."

My counselor regarded me with quiet eyes. He said, "There was a time when I thought I was ready to put all my cards on the table, but, without my knowing it, I put some of them on the table face down. I wanted to please. I was desperately trying to be someone else. Well, I did the best I could at the time, and I believed I was preserving my integrity, my life, when, as I realized much later, I had already sold out at a very young age. I strove to succeed, I pursued the mighty dollar, and at one time I did earn a great deal, as a hot-shot executive, a successful man, as success goes, but the rewards I longed for never came. I never felt whole. I never felt real. *I was living a lie!"*

"Everybody's living a lie."

"Recently, a professor from another city came to give us a seminar. I respect the man. He knows much. I became sensitive to certain aspects of my way of working. Well, in trying to be different, as I thought the professor was suggesting, I got myself mixed up, and the quality of my work deteriorated. When I saw what was happening, I went back to being myself. I'm comfortable being myself. Of course, I'm a professional, but I'm also me. For me, the two don't conflict; they harmonize."

"I like the psychiatry. I have no conflict there," I said.

"I don't believe you do either. Not only that, but you're going to be a much better psychiatrist once you settle down, you'll see life through a different lens. Think about it. Everything will be different. You'll see things differently. You're going to be much more honest. You won't have a secret to carry inside you. In fact, you'll be more open and effective than most people around you. You're a contemplative man."

"I like to contemplate. I do believe there are important issues that only show up in contemplative mode."

"I agree with you, but our society is not geared for contemplation."

"I knew what I wanted until now, but that's changing; I'll give it more thought, I'll put it into words."

On the morning of my departure from the "Rehab Center" I had my case packed, my papers signed and I was ready to go right after breakfast. Marjorie came into my room to help me with the final stages of packing. Suddenly a shadow darkened the doorway to the room; a man stood there; a tall, broad, brown-suited man with a stern look on his countenance. Staff. He spoke to Marjorie in a gravelly cigarette voice: "You're not supposed to be in here." Oh, my! caught us. Caught us in the act of packing a suitcase, no less. Guilty as charged. How awful! What on earth did he imagine we were doing in there? A man and a woman in a bedroom! Outside the door, in the driveway, a car awaited us, and soon we were rolling away, at first slowly, then more rapidly in bright sunshine along a wide highway. It was springtime. The air was fresh.

26: WHAT'S MY SECRET?

In the mountains, a grassy slope, a bright September day, a fifteen minute break from an indoor seminar, and my new-found companion and I lying prone beside each other in the great outdoors, relaxed, comfortable in each other's presence, talking:
"My father was a family doctor of the old school. Do you know what he carried around with him in his black medical bag? You'll never guess. Two things: A picture of a human skull, as in a Skull-and-Crossbones flag, only instead of crossbones, there was a red cross slashed across the skull. Imagine that."

"What was the second thing?"

"A loaded revolver."

"Wow! It's a hard act to follow."

"He loved his work, the people loved him, he was surgically proficient, and he practiced until he was an old man. Yes, my father died with his boots on, and I'm happy to report that he never used his revolver."

"Why the gun?"

"Protection. Why else?"

"From what?"

"He feared robbery; he feared assault, but perhaps I, a psychiatrist, might imagine he feared disability, the inability to be, in other words, he feared the end of his life, as he imagined it."

"Did he ever tell you that's what he feared?"

"No, he didn't. He was a rock."

"So, how do you know?"

"I could read the signs. He was a man of action, externalizing, serving others while ignoring his own need for intimacy. He was always on call for others."

"Strong man; Achilles heel."

"It's as if our culture requires it of us, and particularly of physicians, of those who fly in the face of death dealing diseases and wounds, but, speaking for myself, I have insecurities, but no intense fear, or if it's there, it's unconscious, and, yes, fear can be out of awareness; we suppress, disguise our fears. I love my work. I'm one of the lucky ones."

"So am I."

"Think of the way we talk when we're young. We want to serve the sick, the lame, the down-trodden, and oh, we volunteer our time in serving the underprivileged, and then we talk about 'something happening,' during medical school years, causing us to lose our idealism. We don't change. It's just that we let go of the façade of altruism. We claim a noble calling, many of us aspire to noble labor, and many of us would love to have it so, but it isn't so in any society on earth, and so we have a dilemma. Many of us become disillusioned. Oh, and by the way, we never make mistakes, do we? I mean, we don't admit to making mistakes. If we did, we'd be blamed. We'd be punished. Who dares be honest? Our society penalizes those who admit to making mistakes. In concealing ourselves, we betray ourselves."

"Perhaps the truly courageous in life are those who express themselves openly from the heart, not exclusively intellectually, but by living."

Off came my shoes, my socks, and my shirt. Oh, that grass! Fibrous texture massaging me, tickling me, tingling me, opening up my memory box: The feel of the mountain grass against my skin, the remoteness of the region, the cool fresh air, and the silence, reminded me of my boyhood days in Scotland, with my little dog, Teeni, romping around, cavorting, chasing rabbits, sniffing out mice, leaping after birds, living her dharma. Living her dharma! Imagine that! And she never even thought about it, nor contemplated for a moment. As for the old country, I could never forget it, and I never wanted to, but neither could I ever go back, even if I wanted to, which I didn't. In Scotland, of course, it was heather, grass, and sand that I lay on. So what? It felt the same, the air felt similar, and so, that morning I wanted to curl my toes into the turf, I wanted to feel the wild grass rubbing against my naked torso and legs, and I did.

At the time I was competent in psychiatry as practiced, but I had yet to acquire under my belt years of experience that would provide me with the kind of deep insight and wisdom that makes for a strong professional identity. I knew I was a unique gifted human being with a legitimate claim on life, with a right to be myself, with a right to express myself, but, at the same time, I limited my own potential. I believed the people who wrote the text books. I eagerly sought out the senior experts, the sanctioned leaders. I looked to them for guidance. I imagined they knew the secrets. I longed to be let in on the secrets. Oh, to know the secrets!

What secrets?

Somewhere in the higher echelons of psychiatry, there were experts who knew the secret to insightful psychotherapy, the secret to knowing the human being, the secret to understanding schizophrenia, the secret to understanding depression, the secret to understanding anxiety, the secret of the dilemma of life, the secret to emancipation, the secret to whatever the fashionable question of the day happened to be, bottom line, the secret of life, or so I imagined, and indeed, some of them gave the impression that they knew.

I wanted the secret of life! I wanted to crack the code, but I had no key. One thing I did have was persistence, and I was observant, I was dedicated, not thoroughly playful, perhaps, but ready to play at times, I was also passionately curious, and it all paid off in due course, leading me to the unexpected.

In the work that I did, my colleagues and I assumed that family physicians wanted to be more educated in psychiatry than they were. We assumed that the public wanted their family doctors to be psychiatrically sophisticated. We assumed that the practice of medicine would take a quantum leap forward if only we delivered psychiatric education in an on-going clinical way to medical students and residents who would be the family doctors of the future. It took some courage on our part to do the work we did. We made ourselves vulnerable.

What if family doctors didn't want to learn psychiatry? What if patients who sought out family doctors didn't want psychiatric interventions as part of their medical care? What if, bottom line, we ended up teaching psychiatry to people who didn't want to learn it? Yes, we did talk about these possible complications, and we concluded that over time all involved would become so accustomed to the work that psychiatrists did that they would lose their fear of it. Yes, we believed that people feared psychiatry, that people feared exposure of their inner lives to the light of day.

Who didn't fear exposure of one's inner private life to the light of day? Who among us wouldn't use whatever defensive maneuvers we had at our disposal to protect our secrets? Uninvited intruders into other people's private domains are rarely welcome.

In our vision, psychiatry and general medicine complemented each other, there was a psychological component to just about every disease, and the idea of integrating psychiatry into medical practice in clinics that would also serve as teaching models for students and resident family physicians was a good idea whose time had come, an idea that would benefit future generations. At the time, I was the primary teaching psychiatrist in our program. I saw myself as improving the quality of care for others, and, yes, I made my contributions. Our efforts benefited society, we encouraged psychological awareness, we engaged in comprehensive evaluations and treatments, and I felt good about the work we did. Others followed in our footsteps.

In my conversation with my companion for a day, I said: "Taking the situation further. Maybe Dr. Albert Schweitzer was genuinely altruistic, but most of us are not. Some say that we have 'big egos,' like prima donnas, some say that we like to 'play God,' some say that we try to prolong life because we fear death, our own death, some say that we desperately want to feel needed and loved, that we labor long hours to that end, some say that we harbor secret sadistic impulses that we suppress, hiding them even from ourselves, but hidden or not, we fear our own secret impulses and fantasies, and so we compensate by behaving in pseudo-altruistic ways.

"We labor at fixing others, and, as we do so, we may indeed ignore our own deepest spiritual wants. To the degree that that's true, it has consequences. Over the centuries we have developed societies that require us, if we want to 'succeed,' to fit into pigeon holes, but we feel stuck in that we have life obligations and they are real: If we abandon a job we hate, we fail in our social roles; if we stay with it, we lose out on fulfillment."

"We live in a neurotic dilemma-ridden society," my companion said, "a society that claims to value Christian love, as practiced by Christ, but we don't practice it in our personal or professional pursuits, and, indeed, maybe our secular values, as we live them, are not compatible with living in love as taught by Christ. Maybe the way we define success and love are incompatible.

"An authentic physician is a gem, a treasure, a human being who is living his or her dharma, working honorably, losing personal narcissism in the work. But there is a disturbing potential situation. If it's true that we already have secret sadistic impulses that we suppress, all we need is a major national crisis, a belief that our country is in mortal danger, a strong man to take charge, a malevolent leader who'd tap into our suppressed impulses,-something that charismatic malevolent leaders seemed adept at-and, under social and personal stress, we would regress psychologically, we would give up serving others, we would abandon or efforts at altruism, or, what is more likely, we'd redefine that word. We'd bottom out, act out our repressed impulses. We'd rationalize our conduct by claiming that we were serving our country, that we were preserving our cherished freedom, serving humanity. There is historical precedent."

"It's a mighty big 'what if?'"

"I'm simply suggesting a hypothetical situation. Strange events happen when men and women follow strong leaders."

"There's something about you that fascinates me. Would you like to know what it is?" my companion said.

"Yes, of course."

"Alright, but first of all, before I tell you: Why did you come to America?"

"My father spent time in America, during the depression. He went back to Scotland to marry my mother. I grew up liking America, or at least what I imagined America represented in this world. In Canada, following a car accident, I wanted to know myself. I wanted to know the human being in the best possible way."

"Well, go on."

"The best training was in the United States; I was in Canada. I wanted my share of the American Dream. To me, the American Dream meant working hard in a free society, it meant becoming proficient in my profession, it meant becoming the best that I was capable of becoming, it meant becoming successful, it meant acquiring status in society, and I believed I could aspire to all of that in America."

"Wasn't there some other reason?"

"In Scotland I felt stifled. I didn't like the old entrenched establishment in Edinburgh, and I daresay they didn't like me, a young man who didn't seem to fit in. Anyway, I wanted to cast off the old. I wanted to make a fresh start in America, in the land of opportunity. I identified with the American values, as I understood them. I was passionate about the United States, what it stood for, the idea of liberation from old oppressive ways and values."

"Are you happy living in America?"

"Yes."

"There's something else, isn't there?"

"My mother often told me I that God had a purpose for me,

a specific purpose I would one day fulfill. Maybe that was nothing but an empty fantasy on her part. I don't have a clue, but it's not something I give much thought to."

"Well, do you want to hear it?"

"Hear what?"

"What I find so fascinating about you."

"Certainly, I do."

"It's this. You have something valuable inside you that you conceal."

"What are you talking about?"

"What's inside you is valuable. Others would benefit from knowing about it. I hope you allow it to come out. By holding it inside, you deprive others, but more importantly, you deprive yourself. I know."

What was this man talking about? Silence! There we were, two strangers, essentially passing each other, expecting to never see each other again, touching each other briefly, but I never forgot it.

"I'm good at this," he said. "I can tune into people. I have confidence in my ability to know people. I repeat: Why keep it a secret?"

"I wish I knew what it is I'm keeping secret. All I can think of saying is that, if I had stayed in the Old Country, I would have died, not necessarily literally, but that's not what you're referring to."

"Maybe you have to die in order to live," he said.

With that, he got up and walked away. The encounter was over. We never did resume our conversation where we left off, and a couple of days later, we went our separate ways, never to see each other again. Later, I learned that he had passed away suddenly not long after this.

27: INTENSIVE CARE

At seven-thirty in the morning, the intensive care department smelled of bedpans and of red liquids, orange liquids, of plastic bottles, of yellow rubber gloves, of floor mops, and of wheeled buckets containing mucky water, pushed by a woman dressed in light pink. Maybe an immigrant.
Some clatter around the periphery, but in the center, where the electronic controls were located, where silent nurses and technicians gazed at green flickering screens, all was quiet.

I didn't come with a cheery wave of my hand, I didn't come with a broad smile on my face, I came as I was, a serious minded professional man with important work to do, work not as glamorous as surgery, to be sure, but just as important, and, mindful of my role, I paused in the doorway to one of the treatment rooms, to let the man in the bed see me. He noticed me, we made eye contact, and in his eyes what I saw was anguish, demoralization, but there was more:

"I don't need a psychiatrist. I don't have any mental problems."

The folder I held in my left hand felt clean and cool to the touch. It was an aluminum folder, inside of which snuggled a thin paper hospital chart, clearly that of a recent admission, and, as for the intensive care unit, well, it was not my usual turf, it was not my preferred place in which to do the kind of work I loved to do, but it was where I would be on certain mornings, when I happened to be on emergency duty for the hospital, in order to attend to whatever psychiatric crises might have occurred during the night, any night.

"Excuse me while I get a chair; I'll be right with you."

I knew where to look, in a corner of the room, to my right as I entered, away from the bed, where the only chair in the room, a slim, spare folding-chair, painted brown, was planted and half-hidden behind two unused chrome colored aluminum stands designed to hold bottles of intravenous fluids. Extracting the chair from behind the gadgets, unfolding it, placing it alongside the bed, offering the man a chance to see me moving around, sitting down facing him.

"I haven't had a chance to introduce myself yet. How do you know I'm a psychiatrist?"

"Oh, they told me you'd be coming. I know who you are. I can tell."

"Well, here I am, and I am a psychiatrist," I said, giving the man my name, "Do you mind if you and I have a conversation? Your doctor asked me to interview you. It's important."

"Oh, you're welcome to ask questions, if you want, but I don't have any mental problems. If I had any mental problems, surely I would be the first to know about them, wouldn't I?"

"You might, if you were open to it, but we all tend to hide our painful emotions from ourselves in any way we can, and avoid facing dilemmas, push them down, or sideways, if you know what I mean, and if don't know what I mean, let's talk about that. It doesn't hurt to examine oneself a little."

"So, how do we go about doing that?"

"So, here you are in intensive care, waking up after a serious overdose. A good thing you were rescued, for, if you hadn't been, your brain would probably have shut down, and you might not have made it until morning. Hospital bye-laws require a psychiatric consultation. Now, your overdose was no accident. Would you like to talk about it?"

The yellow fluid dripping from a bottle slung from a tall aluminum pole leaning over the head of the bed hesitated in its journey into the needle that was embedded in a vein in the man's right forearm, then, as the man's arm muscles relaxed again, the fluid resumed its flow. The man's chest heaving rhythmically beneath a pale wrinkled hospital gown; several silver colored metallic electrodes plopped on his chest.

"Doctor, like I said, ...hey, I know you have your job to do and I want to cooperate, so if you want me to talk, please tell me exactly what to say and I'll say it...go ahead and ask."

"Thank you. I understand what you're saying. Now, let's start with one important question: Did you mean to die when you swallowed all these pills, along with the vodka?"

"What's the point of living? They'd all be better off without me. I'd be doing everybody a favor. I'm not worth anything to anybody."

Next to the far side of the bed from me, a dark green machine with multiple knobs and needled dials sat on a tall, spare, two-tiered metallic table. Out of the green machine spiraled several wires that ended in the silver colored electrodes on the man's chest. The curly wires transmitted electrical impulses from the man's heart muscle into the interior of the machine, where a little "brain" converted the impulses into colored wiggles on the machine's white, rectangular face, and all the time the green machine rolled a white paper tongue, decorated with red and black lines, out of its mouth, crinkling in a mild-mannered way like old fashioned ticker-tape.

"You're not worth anything to anybody?"

"She doesn't want to live with me anymore. Oh, she's left me several times, but never anything serious. I mean, I knew she'd come back these other times. This time it's different. She took her stuff with her, other times she didn't. She's into this woman thing, you know, she's a feminist. We used to be comfortable with each other, know each other; now we don't trust each other any more."

"How do you account for the change?"

"All I know is she's different. Where is the woman I married? No more love. I'm all alone. The house is like a tomb. The walls were closing in on me. I couldn't stand it any longer. Yes, I took the pills. I wanted out. Who wouldn't?"

"Yes, please continue."

"I had to prove to her how much I love her."

"Isn't this an unusual way of demonstrating love?"

"She would know I was willing to die for her."

"What if you had died? How would she feel?"

"All I know is I was willing to die for her."

"And you say you had to do this."

"Yes, nothing else worked. I was desperate."

"What does desperate mean?"

"Doctor, I wasn't angry, just frustrated."

"We can help you clarify your life situation, your human relationships, see options and solutions, you'll regain your self-confidence, you'll take action."

Asking for psychiatric help openly wasn't easy in a culture that valued mastery, not even in communities where psychiatric care was fashionable, it being more natural to struggle over mastery, over material possessions, over pride, blame others, blame circumstances, all ego, and, to be sure, this was not confined to any particular group of people. We all, without exception, defend ourselves when we feel under stress. Indeed, the stress reaction is in part at least a biological defensive mechanism with a psychiatric component.

And here was a disheveled unshaven man connected to life-support machines, surrounded by symbols of authority: men in white coats, green scrubs; stethoscopes, needles; nurses; technicians. Not exactly the usual public image of a psychiatrist at work. What! no beard. No couch. No inkblots. No Freudian imagery; no yuppies talking about sex.

Sometimes it would be a woman in the bed, weeping quietly, a box of tissues by her side, more open to the suggestion of personal psychological problems, but also driven to desperate measures, equally alone in her view of the world.

"I can't keep a man. I'm not worth anything to anybody. Who would want me?"

"Please tell me more about that."

"He told me I've let myself go, and maybe I have, but what can I do? I've had children. What does he expect? I'm no spring chicken. I lost all my confidence. I felt drained. Everything looked gray and foggy. We used to have fun together, going places, but as time went on, he changed. He tells me I'm jealous all the time. Maybe I am. I just don't want to lose him."

"Did you tell him you were afraid of losing him?"

"No, I kept it all to myself. I thought it would make my situation worse if I told him. Why, do you think I should have told him?"

"We can help you examine yourself, understand aspects of yourself, to see options."

"I don't know about that. This place is making me depressed. I don't see how this place can possibly help me if it's making me depressed. Now that I'm here, I'm really depressed."

"Now that you're here, you're free to come to your feelings, rather than push them down, and so, if it seems that this place is causing your depression, I suggest that tell me more."

"I feel empty, I can't sleep. Nobody cares about me any more, but, Doctor, I can tell you one thing, and that is I don't get angry. It's not in my nature. I'm easy-going. I try to get along with everybody. I'm pretty good natured. It's the way I've always been."

"It can be a tall order."

"It's better than getting mad and throwing dishes around, screaming and yelling and smashing things. I've heard that psychiatrists try to get people angry. Is that what you're trying to do? Is it? Please tell me. Are you trying to get me to lose my temper? Well, you're not going to get me mad, so there!"

"What if you lost control?"

"Control is all I've got left."

"What if?"

"I'd...I just want to fade away into deep sleep, not come back. Who can I trust?"

"Have the men in your life let you down? Are you afraid I'll let you down, just like the rest?"

Accepting a fresh Kleenex from me, from a box, with trembling hand, eyes moist, eyelids swollen, voice husky:

"I've been let down a lot; betrayed is more like it, and abandoned, more than once."

Under the stress of intimacy and family life, outer appearances fail, old fantasies surface, past lives come into current lives, and so, to those who are close to us, it's as if we change, but, in part at least-this is well accepted by professionals-we all tend to see in the life drama around us themes from the past, dilemmas from the past, we 'create' our life dramas over and over again, until one day our eyes open. And in these human relationship dramas, we defend ourselves in that we approach people with a façade that conceals what we want to not admit to in our personal lives,-out of fear of consequences-for it's usually considered a negative. It is part of the work of a psychiatrist to unravel this.

I don't want to go on like this. There must be something I'm doing to contribute to the problems I'm encountering in life. They keep repeating. I'm approaching despair. I want to examine my life. I've had enough of this. I'll do whatever it takes.

Not very often, but sometimes.

Psychiatric methods did work, not always of course, and, when they did, they were well worth the effort and risk, but then again, there were those-and years later I became one of them-who saw hospital psychiatric units as authoritarian controlling institutions, representative of, and agents of, a controlling authoritarian society, rather than liberating environments where people who wanted help might gain insight into their dilemma-laden lives, see options, and drum up courage to act if so desired. Of course, we prescribed psychiatric medications when appropriate, and, certainly they made a difference in the recovery of patients. We might promise help with the application of assorted methods of therapy, but no one could promise 'cure' to another. No human being had power to 'cure' another, and a good thing too! Power such as that would surely be abused.

Someone knocking at the door. A nurse poking her head in.

An announcement: "The patient's husband is here. He wants to know if he can visit."

"The patient's wife is here...."

"Certainly, I'll talk to both of them together."

And hard lines dissolving from faces, tears of misery and despair becoming tears of relief. A man leaning over the bed. A woman throwing herself on the bed:

"I love you, honey."

"I love you too."

28: RESPECTED ELDER BROTHER

A distinguished Gentleman from the East was visiting California. He was a 'Gentleman' reputed to be of great spiritual insight, a man of integrity, a man whom, the moment I heard of him, I knew to be genuine, and different from anyone I had ever met, although exactly how different, I didn't at that time know. What to do? Without delay, I flew to California to meet him, drawn to whom I did not know, and so initially I refer to him as a 'Gentleman from the East,' although, to be sure, that is not who or what he is, something I'll get to later.

The first thing I noticed upon awakening in California were the golden yellow rays of the recently risen sun shining brightly through the window shades of my hotel room. Then, right away, I noticed something else, and it was fear. I was afraid. I had not been afraid the day before, when winging my way west, I had not been afraid when I went to bed. So, what was I afraid of? I feared a spiritual confrontation with myself, that's what.

There was no organization. There was no group to join. There was nothing I had to swear to, or promise to fulfill. No commitment. No one wanted money from me. No one wanted my signature on a document. Maybe, I thought, I should back out and not proceed any further. I could return home without making contact and no one would even ask me what had transpired. And what did I imagine would transpire? In an honest confrontation with myself, a part of me would die that day. I knew it.

It had to! I was living another's dharma, or trying to, in the midst of living my own past, distant, remote, much of it from past lives, dilemmas, compromises, in ignorance of who I was, practicing ceremonies and rituals, and, as always, there were consequences. Or, to put it another way, I was undergoing karma that was necessary for me to experience as part of my unfolding destiny in my life, to open me up to more life, to the unknown, to the unknowable, to my Self.

The 'Gentleman from the East' I was about to meet had, so I had learned, a rather low opinion of gurus. It was a term that we in the West rarely used in a serious way, although we used it occasionally tongue in cheek, but, at the time, I myself was questioning certain aspects of the role of psychiatrists in western society. Psychiatrists as the gurus of the

West! Psychiatrists as the working arm of Authority! Psychiatrists as professionals licensed by Authority to bring the wandering sheep back into the fold that was an increasingly authoritarian society. Well, what about that? I didn't like the idea one bit. I much preferred to see my work as liberating, offering insight into life, facilitating a maturational process, opening up possibilities, and indeed, it had that potential, but then again, there it was, that nasty notion, wriggling away in some corner of my mind, like an unborn bird tapping at the inside of its egg shell.

I peeked out the hotel window. Outside, a beautiful November sun lit up the city. The dull gray blanket of atmospheric dust that had obscured my view of the city from the oval window of the descending aircraft the previous day was nowhere to be seen in the morning from below, even as I knew it was still there. It had to be. The clarity around and above me that I saw from below was phony.

Surface clarity concealing murkiness beneath, something hidden from view, something that could only be observed if viewed from a special perspective, something symbolic of our way of life.

The 'Gentleman from the East,' the one I had come to see,

would know me, all of me, right down to my core. I was confident of that. I would visit him. I made a telephone call:

"When would you like to come?"

"This morning, if I may. I'll take a cab from the hotel right after breakfast. Is that satisfactory?"

"Certainly; please do come."

A pair of dark luminous eyes, projecting profound all-seeing wisdom, scanning my facade, perceiving my core character, gazed directly into mine as I stood uncertainly in the hall of the house where he resided. An elderly gentleman, dressed in white Indian garments, a khurta and a lungi, which roughly translates into a loose tropical shirt for the torso, and a wrap-around garment from the waist to the calves.

He went by the name of Dadaji. I had been told that the name Dadaji meant Respected Elder Brother to all.

Dadaji halted directly in front of me. He lowered his gaze. He placed the palm of his right hand over my middle just under my heart. He held it there in silence. I waited, not knowing what to expect, aware of the seconds ticking by. Finally he dropped his hand, he looked at me casually, and he asked:

"Do you have a car?"

My weighty sense of self-importance, the weight of the world I was carrying on my shoulders, my self-blame, my self-judgment, that is to say, my egocentric narcissism, vanished; all of it, as if into thin air. No exposure. No rejection. No day of judgment. No demands that I abandon whatever gave me transient security, whatever gave me status, whatever gave me feedback that I imagined I needed. No demand that I identify myself. No confrontation with Authority. No standing alone. No demand that I clarify whatever dilemmas I had in my private life. My mental version of the universe, my splitting of my mind into two, the judgment I had expected, were all fantasies, perhaps based on my self-created images from the past, all the way back to the beginning of my present life, possibly from past lives; yes, definitely in its roots, at least, from a series of past lives in continuum, quite beyond my limited perception.

"No, I don't have a car, I came by taxi," I said.

I had an extended personal meeting with Dadaji that morning. He accepted me as I was in a gentle, compassionate way that surprised me pleasantly, delighted me. Something about this 'Gentleman from the East,' a non-verbal transmission, touched me deeply. I was in the right place at the right time. He didn't question me about who I was, or who I imagined I was. He didn't question whether I was in fit spiritual condition, whether I was sufficiently worthy, or whether I was in any way qualified. This was not what I had expected. I had expected something more formal, perhaps a more organized reception, accustomed as I was to western experts, specialists and speakers.

From an early age, Dadaji had questioned ways of empowering rituals, of engaging in ceremonies, of prescribing rigid rules for living, of accepting dogma, of offering sacrifices, of doing penance, and of submitting to the authority of clergy, wise-men, spiritual preceptors, swamis, or gurus, and, to be sure, at the time, I questioned some of our own socially sanctioned professional methods of practicing psychiatry in the West. I had yet to paint for myself a clear picture of exactly what it was I believed was wrong with our professional institutions, and with our way of life, but it seemed to me as if we created complex frames of reference, in both psychiatry and religion, based on limited knowledge that we then quarreled over endlessly, quarrels that obscured, rather than illuminated, our journey through life.

Dadaji always earned his own living, without trying to acquire wealth, in a number of ways over the years. He was competent in whatever work he undertook. Whatever he did in his personal life, he did so at his own expense. When he traveled, he paid his own way. He never accepted money or gifts from people who visited him, or for his personal meetings.

Later on that day, more people came to join us. These were people who had met Dadaji previously, who came to pay their respects, to reunite with each other, to replenish. I did not know any of them. In the midst of that small group, Dadaji looked directly at me:

"What do you want?"

The question took me by surprise, for I didn't expect to be singled out in a group of strangers. Why had I come? I hadn't come for anything material, or, for that matter, for anything that I could express in so many words. Strange, but true. Later, I imagined it was strange that I hadn't prepared a few questions in advance, which is what I would normally have done if I had been meeting an American expert. Well, why didn't I ask for advice on how to live differently? Why didn't I ask for his blessing? Why didn't I ask for his expertise as a master spiritual psychologist, to help me clarify my thinking, allowing me to live in a more enlightened manner? Why didn't I ask for guidance along a pathway to liberation? Why didn't I ask for wisdom? Why didn't I ask for a better understanding of the human being, so that I could have greater insight and perform my work better, thus benefiting humanity? None of that occurred to me at the time.

I didn't ask for anything.

The vast majority of people who came to see Dadaji, I had been told, came with a hidden agenda, wanting better conditions in their lives, a better love life perhaps, or a better job, more power, more status, or recognition, in short, a better destiny. Of course, some came to discredit him, to find flaws in him, to expose him as a fraud, to be one up on him. He knew. He let them be. That, he had said, was also part of how life was. Not that he didn't clarify and assert, whenever appropriate. He certainly did, and fearlessly.

One of the men in the room took me aside for a few minutes and he said to me: "You would not believe the things I have seen: miracles, happenings so against the laws of nature that even I who have seen these things with my own eyes doubt them. Even as we see such events, we doubt. We cannot fathom what we are looking at." The man told me he had seen the sick healed, matter materialized out of thin air, the local climate altered temporarily, Dadaji appearing simultaneously in multiple places, and much more, all to the bafflement of observers, including respected scientists from several countries and other educated professionals. I listened to the man. I thanked him. Perhaps he believed that that was what I had come for. If so, he was wrong. I did not want any of that.

I had not come to California to see miracles or wondrous deeds, I had not come to listen to inspirational messages or sermons, I had not come to meet a guru, I had not come in search of "God-realization" or "enlightenment," while secretly wanting what I imagined would make my own secular life better. I had grown weary of pursuing goals based on false values, goals that promised much, but left me frustrated. I had had enough of that.

What did I want? Dadaji asked me the question several times. Maybe the question referred, just as much to what I wanted from him on that particular day, as to what I wanted in my life, as my life mission. Was there anything I wanted so passionately that I believed I came into life to find it, to live it? If so, was I avoiding it? Was I sacrificing my life for the sake of living another's dharma? I had time to contemplate, to clarify what I already knew.

I wanted Truth, I didn't know what Truth was, I wanted to know my Self, I didn't know what knowing Self was. I held my peace. Actually, I was there because I was there, and seeking reasons after the event is...Dadaji knew my inner thoughts, he knew who I was, he knew my life dilemmas. It was something I intuitively sensed at the time, something I later on confirmed. But who was Dadaji? Or, who is he? He still is,-that I know-but he remains far away from those who try to understand. I don't understand.

Seven months after my visit to California, I awoke from a deep sleep one morning to find the bedroom quiet, dark and familiar, but also sensing that something was different. I was wide awake. Then there came a scent, faint at first, reminiscent in quality of the aroma of the sea after a long, dusty overland journey. In a few seconds the aroma became strong. It could not be denied. I sat up straight in bed, recognizing the aroma of sandalwood and spices that reminded me of shady tropical trees and the gentle chirping of birds. I greedily breathed in the complex aroma. The scent came from the south-west corner of the room. The six corners of the room were empty. Yes, it was a six-cornered room. But the room wasn't empty for long.

Dadaji materialized, he walked over to my left side as I lay in bed, and he stood there, about two feet away from me, smiling down at me and gazing directly into my eyes. He was dressed in a bright blue Indian lungi from the waist down and a white short-sleeved shirt called a dhoti. For several seconds we remained locked in each other's gaze, then he vanished. I was wide awake.

I swung my legs on to the floor and walked over to the southwest corner of the room, where the aroma was coming from, but there was nothing there except the walls. I examined the other corners of the room, the furniture, the drapes, the adjoining bathroom, and the windows, but there was nothing unusual to be seen. I savored the aroma, enjoying it, wanting more of the same, standing silently in the middle of the floor, but all too soon the aroma was gone. The room went back to normal, but I did not. I felt elated, euphoric, I felt connected to something I didn't understand, I felt a sense of benevolence all around me, and within me I felt bliss. I looked at Marjorie. She was lying on her right side, sleeping soundly, with the palm of her right hand under the right side of her face.

I would be going to India soon.

PART FOUR
INDIA

29: DADAJI

The aroma hit me the moment I walked out of the cool cabin of the India Air flight from Bombay to Calcutta, to begin descending the metal stairs to the blacktop of Kolkata's Dum Dum airport. It was the first of my six visits to India.

A fabulous nation, a complex culture, multiple languages, exquisite beauty, splendor beyond compare, some of which I would see later on. Yes, India was complexity. There was the India of ancient art and sculpture, there was the India of music, there was the India of great modern architecture, there was the India of a motion picture industry that produced more films every year than Hollywood, there was the India of Hinduism, Jainism and Buddhism, there was the India of the Vedas, the Mahabharata, the Upanishads, the Bhagavad Gita, the Dhammapada, the Ramayana; there was the India of timeless wisdom, there was the India of Sanatana Dharma, the Eternal Religion, invisible to those who did not want it, clear and present for those who did.

Mother India.

On my way from the airport, from my seat in a taxi that blew smoke through broken floorboards, I saw in the distance silhouettes of human figures poking around in dark, smoking, surreal-looking mounds. Men and women dressed in loin cloths. The soles of their feet must have endured much over the years before they became thick and insensitive to the heat of the burning cinders, the sharpness of broken glass and metal, and the stress of whatever else impinged upon them.

Rag-clad people eking out a living as scavengers. They were the world's disenfranchised, the helpless ones, the abandoned ones; they represented the down side of what I imagined I was, the dark side of the ambivalence in my intimate human relationships, hidden beneath my social facade. In the psychological mirror they held in front of me, I got a glimpse, during that initial moment when I was open to it, of my own helplessness, of my ultimate powerlessness. What if *I* had been born into...? Who knows but that I might have been at one time in my long history of many lives, long forgotten, blanked out. We were, after all, manifestations of the One, but, with our divisive, dilemma-riddled, splintering minds, we saw separation, all ego.

In the city, the downtown traffic only seemed chaotic to my unaccustomed eye. Actually, it had its own order, and all the vehicles moved around and past each other without incident and without colliding. The sun was shining and downtown Kolkata was beautiful. Indeed, I felt as if I was coming home. Home! What? Yes, Vivekananda Road; Mahatma Gandhi Road; Chowringhee/Jawaharlal Nehru Road. It all fell into place for me. The hotel itself was a well kept, elegant, modern building surrounded by a gated wall, a clean pebbled driveway in front and a bright brass colored doorway. A brightly uniformed doorman sprang into action the moment the taxi squealed to a halt. A marbled lobby, a modern elevator, a spacious room, a luxurious bathroom, clean towels, fresh water....It had been a long journey.

In the hotel room, I picked up the telephone. Kolkata telephones, I had been told, had minds of their own, minds that delighted in playing tricks on compulsive watch-wearing westerners. I dialed Dadaji's number, and, to my surprise, Dadaji himself picked up the instrument on the second ring. Contact was immediate. I was surprised at finding the equipment working so efficiently, I was surprised that he answered in English, for, after all, the people of Kolkata spoke Bengali or Hindi, unless there was specific reason to speak in English.

"My name is Donald...."

"Yes, come; come now."

I hadn't expected a personal invitation to visit Dadaji's house that day. I had expected to ask for directions to where a gathering of international visitors would assemble on the following day, but, of course, I happily accepted. A car and driver were readily available at the hotel door, and within 15 minutes I was sitting in the back seat of an olive-green Ambassador, driven by a young man with a ready smile and a limited but adequate command of the English language. I was excited at this unexpected turn of events. I also had a comfortable feeling that everything was going to be alright. A sense of equanimity.

Out in the street the air was humid, and dust blew in through the open windows of the Ambassador, bringing with it a rich, sweet, pungent aroma of humanity, fruit, vegetation, drain water, and also of something complex and mysterious of no specific identity. It was the same complex aroma that had greeted me the moment I stepped out of the aircraft door, on to the platform of the ramp. Several times the Ambassador halted, caught in traffic. Once, a boy stuck his head in through the open window next to me and stared silently at me all the time we were stopped there. The boy didn't ask for money. Dusty hands, bare-chested, bare-footed, torso covered with a fine layer of dust; despite that, an impression of cleanliness. Maybe it was his eyes: wide, moist, dark and limpid. Behind these eyes was a complex human being, learning to become a man while running around the streets of Kolkata. Relative to the boy, I was affluent, well-fed and privileged; relative to other Americans, I was middle-class. The boy let go of the vehicle only when the wheels began to roll again. Was everything in this world exactly the way it was supposed to be? From one perspective, things were the way they were supposed to be, but that was no prescription for passivity; on the contrary, we were to do our best in our activities of life, avoiding exploitation, either as perpetrators or as victims, and, for those of us who had eyes to see, there was much to do in our world, according to whatever talents and desires we might have. Work was important.

Fantasies from the past flashing on to the screen of present encounters, attempts to fulfill opposing desires simultaneously, dilemmas, ignorance of authentic identity, ignorance of why we are in this life, superstitious ceremonies to 'liberate' us from that which we fail to understand, increasing anger at entrapment in the neurosis,-an endless struggle to serve two authorities, resentment, suppression, a 'dark side,' *the war within*, anger at entrapment in situations where our only options seem to be one of two undesirables, enemies all around-war without.

Dadaji was different. He was without social, personal or psychological façade, beyond mental defenses, beyond human dilemmas, beyond mind: So I had learned; so I believed, and so I knew it to be. I felt my chest unwinding as if blood vessels were opening up spontaneously, as if my chest muscles were relaxing, my bronchial tubes widening.

A gentle breeze blew through the wide-open windows of the room I found myself in late that afternoon. It was a warm tropical breeze that was comforting and dry, that carried with it an occasional human sound like a shout, and a couple of times a sound like something metallic falling from a height, and of vehicle horns blowing in the distance. Kolkata hummed and throbbed with vitality.

Dadaji's hair was fine, firm and dark, receding on top at the sides, over the temples, but still prominent at the middle. His smooth, delicate skin was remarkably free of stress lines. Clean dark eyebrows curved upwards over the eyes; the bridge of his nose was wide, and beneath, his mouth curved upwards on each side in a smile. I felt a tingle in my middle, tears of tenderness. He reached out towards me, placed the palm of his right hand under the base of my heart, and we sat there in silence for a few seconds. I became aware of my heart, the center of my being. I became aware of its rhythm, its lub-dub sound, its significance as a vital organ. In India, the heart was considered to be the center of one's being, where the essence resided. I leaned slightly forward, revealing myself from my inside, allowing him access to whatever I had in there, including the structure of my character, and the way I operated in life, the way I made myself appear morally superior to others, the way I saw my own flaws in others, the way I passed judgment upon others, and the degree to which I was unforgiving of those who had 'done' to me! Despite insight and experience. As a member of my own profession, Psychiatry, I defined, diagnosed and claimed to have methods of curing, disorders of that intangible ethereal function called mind that we spoke of and wrote about in metaphoric terms, or by using analogies. All mind. Mind evaluating mind. And what was mind if not fleeting and capricious? Ego examining ego....

Of course, we had our learned disciplines, we had our diagnostic manual, our books, our journals, we had our technology, we were socially designated experts, we had medicines to prescribe, and, to be sure, society rewarded us with success and status. But what, bottom line, did society want from us? It was a question I seriously considered on a daily basis at that time in my life, a question the answer to which would only later come to me.

Dadaji dropped his hand.

As an experienced American psychiatrist, I was accustomed to formality, ritual and the aura of importance that a "great man" generated around him-after all, we had many "great men" in the profession-and I had expected Dadaji to behave like a "great man" of the West. I had expected him to be protected by underlings, assistants, possibly a secretary. I had expected barriers. I could not have been more wrong.

"What do you want?"

What did I want?

I imagined I pursued exactly what I wanted in life. Did it present any dilemma? Was there compatibility between exactly what society wanted from me in concrete terms, and exactly what I wanted for myself in life? For a time, I imagined I would find the secrets of the mind, possibly the secret of life, in my medical studies, in neurology, in psychiatry, but alas, it was nowhere to be found in my pursuits, and the years were rolling by.

I suspected that something in my work as a psychiatrist was inconsistent with spiritual authenticity and integrity, and I was slowly pondering whether or not we psychiatrists would be far better off if we simply practiced getting to know the human being, using the frames of reference that worked, exposing and clarifying dilemmas, promoting self-examination and self-knowledge, reviewing options in those who wanted that, and only in those who wanted it, for, after all, 'cure' came from within, and no 'cure' could be delivered from without by another, as if it were some message, although "recovery" in the motivated could be encouraged and inspired, even if "recovery" meant acceptance of what was and living in the inevitable, but I didn't know exactly how to explain all that in words at the time, for it was a long involved story that I had yet to complete for myself in words, and, bottom line, it had no *direct* relationship to what I was as I gazed at Dadaji.

After some time I offered to leave, so as to make room for others who were arriving at the house, but Dadaji said, "No, stay here."

Somewhere inside me was a warm-hearted, dedicated, conscientious human being, a mystic, my heart almost ready but not quite to open, but I didn't try to say so, which was a good thing, for if I had, I would have reduced myself to some intellectualized summary, I didn't attempt to 'explain.' At that time, I knew intuitively but didn't know intellectually whom I was addressing.

My visit to India was not about intellectual understanding or psychological insight or the receiving of advice or the drawing up of a psychological contract, or about some esoteric religious rituals. It was about Truth. It was a term I was unaccustomed to, but it had a ring of authenticity to it, and it felt right to me. I believed that Truth was at the core of the Eternal Religion, the Sanatana Dharma, immanent and transcendent, the core, so to speak,-and here again, speech is limiting-of the universe, indeed the universe, and Dadaji was Truth, Creation, which is not to understand Dadaji, far from it, only to acknowledge.

In India, no one imposed conditions on me, no one required me to undergo purification ceremonies, rituals, steps, prayers or efforts to prove myself, no one suggested that I was inadequate as I was, that I had "a long way to go," that I was "not in fit spiritual condition," that I should take classes, or undertake meditations. No one suggested that I should abandon a church or a religion, or that I should join a group. No one wanted donations. No one wanted money from me. No sales pitch. No one wanted anything from me. What a surprise! How novel.

My way of life may well have originated as my solutions to, or compromises in the face of, my early life dilemmas, dilemmas that reactivated and confronted me when I wanted to emancipate. Or maybe my dilemmas came with me into this life, or possibly there was a bit of both. Life unfolding as destined. In any case, I had had enough, and, despite my fear, I wanted to have my eyes opened, I wanted to see through the idiosyncratic perception that I generally accepted as reality. Actually, my efforts at explaining by writing are after the event egoistic mental manipulations, and, it might be more accurate to simply say I was drawn to Dadaji by Dadaji. Yes, bottom line, that was it, and the rest is mind stuff!

Some came to Dadaji seeking solutions to their self-identified problems. I could tell that much without understanding the Hindi or the Bengali they spoke, by reading the cues in their eyes, faces, gestures, and in their body movements. As if they were saying: Is that your answer to our problems? We were expecting a solution. Are you not going to solve our problems for us? Can't you see we're in great need? Tell us what to do to make our problems go away.

And was I not familiar with that expectation? *Tell me what to do.* As if religious teachers historically hadn't already done that as recorded in the scriptures of the various religions world wide, and with what result?

"How about a cup of tea?"

"Yes, thank you, I will."

A young woman left the room, returning soon afterwards carrying two cups of tea and some Bengali sweets, which she laid on a small table in front of us. Bengali sweet was a cookie that had a white flour-like exterior, that was round in shape, and that had a delicious juicy interior. We drank our tea in relaxed silence, Dadaji sipping his like a refined gentleman from the old days of elegance.

"There was a vision, or was it a vision? I was awake. It was a strange experience," I said.

"Yes, it was. I was there. I know all about it. I am with you, always."

"You were really there?"

"Yes."

"And you are with me always?"

"Yes, always."

What!

My bafflement must have shown on my face, for Dadaji quickly averted his eyes, while giving me time to absorb this. It wasn't easy for me. My orientation in life was turning inside out. I had never encountered anything like this. I was intellectually overwhelmed, for my intellect failed at the end point of what was deemed to be rational. I was blinded by my own ego. I was trying to understand Truth with my mortal mind, with the very equipment that couldn't possibly perform the task, and the more I tried to understand, as I was wont to do in the course of my life in America, the more bewildered I became. Dadaji had said that our human mental processes, especially our conviction that we ourselves were the creators of our destinies, that we were the ultimate doers in life, got between us and Truth or God, but, at the time, I did not know how to let go of my psychological modus operandi. Partly, it was out of fear, as if of stepping off a window of a burning building, unsure of whether the supposed safety net was really there, and partly it was out of ignorance. I knew so little. I knew one thing that day, however, that, without a doubt, my vision was real, and here was proof of that, but that was as far as I could go at that moment.

"What's that?" he asked.

"It's a camera. May I take some pictures?"

I opened the camera case and took a few pictures, but after a few snapshots I suddenly felt as if my heart wasn't in it, and that, in the presence of Truth, picture taking was inane. I put the camera away. I hadn't come to India to take photographs, any more than I had come to view a spectacle. I hadn't come to view the street scene, I hadn't come to elevate myself by feeling sorry for "those less fortunate," I hadn't come to photograph the wretched. Nor had I come to photograph the Marble Palace, the Jain Red Temple, the River Hoogli, the Howrah Bridge, and certainly not the Victoria Monument, no way, that. We continued communicating in silence.

A stranger approached, a slim, mature-looking man with gray hair, dressed in white Indian garments, with a strong bony face, handsome in an elegant kind of way, quiet and steady looking. He spoke in Hindi or Bengali. This was no needy man seeking personal favors, a better job, a better love life or some self-directed life transformation that he might imagine would suit him. He was in no danger of egocentricity. He was a man in balance, a man comfortable with his life role, according to his destiny. How could I possibly take in all that in the brief moment I had to observe him? Well, I did. As he walked by me, I felt a draft from the flowing of his garments. The newcomer sat down on the floor beside me, crossing his legs, flexing his knees, and straightening his spine, all in one smooth effortless motion.

"You may go now," Dadaji said to me.

It was then I became aware of another man who was standing behind me, and who seemed to have been there for some time, observing me in silence. The moment I stood up, he approached me and spoke:

"You are Donald?"

"Yes, I am. I come from America."

"I know. I am Abhi Bhattacharya. Please come with me."

Abhi stood tall at five feet nine inches, a thoughtful-looking man with a broad forehead and thick rimmed glasses, the ready smile of a man of the world and the cool, casual look that clean, white, Indian garments gave to a tawny-skinned man such as he was, and indeed he wore them well. He carried himself like a gentleman. I had not expected to be acknowledged in any particular way, far less receive personal attention. I followed him into the next room. He handed me four small books, a rolled up paper about 14 inches by 20, a plastic wallet card, and a small circular medallion.

On the rolled up paper was the portrait of a mature looking man, of no particular race, with short white hair, a neatly trimmed beard, wearing a loose white cloak. He was seated on a solid rectangular block of wood or stone, his bare feet resting on a disc that was decorated around its perimeter with flower petals. A halo encircled the man's head. He had quiet eyes, an air of gentle dignity, and the appearance of immense wisdom. Beneath the image were inscribed the words Sri Sri Satyanarayan. The same image was on the medallion and on the wallet card, with the same words written underneath: *Sri Sri Satyanarayan*. Sri Sri Satyanarayan means Much Revered Existence Itself Truth Internal.

"I am a film actor, now retired for the most part. I devote most of my time to informing people about Dadaji, those who want to know, that is."

Dadaji never accepted for himself a title, such as Maharasha, Mahatma, Bhagawan, or Guru, for, according to him, all affectations, including the identifying clothes worn by holy men, were ways of suggesting to others that one was elevated spiritually, that one had power to lead others to God, that one was specially favored in the eyes of God. He never accepted an ashram in his name. Our bodies were our temples. Truth could not be debated, written down, elaborated into a philosophy, or taken into an institution as a theology. Truth expressed was Truth expired. Truth could only be lived. And each one of us was assigned a destiny that unfolded during the course of our lives.

"*I cannot give you anything. I cannot take anything away from you.*"

More people were arriving and the hum of conversation became louder. Many of the people seemed to know each other. They smiled at each other, they greeted each other, they spoke to each other, and, as the room filled, it became clear to me that my companion was the kind of man who had a distinguished presence. People knew when he was in the room, people approached him, people wanted to stand beside him, perhaps considering it an honor. But on that night, the people were talking in a language I did not understand, which was not surprising, but Abhi was kind to me and he looked after me by escorting me around. I was sure he would have continued keeping me company for a long time, but everything was so new to me that I was running out of casual conversation, and I didn't even know enough to ask questions. I wanted time to review, to think, to contemplate. I wanted time to myself. I wanted to sleep.

"I don't know what's going on tonight, I feel lost. I've just arrived from America. It's my first time in India," I said.

"You're going to be alright. It will all work out for you."

"Where exactly are we in Calcutta?" I asked.

I had no map of Kolkata and none was available either at the airport or at the hotel. I had no mental picture of where I was in that huge, sprawling, strange city. It was dark outside, I had crossed twelve time zones and I had entered a culture vastly different from my old familiar one. Suddenly an immense fatigue gripped me. "Right now I want to go to bed. I'm tired," I said. I wanted to slip between the clean sheets of a warm, cozy bed, and allow my eye-lids to droop. It was time to return to the hotel.

My car and driver were there on the street outside the house, where I had left them. This was India, where, at least at that time, drivers were glad to get the business and were also polite. Private drivers had relatively good jobs in a poor economy, where many Indian citizens were unemployed and where many lived in abject poverty. As viewed from inside the Ambassador by me, the street scene seemed strange, but not nearly as strange as it looked to me on another night when I was a passenger in a rickshaw that took me through the slums, along narrow dirt roads alongside ditches that were half-full of oily-looking liquid delivering six feet of smoke into the air above. Slim silent men and women and wide-eyed children gazed at me as I rode by in the pale soft light of the moon. A fairy-land! Well, not for those who lived there. A moon-lit community of impoverished people, looking to me, with my splintered vision, like a fairy-land.

Many of the men who labored on the streets pulling rickshaws were sick with tuberculosis and other chronic debilitating diseases. There was a law on the books against that form of labor, but it was a law the authorities ignored, not because they were uncaring, but because the rickshaw men had no other way of scratching out a bare existence.

The Kolkata rickshaw drivers made no effort to flatter me. They were quiet, lean methodical men. They were eager to work. They never groveled.

They labored in silence.

30: WHY AM I?

A lively, merry-looking man approaching, hand extended in greeting, a greeting I accepted; a firm grip, eye contact steady, exuding confidence, and, to be sure, the merry man arriving at precisely a time when I wanted something he had. What could this stranger possibly have that I wanted? Not merchandise. No way, not that! What I wanted was information, experience. I had, still have, a passion for learning. Nevertheless, I had mixed emotions.

"Perhaps you misunderstand something about me," I said, "Or perhaps you mistake me for someone else. I'm not here on business. I'm not buying," I said.

"Why are you in Calcutta?" he asked.

"I'm here to visit someone special. I'm exploring my spiritual life. As a man from India, I'm sure you know what I mean."

"At least you're not a tourist. No tourist ever comes to Calcutta."

"No, I'm not a tourist. My visit is personal."

"I'm curious. Is that what you really want in Calcutta?"

"Yes."

"A few years ago," he said, "I met a senior Christian clergyman who was visiting Calcutta. A charity-minded man. We had an interesting conversation. I remember it well. Anyway, what are you doing for the rest of the day?"

"I have no engagements, but first I want to go back to the hotel to wash and rest."

"I'll take you in my car. I'll show you around; later we can eat dinner at a place I like."

"I don't want to inconvenience you," I said.

"You wouldn't be inconveniencing me; not at all. I'm asking you,"

I hesitated, but then my curiosity about Calcutta won, and I agreed to go with him, and so, off we went in his dark-green oven-hot vehicle, humid air blowing in through the open windows. After driving around for some time, he parked the car in a wooded area under some trees, and we walked: "I want to show you something of interest. Look up right above you," he said, and I did.

"Oh, what is it?"

"What do they look like?" he asked me.

"I've never seen anything like it. Are these bats?"

"Yes, they are. That's what they are. They hang upside down in the trees, and they come out at night to do their prowling."

"Wow! They're huge. What do they eat?"

"You'd be surprised what they find to eat in Calcutta."

"You don't have to tell me."

He took me to a few other places that only a familiar local would know about, including a forest outside the city. We parked; we walked. A tiger had his lair nearby. We halted. Don't go any more in that direction! There was a narrow creek between us and the tiger that stepped out to greet us, right forepaw in front of the left, two rear legs flexed, ears back; eye contact. Eye contact. A close encounter. The strong face of a territorial animal, a beast that knew the boundaries of its property. We knew. We knew the tiger knew. We withdrew, happy to put trees between us and the tiger.

"Will you accompany me to dinner?"

"Where would we go?"

"It's a beautiful restaurant. It won't cost you anything, and the sea-food is the best in the world."

"OK, I'll go with you."

"Good, now let me tell you something: I ask directly for what

I want in life. I know exactly what I want. I find that many people also want similar things, but they're afraid to let other people know; they're afraid to ask, so they don't make clear what they want in life. Everybody wants something. Don't tell me you don't want anything. People are inhibited. Are you inhibited?"

"Yes, I am inhibited."

"You Americans! You're jaded. You have affluence, you have the things that money can buy, but still you're not satisfied. Some say you have too much, that you want endlessly, that you'll never be satisfied. You're unhappy, so now you want to go back in time. You imagine you'll find satisfaction in intangibles from the past. Well, we want to go forward. We're in this life to enjoy what life has to offer. I told the Christian clergyman exactly what I'm telling you. He disagreed with me, quoting scriptures, but, you know, several months later he wrote me. He had changed his mind. He told me I was right."

"Some of us seek roots, solid roots, Truth, the core of existence. I don't want to go back in time."

"Imagine a leading Christian agreeing with me, but he had to go home and think about it for a while. Do you know him?"

"No, I don't know him."

He blew his horn three times and laughed. "Why are you laughing?" I asked him.

"There are many people all over the world who want to be miserable. Well, they get exactly what they want in life, and they are miserable. I don't waste my time on people like that. I live my own life to the full. I tell people what I want. They can agree or not. I ask others what they want. I don't force anything. I don't persuade. What could be more honest than that?"

Did unfortunate people really want to be miserable? Or were they caught in some destiny they little understood? Exactly what did the term 'want' mean in a bottom line way? Was there something in us that made us 'want' our destiny even as we protested when we didn't like it? Or, were remarks such as these rationalizations designed to establish distance? There were aspects of life that were impossible to reduce to words.

By this time we were arriving at our destination for the evening, and my new friend tugged at the steering wheel, bringing the car out of the main thoroughfare. He led me to an inconspicuous door in a solid stone wall with no visible windows and he rang the bell. In a moment the door opened and a tall, dark-skinned man with snow-white hair appeared. The man wore a wide droopy beard that flopped over his mouth and down the sides of his lower jaw, and he was dressed in sandals, floppy gray slacks and a long loose shirt that hung almost to his knees. After giving me a not-too-friendly stare with cold eyes that had ivory-white rings around the corneas, he spoke in Hindi. His eyes looked like tiny white-wall tires. My companion flashed a card, said something in Hindi and we were allowed in.

What a mess!

Tables, chairs, brass lamps, large ashtrays, electrical cords and other debris were scattered all over the floor, as if a tropical storm had blown through and no one had cleared up after it. We walked in single file through the shambles into a back barroom where several men and women sat at tables drinking, smoking and talking. We sat at the bar and a middle aged barkeeper approached to serve us. A single gold tooth gleamed as he spoke and my companion ordered drinks for both of us. Behind the bar, a mirror.

Bottles: Old Times Gin; Old Smuggler Rum; Johnny Walker Red; a quart bottle of single malt Glenfiddich; much more.

Several men approached, some sat to my right, some to the left of my new friend, and a couple stood behind me, and soon, the whole group, except for me, were talking loudly in Hindi or Bengali, laughing and back slapping like old friends at a twenty-year reunion. After a while, my companion said, "Meet my friend, Donald. He's psychiatrist."

"A psychiatrist!"

"He's needed in this place. You need him. Is he here for you?"

"No, you're the one who needs him."

"Don't listen to him. Everybody here needs you. Everybody here is crazy. You have to be crazy to be here."

"We're all crazy."

As if I didn't know the insanity, but it wasn't what they imagined, nor did they know that the same applied to other and more elite social establishments, all the way up to and including the chambers of rulers of nations. Their kind of laughter was common enough, suggesting a cover up for terror arising when one's inner life, with all its frailties, its fragility, its inevitable unaddressed dilemmas, and, yes, its apparent futility, that is to say, its demons, flashes into consciousness momentarily. In any event, soon the exhibitionism petered out, the place quieted down, the new arrivals ordered straight whiskies with beer as chasers. The men tossed the whiskies back, they shook the last drops of liquor into the beer. *Slainte!* What about a refill? The man sitting next to me asked me, "What are you doing in Calcutta?"

"I'm here to meet a certain man called Dadaji."

The man took a long drag on a cigarette, he shook his head, and he smiled, more to himself than to me: "Da da ji!" He repeated. On his head he wore a dark blue hat tipped backwards to reveal a mess of thick black hair. A middle aged man with a strong-looking face, a straight nose, good teeth. An intelligent man. A comfortable man, a man of action, a risk-taker but not a gambler, at that moment contemplative, still in character, gazing beyond the bottles, into the mirror behind the bar, beyond the glass, into himself, exhaling smoke.

A skinny, gangly man with a receding chin and lank hair, wearing a long, ill-fitting shirt and slacks at half-mast, revealing bony ankles and bare filthy feet in scruffy-looking sandals, approached. He was smoking a flat cigarette called a Beedi. Where had he come from? Out of the crowd. The place was filling up. The noise level was escalating. A little smoky.

The sea-food arrived, expertly laid out on heavy plates by someone who knew how to please aesthetically, and how to cook. This was culinary excellence, here was authentic cutlery, and linen napkins. We ate sitting at the bar. Excellent!

Finally, it was time for me to leave. I had had enough. I had other things on my mind, I pulled out of my pocket a business card I carried, the card of someone I had met the previous day, a card I knew would have an effect: "Do you know this man? Well, I have an appointment with him early in the morning. I want to return to the hotel. I'm tired. How may I call a taxi?"

My companion interrupted the loud conversation behind me, he addressed the lanky man, who paid immediate attention, and he handed him his car keys. He spoke to the man in Hindi; after a while he switched to English: "...and be sure to take him straight back to the hotel. Don't take him anywhere else. Know what I mean?"

"Yes, straight back to the hotel."

Where else were they thinking of? I hesitated about entrusting myself to this stranger whose external appearance suggested a separation from what I was used to, for, to be sure, he was no executive, no diplomat, no country club aficionado, no psychiatrist, and, not only that, but he smelled of the Bay of Bengal. My hesitation was brief, however, and once again I was a passenger with a stranger behind the wheel.

My driver was solicitous, making sure I was comfortable in the vehicle, driving like a man familiar with the streets, carrying on a pleasant conversation with me as we drove back to the hotel. I relaxed. What a beautiful aroma was from the Bay of Bengal! Soon, we were back at the hotel, and soon afterwards I was lying in a comfortable bed, where I fell asleep immediately, and the next thing I knew it was a bright sunny morning, with sunlight shining in through the window of my room, and immediately I remembered something I had been told:

"If one judges Him, He is far away. With the simple approach, He is there. It is difficult to be simple, but you are simple."

I was learning.

The differences that I classified as racial, religious, geographic, educational, or as degrees of success or affluence, were mental fictions, fictions based on my own idiosyncratic perception of life. Truth was beyond all that. Truth was one in all, the life essence in all existence. The Lord, the Infinite One, created manifestations of Himself, and all of us were His manifestations. He comes with each one of us into life, giving us minds and bodies for His play, but we forget who we are, and behave accordingly. Hard to grasp immediately because it required a switch in the style of thinking. It would take time, but in the meantime, there was nothing I had to do to earn His love. I was already loved. Of course, my thinking changed as I absorbed all this, and my worldview changed, but internalization was slow, in my case taking years, as my perception altered. *Love!* I was expected to do my duty, which in that context meant, as far as I knew, simply working according to my given aptitudes and potential and deepest desires, *while remembering Him, the Lord, as the ultimate doer in all I did, doing it in His name.* True worship! I was a human destiny of Him, a manifestation, but then again, it was all beyond my intellect, and my efforts at understanding or knowing were futile.

If we don't have desires, how can we realize their nature and purpose? If we don't satisfy them, how can we get rid of them? And, why has God given them to us?

Man is a helpless being....The seeker and the sought are one.

What about all the misery in this life? Why did God allow suffering? Relax, ask yourself: Who is suffering? We are all manifestations of God. His destiny. *Who is doing what to whom?* Are we not one at the core? And what we call suffering, what we call pleasure, is of mind, although, to be sure, we have destinies to fulfill, and fulfill them we will, in one life or another.

The Lord was beyond our mental processes, as well as beyond all differences, present in all beings as one. Whatever learning I acquired was inevitably biased and limited owing to my mental processes, and learning, as we experienced it, encouraged argument, based on opposites, such as vice and virtue, up versus down, good versus bad, old versus young, one chemical versus another, one medicine versus another, medicines prescribed by legally sanctioned professionals versus medications self-prescribed, yes, and even on a certain level, sanity versus insanity.

Was the Lord partial? Surely not. All biological life was significant, and we 'fought' microbiological organisms so as to acquire our own health, we 'fought' disease cells within us for the same reason, but if these cells could talk, maybe our health would spell disease for them, our disease prosperity for them. Just a fantasy! I know.

I had lived in the shadows all my life, or worse, in darkness, blind, adjusting, afraid to open my eyes, afraid that what I might see would require me to sacrifice my little sack of self-made security, my ego:

"The bridegroom has come to lift away the veil that obscures the view of the bride, but the bride fails to recognize the groom."

...*sacrifice the ego*....

That morning, the morning after my night out, I went to Dadaji's house again. It was quieter than it was the previous afternoon, but Abhi was there. He said:

"Now I get what I need, without sense of wants or expectations. You will feel it also. This is called natural living in Him, living where there are no complaints, and everything is loving and beautiful. In the future, all will be like this. It is difficult to be simple, but you are simple. It is His choice."

* * *

Dadaji came into this life in human form in order to establish Truth. What is Truth? Truth cannot be defined. Truth cannot be explained in words. Truth expressed is Truth expired. But the Supreme is inside us, chanting 24 hours a day, as a core identity, and so it isn't possible for us to be forgotten, not for an instant, even if we, in our mental mode, forget, and we do. Is it possible for us to live Truth? If we do, we'll know it when it happens. As for organization in religion, well, there are problems.... The danger is that we may conjure up images of God, of righteousness,-psychological projections-that we as groups quarrel over, splintered visions, or we find a 'strong man' to follow, we create politics, we create institutions, business, power. Why join an institution to get what I already have? I am His manifestation. I am in you, Dadaji has said repeatedly, and you are in me. We cannot be separated. All is the Supreme. He alone exists, and all that we do is Supreme Being. We are in this life in order to enjoy His play, to get a taste of His love, and we will enjoy His love if we abandon ego, which separates us from Him, and bear with patience the respective life roles we are assigned, doing our duties, while remembering Him, but no mortal being can ever be a guru. To repeat, no human being can be the spiritual guru of another. Dadaji had no disciples, he refused to be the guru of anyone, but, of course, he spoke to us, as an elder brother might.

31: MANIFESTATIONS OF THE ONE

Dadaji refused all gifts, he refused all honors, he had no ashram, no temple, no institution, no official building, no disciples, he accepted visitors in his house where he and family lived, he supported his family by working for his living, the implication being that we should all work for our living, that all work done in the Lord's name was worship, and that no one should make a business out of God.

All work done in the Lord's name, while remembering Him as doer, is worship! *When those who make a business out of God realize Him, they are out of business.* What took me so long to open up my heart? Ego. *It is the ego that separates us from each other and from God.* It is ego that burdens us with problems, social, cultural and psychological. It is from ego that we close our hearts, it is from ego that we cling to dilemmas, hoping to have it both ways, have our cake and eat it, so to speak, it is from ego that we are self-righteous, but: *If you don't have your mind and ego, how will you relish His love?*

I would open up my heart in a spiritual way to the Lord, not to some human guru who knew not what he was doing, whose perception was splintered, limited, limiting, who would have conflict of interest, caught in personal dilemmas, as all human beings are, but, unwilling to let go, I was like those, who, when called, had some other "obligations" to complete, which made me no different from millions of others, but there I was, in India, seeing myself in a new light, and millions of others were not. What was I supposed to do?

"No need to do anything...," Dadaji said to me, after taking me aside. "You...me. *I will visit you in your house."*

What did he mean? I felt bewildered at the remark. My mortal mind entrapping me, vise-like, separating me from Truth, wall-like, between 'me' and the Guru within; my psychological sense of self, my ego, getting in the way, an obstacle that could not be fought successfully by direct confrontation, for direct confrontation would mean fighting mind with mind. Wrestling an octopus in a barrel of eels! Hopeless. A struggle that would inevitably wear me down. I engaged in that struggle. I imagine we all do. Only one way to 'win': Surrender ego; let go; abandon the futile struggle for control, accept destiny, accept the Lord as the ultimate doer in life, for the events in my life were all His, and I was simply the actor, free in my spiritual pursuit.

Simple, isn't it? But letting go of ego is by no means easy, and may indeed, when it happens, be a spontaneous event occurring from within, expected or unexpected, not subject to mental manipulations, not the result of formal education, remarkable in its simplicity when it happens, but, be that as it may, I surrender ego!

A God beyond my understanding, a God beyond my knowing, a God I may remain in tune with by simply remembering Nam, but a God whom, when I try to know intellectually or explain, I, with good intentions, reduce to mental imagery, mental imagery that may well become idolatry, even as I deny and rationalize it, and idolatry is more ego, a formidable barrier.

God, the Lord, the Almighty, The Creator, as mental constructions, psychological fantasies, social images, words helping me to communicate with others, to be sure, but with a down side, in that I might forget, or fail to know consistently, that I am talking in the metaphor; story-telling, regaling others, comforting myself, while somewhere within myself I know that something is amiss, as otherwise I would not be so ready to take umbrage, to be prepared to fight to defend, forgetting that Truth needs no defense, cannot be debated, can only be lived.

Debate in spiritual matters seems to lead to more splintering, more divisiveness, more anger, more defensiveness. Isn't there enough of that already? Friend and foe alike share a common core, we are one, the divisiveness is of our own making, at least mine is, I transcend my old way of perceiving life, I accept all of life as multiple manifestations and multiple destinies of the Lord.

One day Dadaji took me aside into a quiet room, as he had done previously, he stood in front of me, laid his hands on me and uttered words in Bengali. Exactly what words he used, I do not know. He was blessing me.

Historically, certain wise-men of India had spoken of the oneness in multiple manifestations of God, they believed that the Self was a manifestation of the Lord within each living being, and that the Self within, the Atman, was one with Brahman, the Lord. But many of these wise-men or gurus also taught asceticism and withdrawal from the world as well as many esoteric rituals and practices, as a way to mukti, moksha, or liberation. But, why withdraw from the world? Was the world not also a manifestation of Him? If we are actors and actresses in the drama of life, players in a Grand Play, as Abhi had suggested to me, surely we are to take part in life, including family life and work. Surely we are not to shun our designated role. And surely the best way to know others is to know ourselves, surely the way to be of best service to others is to be true to ourselves, behaving according to our given aptitudes and deep desires, living our dharma. I had enslaved myself to a worldview in part non-verbal, pre-intellectual, with its neurobiological concomitants, that I was just about willing to give my life for. *I didn't know any better!* It applies to all of us. I knew that running away from fear empowered fear. No more running away. As for doing "God's work" versus any old work: Who among us could legitimately claim to be doing the Lord's work? while implying that the work done by other people, who might be equally conscientious, equally honest, was not God's work. Was not all non-exploitative work, for which we had aptitude and passion for, equal in the Play of Life, the VrajaLeela? And maybe all work! What did I know?

Dadaji did not promote organized groups either in his own name or in God's name. *When those who make a business out of God realize Him, they are out of business.*

I observed that on-going groups suppressed free thinking and open-mindedness. I had grown up in a tightly knit culture, and, in my adult years I had been a member of several groups, and, from my experience, I concluded that groups did not tolerate independent thinking by individual members, and groups especially did not tolerate their group values questioned. Yes, groups had values, and each group had an agenda. Regardless of what group members claimed, regardless of how much they claimed freedom of speech, every group generated a leader, "senior members," "old timers," that is, a hierarchy, and every group had a history with "founding fathers," expectations of members, and those who deviated were persuaded to come back into the fold, or, if that failed, those who strayed would be punished, usually, to begin with at least, by withdrawal of emotional support, later by more confrontational methods.

A microcosm of the larger group called society. Groups, organizations, institutions, and societies developed rituals that took on meaning and sometimes autonomous properties that lasted long after their usefulness had receded or had worn out. And just as individuals created behaviors to cope with dilemmas in their own lives, behaviors that served some survival purpose in childhood, behaviors that we psychiatrists classified as childhood neuroses, behaviors that became more problematic as individuals aged, so did groups! Could a group be neurotic? Could a whole society by neurotic? The whole world? A world mad! Yes, and all of us blind to our own insanity. No use blaming designated leaders, no use blaming anyone, I am responsible for the manner in which I confront the dilemmas in my life, the degree to which I compromise, the degree to which I try to accommodate two opposing sides, if I do, the degree to which I act or fail to act upon the power given to me.

Of course, certain people in psychological distress or addicted find help in groups that they attend freely, where they find release from loneliness, fulfillment in intimacy, reinforcement of human identities, and usefulness, all of which might be lacking in their lives as lived. And, to be sure, they live better lives as a result or concomitantly.

In India I learned that God did not divide human beings into groups whom He favored versus groups whom He did not favor, that He was not subject to one group's prescription as opposed to another's, that He was always the same in every man, woman and child, as well as in all of life, and that it would be a serious mistake to reject the world, of which we are all a part, but not apart from. It's because of our limited and splintered perception that we see the world from different perspectives, and all too often in ego-centric, self-serving ways that encourage divisiveness and drama, but that does not mean that the world is an illusion. No, the world is not an illusion, we ourselves are not illusory, and God is not an illusion. Neither is the world what it appears to be as seen by mortal men and women.

As players in the life drama, in the life comedy, in the Play of Life, in the Vrajaleela, we are all needed, and we all have destinies to live out. We are also in each other in some mysterious way, we are in the Lord in some mysterious way, and He is in us, and, sooner or later, in this life or another, the Lord will bring us into Him, so that no one of us will be abandoned, although, to be sure, nature has a way of bringing responsibility home to us, and the consequences of our actions came back to us. Humility helps, as does a sense of humor about the whole comedy of life-as opposed to humor that is hostile to others. Somehow, non-intellectually, I absorbed this and more, I who was and still am an empty vessel, a passionate learner, my "reality" turning upside down and inside out.

* * *

One afternoon during the cold season, my clinical work tapered off to a conclusion earlier than usual, and even my paper work, which often seemed to have no end, and to take on a life of its own, like some extraterrestrial organism from a late-night movie, was complete. My desk was clean, no one called me requesting service, I sat alone. What kind of activity was that? I wasn't contemplating. Being alone in my office with nothing to do felt to me like a threatening situation, I had had no recent experience in simply being alive and enjoying the Play of Life, although I had had many such experiences in my boyhood days, such as, for example, lying in a green hollow listening to a lark warbling far above me in a clear blue sky, swimming alone in the buff, and rambling beach-combing, but, in my journey through life into adulthood, I had forgotten the simple art of being alive, of being innocent, a part of me had frozen.

While sitting in my chair that afternoon, an immense weariness arose within me, beginning in my middle like a heavy load, and spreading throughout my whole body, so that soon my eyes felt weary, my head felt heavy, my thinking slowed down, all to the point that it began to overwhelm me. A ringing arose in my ears. My head sank forward as my neck sagged under its weight. The silence in the room intensified, my legs seemed to weaken, and they felt clumsy, as if partially disconnected from the rest of my body. My attention wavered.

I had slept well the night before, I was not sleep deprived, nothing unusual had happened to me that day, I was not overworked, there was no particular stress in my life, and my health was good. I wasn't used to unexpected attacks of weariness. It was like a visit from Old Morpheus himself. Well, I would obey the call.

There was only one sensible thing to do, and that was to leave the office early and go home, and that was what I did. As I approached the house, I noticed that the whole neighborhood seemed to be deserted. Why was everything so quiet? Where was everybody? Were they all at work? What were they doing? Were they all busily performing, gathering, accumulating, producing, competing with each other, wanting desperately to succeed?, earning, purchasing, spending, borrowing, getting deeper into debt? As I walked through the front door of the house, the feeling of desolation intensified. No one was home, but it wasn't only that, it was that the house seemed to be devoid of movement, essentially quiet; not even a clock ticked, no refrigerator grumbled, no heating system blew air through the vents.

Was this really my home?

I took off my overcoat, hung it in the closet and walked into the bedroom, and, yes, the bedroom seemed the right place to be at that moment, the ambience seemed right, the shades were still drawn the way Marjorie and I had left them that morning when we left for work, and the room was dim to half-dark. I removed my jacket, opened my tie, shook off my shoes and lay down on the bed, whereupon I immediately sank into comfort.

In a moment it happened: My fatigue vanished, I felt unusually alert, lively, full of vigor, my consciousness and my awareness altered, my surroundings change in light and color: The dim lights brightened up remarkably, the shadows vanished, and the room began to shine with vitality, everything snapped into sharp focus, and my limbs, which only a moment before had felt leaden, felt strong and athletic.

A mist came out of the wall, from the East; a swirling, gray, cool-looking fog like the fog that might come out of a freezer when its door is opened in a warm room. I felt at peace with the world and with myself. My mask of ordinary life vanished, a weight fell off me, I felt as light and fresh as a breeze on a spring morning. I had no need to suppress, no need to say anything, no need to ask for anything; there was nothing to fear; I had no desire to control my situation. I was light-hearted, happy, serenely at play in my heart.

My ego was out of the way.

"The Word" arose within me, like a beautiful flower opening up its delicate petals and releasing its lovely fragrance into the air. "The Word" was like pure cool liquid that arose, as if from a fountain at the top of my head. It percolated through the tissues of my scalp and face, then down through my neck, arms, body, legs, and finally into every cell in my body.

"The Word" became thought.... And it was love....inspiring love, universal love beyond words.

A powerful aroma of sandalwood and assorted tropical spices filled the room. It was an aroma usually associated with the presence of Dadaji. I sat up. I sat on the edge of my bed savoring and enjoying the aroma as much as I could for as long as I could, but, inevitably, in due course, as the aroma faded away, so did "The Word."

32: SEEKER AND SOUGHT

A balmy winter morning in Calcutta, a cloudless sky, the downtown streets freshly watered, aromatic and colorful, pedestrians relaxed looking, no outward signs of anxiety, crowds but no rush, and gone was my own insecurity about being the only Caucasian on the street.
Strolling casually along the sidewalk, ignoring the ten or twelve youths who followed me around, possibly out of curiosity, perhaps hoping for a handout, knowing that, despite their proximity to me, none of them would touch me, and none did; enjoying the warmth, the color, the crowds, the esoteric aromas, the pleasant sounds. At peace with the world, at peace with myself, I felt like smiling, pausing at a street corner, feeling innocent and alive.

A stranger dropped out of the crowd and halted in front of me. He was well-dressed in fashionable slacks, brown shoes and a white shirt: "Good morning, Sir, may I introduce myself?" he asked, in the delightfully musical accent of Northern India.

"Who are you?" I asked. I didn't want any hassle that morning, I wanted to keep my peace of mind, I was in no mood for negotiating whatever he had in mind. I wanted to be alone.

"I'm a shopkeeper. I sell silk. My shop is just down the street from here. Please let me show you my collection of beautiful silks."

Just as I suspected, the stranger wanted something from me. No free lunch! And no free friendship even. Don't we always want something from each other whenever we approach each other, professionally, socially, even casually? It keeps us on guard. It keeps us at a distance from each other. It keeps us from revealing our true selves to each other. What does he want? What does she want from me? If I reveal myself, I'll be vulnerable; if I don't reveal myself, I'll miss intimacy. Human love is fraught with complications…what? Well, that morning I didn't want to haggle with merchants over "bargains," I didn't want to take any more trips with strangers, and, in any case, I had only limited time before my appointment of the day.

"I'm just going for a walk," I said. "I'm not here to buy silks. You'd be wasting your time with me."

"Not at all, Sir; not at all. On the contrary, I'd be delighted. Please be assured I would not be wasting my time. To me, time is not a commodity. I am here. You are here."

"Are you sure?" I asked, referring to the first part of his remarks, and not to the last part, which I ignored but remembered.

"Of course, I'm sure.

"Very well, I'll go with you."

The store was modest in size, but clean and airy, and the shopkeeper did indeed have many silks available. Rolls of silk were stacked on the furniture, some were stored on shelves, some rolls stood up against the walls, and some were scattered all over the establishment. A delightful aroma of fresh, recently watered flowers pervaded the room. The store was a pleasant comfortable place.

"I don't want to buy silks. Please understand that. I'm in Calcutta for personal reasons, not related to business. I'm not here for shopping. There's no need to show me anything. I don't want to take up your time. I don't want to burden you."

"Will you have a cup of tea?"

"No, thank you, I just had breakfast at the hotel,"

"Well, then, please sit down, Sir, and make yourself comfortable, while I show you my silks."

I took the proffered chair and watched the man as he unfolded roll after roll of lovely silk, each one as beautiful as the other. He did this while sitting on the floor directly in front of me, loose-limbed, relaxed and comfortable in the oriental lotus position, and all the time delivering a running commentary on the origins, qualities, colors and potential uses of the materials. The salesman's eyes widened visibly as he became more and more enthusiastic about his work and more engrossed in what he was doing. I knew next to nothing about silk, but I was sure that if I wanted to learn, if I had any questions, this intelligent man would be the right person to ask, and he would happily supply answers.

I smiled at the thought.

"You like my silks....You are smiling," he said.

"Oh, your silks are beautiful."

"Your misses will surely love them. What's her favorite color?"

"I already have silks at home from previous trips, my needs are limited and I don't intend to buy any more silks."

"Then let me teach you about silks. You like to learn. I know. I can tell."

"You have a lovely shop, I can see that you enjoy your work, and that's good, but why do you insist on showing me so many silks?"

"Because it is my duty," he said.

"Your duty?"

"Yes, my duty."

"I understand," I said.

I was just beginning to know that, in the context in which he used the term 'duty,' it meant an aspect of dharma. Dharma! What? In my buttoned-up Northern Presbyterian Calvinist Puritanical way of looking at life, I was actually contemplating the meaning of words like 'dharma,' and 'sanatana dharma,' and not only that, but I seriously wanted to enjoy a way of life that included such ideas. Living my dharma, as I understood it, meant living according to my deep desires, utilizing my aptitudes, and fulfilling my potential, according to my given destiny, and doing all that while accepting God within as the giver of destiny, and also as the ultimate doer in life, which meant that I would leave the outcome in His hands, and not worry about it-simply being in life, accepting its multi-dimensional non-linear complexity, delighting in life's VrajaLeela, accepting myself as an inseparable part of existence, at one with others and with whatsoever I happened to observe. I was abandoning my old ideas of who I was.

Was I one with this silk merchant? Yes, I was, at some deep spiritual level that was beyond the barriers of intellectualization, race, religion, language, geography, and possessions, not even explainable as "non-duality," beyond the barriers of species, as manifestations of the One, and that morning I felt some of it within me.

I wasn't entirely there yet, however, and I felt obligated to him, I felt guilty about "taking up his time," and accepting his hospitality, I felt indebted to him, but he didn't express any disappointment when I got up to leave. He simply accepted my decision. I thanked the man and walked back to the hotel. To be sure, the culture of India was different from that of America, and Kolkata had a unique culture of its own. The people of Kolkata had a reputation for being spiritually oriented abstract thinkers, they had a reputation as raconteurs. I saw much laughter among poor people, strangers to me, some of them greeting me with smiles. I was amazed at how much laughter I saw in the streets.

I was learning that living my dharma, which included undergoing whatever karma was due to me in my life, was necessary for me, opening me up to emancipation. I had never found emancipation from my numerous attempts at changing my nature or character by psychological manipulations to what I imagined would be better, but I had gained insight, and I came to accept my own nature, which in itself opened me up to more acceptance of mystery. As for a psychological self, it didn't exist in isolation, except as mental conceptualization, but my Self, my true identity, was the God presence, universal, immanent, transcendent, that made all of us living beings one at the core.

And, as for rituals, ceremonies, programs, meditations designed to promote self-realization, self-actualization, liberation, emancipation, Self-realization or God-realization, I was losing confidence in all of them. In India, no one ever said anything to me about psychotherapy, but I myself saw flaws in our processes, I saw pomposity in us who undertook the work of exploring the psychological lives of others, I saw an assumption of the moral or spiritual superiority of the therapist over the patient, or the client. Over the years, I had known many psychiatrists and I saw in them the same tendency towards judging others, towards defending themselves psychologically, towards one-upmanship and towards retaliating against those who had offended them, that I saw in most lay people, and that I knew was also in me: action-reaction.

None of which is to deny the potential benefits of psychotherapy freely engaged in, for I have personally seen it as helpful many a time.

What if my enemies were in my life to help me? How? To offer me an opportunity to confront hostility, my own as well as that of others, to offer me an opportunity to practice patience, to offer me an opportunity to forgive, yes, to forgive all the way back, to offer me an opportunity to transcend the idea of forgiveness-more on this later-and put the energy of mental maneuvers to good use, to give me an opportunity to come to my Self. No one said that to me in so many words, but it made sense to me. After which it made no sense to hate my enemies, or to retaliate in kind, as in action-reaction. *Patience is the only virtue.*

Through all the afflictions of life, only he can live in peace and happiness who can surrender all his fears, thoughts, desires, expectations of loss or gain to the Will of the Supreme Lord.

My mental processes limited me. Was it possible for me to escape from my limiting mental processes? I needed my mental processes to enjoy the Play of Life! Abandon ego and you shall have a powerhouse of energy...spontaneous eye-openings-simplicity.

Every night, in deep dreamless sleep, my conscious mind out of the way, beyond time and space, I was being replenished by my Creator. How do I know that? I was told it was so, it made sense to me immediately, I believed it, I found the idea refreshing, I still do.

Some of India's spiritual teachers taught that the world was an illusion, but I was never told that the universe was an illusion, and I didn't believe the world was an illusion. We ourselves were part of the world, we were not illusory, God was immanent and transcendent, in all and of all, and we-indeed the universe-manifestations of Him. But I couldn't possibly know what was beyond mind. As mortals, we are limited. I was to do my duty in life, and enjoy the love of the Lord as I went about doing my duty, by remembering Him as the doer-simplicity.

There were no paths to salvation, no journeys to undertake, no quests to worry about, no pilgrimages to prepare for, no steps to master, no institutions to belong to, no groups to join, no money to collect. What, no money! Surely money was necessary to do God's work. Well, I could give away my money if I wanted to, but not as bribes to God! God didn't need my money. There was no conflict between the secular pursuits I undertook and my spiritual pursuit, no conflict between worldly activities and Sanatana Dharma, the Eternal Religion. The whole thing was one, but that awareness was important. If I saw any conflict, it was mind-created, and, of course, in my mind, I projected internal fantasies on to aspects of the universe, on to my perception of my parents, on to my perception of authority figures, on to my sexual and marital relationships, on to my work relationships, and on to my image of God, and I defended myself against open honesty in such fantasies. In so doing, I recreated situations I experienced in my early years, or brought with me into life, based on old themes, imagining them as solutions to old dilemmas, but the solution was itself a neurosis, and, seeing that it appears to be universal it generalizes into a global 'neurosis,' to which we remain blind, and it is where we find our enemies.

Would I love my enemies? Would I remember that they too were manifestations of God? Would I remember that, without my enemies, I would be lost in my own narcissistic fantasies? Would I remember that there was no distinction between one human being and another? Except as imagined by culture creating men and women. Would I love those whom society despised? Would I blame no one for whatever events happened in my life? Would I transcend human action- reaction?

Would I abide by my spiritual compass within, and decline all external guides in my spiritual pursuit? Knowing that what I was looking for was already mine, that the only sacrifice required of me was of ego.

Everything was already within me. Everything already was as it had to be. Professionally, I was in the business of treating others, and, to be sure, there was much to be said for helping others, which was my destiny, but I had room for knowing myself, coming to myself, remembering that the inner eye's opening did not translate into saving the world.

The seeker and the sought are one!

33: DILEMMA

A tall, cylindrical, windowless building, smooth curving wall mirroring itself in infinite reflections in dim omni-directional orange light, light emanating from nothing in particular, light coming from all matter.
Was this the shell of a lighthouse? It could be, but what a lighthouse, made of expensive polished gleaming Italian marble, with no visible door. And where were the internal structures that could not have been removed? This gigantic empty cylinder rose up and up until it vanished, not into shadows, but into a region of violet, blues and reds, where everything was relative, interchangeable, visible, invisible. The cylinder was furnished with a series of three perfectly carved off-white marble couches arranged symmetrically at regular intervals against the wall.

There were three of us inside the cylinder, two women and I.

"We're doing it all out of love," said the older woman.

"Needless to say," said the younger woman.

"Why do we have to do this right now?" I asked. "What's the big hurry? I'm just beginning …."

"Now's the time to make a commitment," a woman said. "Society expects it of you, as the least of your responsibilities, after all you've received. Quid pro quo!"

"It's my mission, actually, it's more than a mission, it's a calling," the other woman said.

"Yes, indeed, it's from the depths of our hearts."

"All we have to do is sign this official paper, then we'll be free to live, we can do plenty, we can go about our business."

But I knew something they didn't:

If I signed, I would be denying my dharma, I would be abandoning Sanatana Dharma, I would curl inside my shell, I would hide, I would deny myself, I'd see my own flaws in others, I would rage and hate, unforgiving, living in action-reaction, bouncing from pillar to post, and the war within, the war between my mind and my senses, the Kurukshetra War, would break out again in all its fury, just as if it had never gone into remission, and, in my loneliness, I would grovel for love, sinking slowly but surely into despair. Alienation from Truth.

"Please sit down and listen to me," I said, sitting on a couch that was against the circular wall, and the women sat down, one on each side of me. "Do you realize what we'd be letting ourselves in for?" The two women smiled, first at each other, then at me, indulgently, as if ridiculing what they imagined to be the ultra-serious obsessive nature of one who was overly concerned with ego-centric responsibility, one who intellectualized so as to spare himself the pain of authenticity in full poetic bloom, sensitive creature that he was, Womb-man, ambiguous symbolic imagery.

"We're busy. We have work to do. We must go soon."

"We want to put our education to work. We want to make the world a better place. Those who don't go forward slide backwards."

"Our time is valuable. We can't afford to waste it. What's he so concerned about anyway? It's only a contract to serve one another. Love one another. After all, certain conditions are essential."

"If he got busy with real work, instead of all that mental psychological introspective pseudo-intellectual gobble-de-gook, he'd come clean, clean as the cascading creek rolling the old mill wheel."

"I'm a doer."

"We're both doers."

"Thank you," I said. "I'm learning."

"It's not over yet," said the women in unison. "Look who's here!"

Solan Solaire appeared, clean white body, two black and white wings, long lean legs, and beautifully coordinated, large Atlantic gannet that she was, one with a unique history, no less, which was why she got momentary glimpses of past lives, and of one past life in particular, although her visual field these days was non-contemplative sharp crystal-clear monocular. Being of an aristocratic disposition, she cared nothing about fish guts, seaweed, old sea shells that crawled with bugs of assorted sizes and colors, nor about decaying fish carcasses.

Aware of more ways than one to communicate, aware that speech, the usual and customary, was cumbersome when it came to certain nuances, essentially spiritual nuances, and that speech was subject to the wiles of charismatic rhetoricians, of whom she had ambivalent unconscious memories.

Solan strode with her skinny legs tipping and tapping on the gleaming reflective floor, and with each step, the marble echoed and re-echoed in a musically weird way up and down the cylinder. There came a whoosh of diminishing light, almost but not quite to the point of darkness. Shadows moved eerily. Don't look at the shadows, Solan! And mind the smooth surface. It's slippery. Solan pranced around until her outstretched right appendage touched cool marble.

The cylinder shuddered at the touch of Solan's appendage, a door opened with a faint moan, which was when any sane creature would have taken stock and flown, but Solan didn't qualify for that descriptive term. The neurosis of life was not confined to humans! Once inside, she found herself in a circular stone-walled room exactly twelve feet in diameter. The room was dimly lit by a purple glow coming out of the ceiling, and, to the east, there rested a huge sea shell, white and sturdy looking, like a piece of ivory. Solan tapped the seashell thrice with her powerful beak and waited. The shell opened, and out came an octopus that wriggled and twirled in the air. The shell vanished. The octopus shrunk. The octopus became a belly button.

Solan snapped up the belly button in her beak and swallowed it. Of course she herself had no belly button, seeing that she was a bird, and not a woman, but not to worry, for the belly button immediately appeared on her breast. Preening herself, standing upright on her two elegant legs, she asked herself the following questions: Who am I?, who is called Solan. Who am I? What do I want? Why am I in this life? No answer. No words of wisdom. Nothing.

Solan, emboldened by the presence of her newly acquired belly button, flung a gleam from her eyes, actually two horizontal glances, owing to Solan's habit of cocking her head to one side, a maneuver that, however, gave her a noble, dignified appearance, reminiscent of Regal Beak. Bird-brain she might have been, but she was no slouch when it came to crystal clear non-verbal communication, and so, when she opened the lid of her long-term memory compartment, hidden in her diminutive neurophysiology, she broadcast her vision to the world.

She had once been a man and a philosopher, although only a lay philosopher, not a *salaaried* one like those who had lots of formal education in the hallowed halls of institutionalized learning, and whose office walls were plastered with fancy diplomas. Yes, she had indeed been a male! A real live man, a man affectionately known among his friends as Saorsa, a Gaelic word that suggested one of cheerful independent ways, strolling his way through life on the fringes of society. Not a middle class money-grubber; oh, no, not he. Well, it so happened that, one cold moonlit night Saorsa made a discovery. He had found the elixir of wisdom and serenity, a sort of philosopher's stone, so to speak, but, being of an impatient, excitable nature, despite his independent ways, he went around gabbing about his discovery, rather than absorbing it into himself, such as it was, instead of living it, instead of being.

His friends, who had previously ignored Saorsa because of his low status on the social ladder, he being barely on it, because he had no membership in a country club, (You couldn't take him anywhere) and because he had no government grant to his name, began to remember him again once the word got out that he had stumbled upon a concoction, and so, to hide the amber frothy brew from friends and agents of Authority alike, he swallowed it, all of it, the whole bottle, whereupon he immediately turned into a large female bird. The first thing the bird did was to fly halfway up a steep cliff and lay an egg. After depositing her egg, she took off into the air and flew across the meadows, beyond the beach and far out to sea, where she remained for days, enjoying her skills, and, what do you know! She forgot where she had laid her first and most precious of eggs.

And without the egg, her first born, she could never acquire human status again, at least not for many lifetimes to come and much prarabda, much karma, to endure, and no ego abandonment in sight at all at all.

The "brew" had been a false one, deceptively elegant, to be sure, but bottom line, nothing but manipulative psychobiological ceremonial spiritual quackery that, at best, served to seduce its practitioner into believing that it had intrinsic merit and power to elevate spiritually.

In her palmier days as a philosopher, or should one say?, his palmier days, Solan had often contemplated his belly button while sitting under a bridge alongside a flowing brook, with a long pipe in his mouth....patience facilitating dissolution of egocentric limiting fragmenting I-thou mental processes. But then, just when he 'knew' that he was 'enlightened,' having concocted that fateful brew, the unthinkable had happened, and now he was a female bird with a mind too limited to contemplate, and she was compelled by her nature and destiny to repeatedly take off, climb, swoop and dive straight down, down, until she hit blue green water in pursuit of silvery food called fish.

The two women and I internalized all this easily in playful mode. One of the women spoke:

"*Saorsa's* independence was a façade."

The woman tossed her long brown hair in the air, as if she knew that it would, and indeed it did, fall over her fresh-as-the-morning face, partly hiding her sparkling bright eyes. Clear eyes, and so innocent looking, and how like the other woman's eyes they were! Indeed, the two women resembled each other closely in many respects, and so they should, for they were sisters, gene pool sharers, not necessarily precise pattern sharers.

"Well, I'm not surprised," I said. "Isn't that exactly what comes from being consumed by ignorance of who he truly was, and still is, for that matter, from his superstitious belief in the power of rituals and ceremonies and formulae and concoctions, from his belief in programs, no less? What have I said? Are you two there yet?"

"We two have no time to waste on matters that might concern contemplatives with their not un-nerd-like bent frames, their pallid faces and their cold wet drippy noses poking around in dry library tomes."

"Dry library tomes, and Eastern Scriptures too, no less."

"Tedio; tediai; tedium!"

The two women glanced down at their stylish high-heeled shoes, gleaming black shoes that moved easily below elegantly swinging dresses, and, to be sure, the women were dressed suitably for the highest board-rooms in the land; ah, yes, dressed for it, but not destined for it, not unless they moved beyond sitting on aluminum chairs in roofless cubicles under unadorned electric lights, hoping for praise from Authority, curricula vitae.

They giggled in unison. They then rose up from their seats and began to look busy, tending to papers, photographs, shuffling them, stuffing them into huge handbags, discussing upcoming agendas and visions of the future, talking about being productive, then:

"He spends a lot of time by himself, too much if you ask me. What has he ever contributed to society?"

"How will he ever cut the mustard while his head is in contemplative fantasies and fairy tales?"

Cut the mustard, indeed! Well, I knew the game: First, they would seduce me with caresses, flattery, flashing eyes, strokes, then they would betray me, denounce me, yes; sell me down the river, the bitches! Well, so what!, let them. So what if Authority gave me a one-way ticket to the Cultural Chamber of Socio-biological Liquidation, where religious conversion in public might seem a viable option. Anyway, were birth, life and death simply not phases of the one? Of course, they were. I knew. Yes, but I had my lapses, my 'regressive episodes,' so to speak, into splintered I-versus-thou perception, ego-generated ways, and struggles against destiny, and, in remembering, I made my decision. I would not sign, and immediately I felt energized, fully alive, I smiled.

But wait; true, I had made my decision, but what if there was a complication? Death itself was not a problem for me. Death I could handle easily, but what about the manner in which death would be delivered to me? What if I were grabbed and bound, what if I were to be stretched naked on a long cold steel machine, my flesh squeezed and torn away from its roots against my bones? What if I were bled, my eyes stuck with red-hot tongs, my limbs cracked out of their joints into ugly unnatural positions, my testicles twisted with red-hot tweezers wired to electric generators?

In a situation like that, my tormentors would nod wisely to each other, they would tell each other that my weeping and moaning was self-serving, that I was shedding crocodile tears, that if only I had accepted the earlier recommendations, I would have adjusted, and I would never have brought such miseries into my own life, for, they would agree, I had the potential for obedience within me. They would remind each other of similar examples they had encountered in their illustrious careers, and each one of them would remember a "case" in which a subject had adjusted and gone on to a notable career in The Firm.

The two women looked at each other, they laughed and they laughed, and, as they laughed, they revealed sets of clean white teeth, the kind of teeth seen in television commercials for toothpaste, the kind of teeth associated with the aroma of mint, fresh air and the crying of seagulls.

"I have materialized into this life, from another existence, certainly not from nothing, with a destiny that is mine to act out and fulfill, indeed, to *be* what I am to be, *while remembering Him,* remembering Nam, living in His Name, regardless of obstacles encountered, including the resistance of others, and accepting all as manifestations of His love, and eventually, when my own part in the Great Play is finished, my biological body will melt away and I shall return to where I have come from."

The two women strolled casually towards the middle of the floor, side by side, almost touching each other, and, once in the center of the cylinder's floor, they paused momentarily, they swirled their dresses, they flashed bright-eyed looks at each other, they walked towards the circular wall, where a door opened silently and smoothly for them as they drew near to it, then closed behind them.

As the door closed behind the women, its outline vanished from sight.

34: BEYOND DILEMMA

Beginning in my middle, spreading throughout my entire body, to the top of my head, to my toes, a tingling of beauty, love in its purity, and to be sure, I was not alone, which I never am, of course, but this was different; a presence.

Up through the ceiling of the room I went, through the roof of the house, and far beyond, in silence, so that in a moment I was outside the earth's atmosphere, indeed, far from planet earth, out in the space of the solar system, and all without benefit of, or need for, oxygen or a pressurized space suit; at peace, at one with the universe.

Climbing, circling, swooping, roaming the solar system, planet earth a blue globe, earth becoming a tiny dot, earth vanishing, the mighty sun a remote splash of cold yellow light, then from the outer reaches of the solar system, back I came, back into the interior, closer to the sun, giver of energy, sustainer of molecular motion, energizer of biological life, manifestation of Him, bursting with love, brimming over with love, no concern about my past, no fear of the future, no desire, like a new-born babe in a crisp clear universe where time and space were and were not, and where, wanting nothing, I had everything.

Returning to earth as effortlessly as I had left, entering all of the countries of the world simultaneously, where all the people on earth were for me to observe at one time, and all was rare, of exquisite beauty, beyond space, beyond time, moving in multiple directions simultaneously.

Creation in all its glory sparkling pristine, the full spectrum of the rainbow spreading out around me, each color crisply clear, separated from each other by lines as sharp as slashes made in glass by a diamond cutter.

Music from many sources, in perfect harmony, also in harmony with multiple aromas, a gentle rhythmic motion of the whole universe alive-a sensory banquet! A delightful cosmic orchestra at the root of existence, beyond the limitations of human mind; liquid gold.

All over the world, which I was a living part of, not in any way separate from, men, women and children went about their affairs: some awake, some asleep, some happy, some sad, some healthy, some sick, some in pain, some laughing, all of them living their lives as best as they could, destinies unfolding, unaware of my presence as a silent ubiquitous observer, at one with what I observed, indeed, in oneness, with nothing of my own.

Two people next to me, a man and a woman, Eskimos, dressed in leathers and jeans, walking along a snow-covered road, the man waving his arms, talking loudly, shouting. They were quarreling over something important in their lives at that moment, an affair of the heart, perhaps, or concern over inadequate resources, but, whatever it was they quarreled about, the quarrel was intense and personal. Both were angry and afraid. The snow on the surface of the road was frozen hard, the brown fur-lined boots of the two made mild scrunching sounds as they walked, and the village smelled of cold air, wood burning stoves, electric fires, and of men, women and dogs. From the roofs of houses, television antennas snarled at the sky. Trucks were parked here and there in the neighborhood. Two diesel trucks had motors murmuring serenely.

In sun-warmed lands, dark-skinned, scantily-clad men, women and children went about their business, reacting to whatever pleasures and sorrows, gains and losses they encountered, and, all over the world, all was in perfect harmony: wealth, poverty, cities, villages, age, youth, health, sickness, vice and virtue.

And my heart was at peace.

Jungle all around me and a lion came out of the green, head rearing and mane flying, smelling of warm belly, warm breath and green grass. The beast was a male, he looked angry, he looked hungry and he opened his jaws, baring yellow-stained teeth, fangs, rolling a saliva-dripping tongue, ridges on the roof of his mouth. He placed his front paws on a large, round, brown rock that lay between us, and there he stood, silhouetted against the dark of the forest, swirling his tail majestically, as one who knew he could swirl his tail in full view of anyone as a gesture of mastery, giving a blast of his fearsome aroma to any warm blooded creature in the way.

No, I was not his prey, not at all, he wasn't even interested in me, and, in fact, he gazed right through me, beyond me, at something else, at another creature, a small furry animal whose purpose in life at that moment was to exist, die, be eaten and vanish into the great fire of life. No sorrow at the loss of the biological body. It would be false sorrow anyway, sorrow based on ignorance, for, knowing who I truly was, I regarded death as simply the separation of the God presence, the Self, the Atman, from the biological body that served as a temporary temple for the One within, because that life role was finished, and whatever was necessary was to be absorbed into the mystery of existence, beyond my limited perception, from which I had also come, out of my before-birth existence.

Salt water all around me, in the depths of the sea, breathing easily, no danger to my existence: fish, lovely multi-colored fish of many shapes and sizes swam all around me, while above me blue-green sunlight filtered through the water, and below me the dark belly of the ocean swayed gently: a bird dove into the surface, chasing a fish, splashing water, sending vibrations of sound like heavenly music into my whole being, and, in the air, birds wheeling, chasing the bird with the fish in its beak, squawking, threatening, cajoling, demanding, whining, whirling. A second bird dove into the water, then a third, they each got what they wanted. They wanted food, but some birds didn't get enough, and some were ageing and incapable, some didn't "know" what to do any more, some died, but then again no sadness, for the dead were, and the living were.

On land, birds chirping, warbling and tweeting, perching in tree-tops, on buildings, on high wires, and I gliding effortlessly, serenely through the air, savoring within me and around me life in abundance, in millions of forms, in multiple mediums, and it was good. In all the complexity, I questioned nothing, all was what it was designed to be, everything was complete, the universe was alive, all of it.

And all human beings were one. No racial differences. No separation based on wealth, national boundaries, formal education or religion. All manifestations of the One; yes, even the insects, the fishes, the birds and animals, and all forms of biology we called life, although, at a certain point of reduction to part protein, organic and inorganic segued into each other, as did psychological processes, biological chemistry, metabolism.

Into space, as if simultaneously, remaining next to earth's upper atmosphere, keeping the planet in full view, relatively close, and, over Africa, swooping down to earth, landing effortlessly on a grassy slope among a group of Africans camping around a fire. A wood fire, fueled by tree branches, some of which protruded in part from the flame that took their energy into itself, consuming them, giving out warmth and a dancing leaping light. A smell of burning wood, ashes, smoke, dry grass, of bare feet and children running around squealing and shrieking at random and to each other, to siblings and to their mothers.

Lean lithe men strode and strolled around the fire, with the easy confident motion of men who knew they were at home, in their own territory, in their own group, acting out their socially designated roles. Some dragged dry branches from a nearby cluster of trees towards the fire and tossed them into its blazing center, sending smoke billowing into the air and sparks glittering, and the fire's center sputtered and flamed as if in appreciation of the hearty meal, as if thanking the Big Nuclear Fire God of the universe for the opportunity to play for a while, the same nuclear fire that energized our own biology for a time, biology that would one day be reduced to its constituent particles, once our Selves, the Self, the God presence, separated, and always, I imagined, there was the potential to take up with another body in another life.

The campfire crackled crisply, the brightness of the sky retreated steadily into darkness as the side of the planet where Africa clung to earth's crust rolled out of the sun's light at over one thousand miles an hour.

Beside me a man, tall, lean, muscular, dressed in a gray shorts and a tattered khaki shirt with two breast pockets, so close to me I could have touched him, but then again I couldn't have touched him, because, although he and I coexisted as fellow human beings, sharing the same time on earth, we were, in that experience, in that vision, in separate "realities," with him totally unaware of me, and, to be sure, I didn't try to walk through him.

The man spoke in a language I didn't understand, all the while gesticulating with both arms, then, in one swift graceful movement of his lithe, powerful body, he flexed his knees, rested one knee on the ground, picked up a piece of timber that lay close to his feet and flung it into the flames, where it crackled and threw a galaxy of yellow sparks into the sky. Thick clouds of smoke arose from the flames. A thin column of gray smoke curled its way aloft out of the top of the conflagration, vanishing slowly into the sky. The flames lit up the man's cheekbones and teeth-he had two missing teeth in front-and the flames occasionally flung light into the man's eyes, eyes that reflected the flames, flames that never lit the man's face entirely at any one time, so that, always, some of his features remained in shadow.

Scarlet streaks from a rapidly sinking sun spread a thin rim of fire over the treetops, leaving the rest of the sky a vast eternity of deep dark, except for millions of tiny stars that winked a remote message. The presence of the One was ubiquitous, imminent, transcendent, and "I" in the Presence, visibly accompanied, warmed by the fire, among people, but not too warmed, only comfortably, in fresh air, I felt the grass beneath my feet soft, rich and springy; tiny electrical impulses tickled the skin of the soles of my feet.

Some women wore long dresses, some spotted, some striped, some patterned with squares and rectangles, and all of the dresses brightly-colored in red, blue, green and violet, and white ivory earrings dangled from the women's ear lobes, rocking gently as the women busied themselves over pots that sat by the side of the fire, using long slim wooden handles to stir the food within the pots; tall cooking pots, curving from round bellies below into long graceful necks ending in small spouts, out of which came a delicious aroma of stew, and handles rolled elegantly out of the sides of the pots, one handle on each side. Graceful women, moving efficiently, preparing communal, nourishing food-serenity.

Strolling through the throng of people, at ease, secure in the knowledge that I was in my place in the universe, that others were in their proper places, that the universe was one, that there was no separation, that all was One, that the One was the universe, I saw people, some frowning, some smiling at their lots, some working productively, some resting, some lazing about, some sleeping, some laughing, some arguing, all in complexity, and, whereas I was within inches of people, I was as if in another and parallel universe.

Over to the side, a little bit away from the fire, several small groups of men sat in serious conversation, sitting with their spines erect, knees flexed, and their legs folded beneath them. What a congenial lively company of barefooted fellows they were! And I was in *moksha*, simply being, not trying to do; not wanting to "help" others who didn't want my help, no desire to meddle uninvited in the lives of others, no desire to keep busy so as to avoid meeting myself, no desire to rescue people from themselves.

I sat down on the grass, I stood up, I strolled around the fire in a complete circle feeling quiet and complete, brimming over with love, secure, with no intellectual questions pending, no inhibitions, desires or fears. The tropical air was rich with the multiple aromas of grasses, shrubs, leafy trees, flowers, insects and village huts all around, in turn surrounded by wood fabric fence. Out of the cooking pots arose a delicious aroma, a column of blue-gray smoke spiraled silently skywards; night lowered its lid on life.

In India, all over India, time was not, for I was beyond time, and I knew of remote villages where lean, bony-faced, dark-eyed men and women lived lives that on the surface seemed simple, but that I knew were as complex as city lives, of course in different ways, for no human life was entirely simple, no human life was entirely complex, no human being was entirely what another was not, but, to be sure, money was scarce in villages, as were fine clothes, and when villagers traveled, they walked or hitched rides on slow-moving trains that rumbled by on tracks outside the villages, or they clambered on to lurching brightly-colored buses with open windows, buses that were invariably overloaded, but no matter, for the people on the buses were happy, and there were children in abundance, romping around, laughing and shrieking.

Something beautiful was happening globally.

Here and there, in assorted places around the world, individual men, women and children were "experiencing" Truth, but of course, God was in no way becoming visible as some kind of being, God was not a psychological projection, for He had never been separate from us, except in our imaginations. What were these "spiritual experiences?" Always private, always personal, never group-related, Truth manifesting without being called, the Great Will, the Creator, awakening people to knowledge of Him, one at a time, in His time, so to speak, although time in human terms was not relevant, and Truth never arose in more than one person in the same "place" at the same "time," only in whomsoever it arose in, without preamble, wherever people happened to be, on the street, at home, at work or at play.

Truth brought tears to some, laughter to others, it brought

amazement to all, and out of each being came a spontaneous outburst of love. Each one halted whatever he or she was doing, joy came out of each one's eyes, happiness out of each face, and some held their hands in the air, but in all this, other people didn't notice anything unusual in the ones experiencing Truth, and only the subjects knew.

How would the lives of these people change? Details were not for me to know. Sincere people with open hearts; simplicity. Meantime the multitudes of the world-and I was both of them and not of them-lived their lives as usual, totally oblivious to the manifestation of Truth here and there, seeing nothing unusual, following leaders, bound by cultural mythologies, caught in the clutches of mortal conditional love, never suspecting that what we all sought was already within each one of us, patiently waiting, waiting, until one day, ego relaxed.

Education, social status, material possessions, religious affiliation, power in society, intelligence, gave no advantage; neither did religious rituals, ceremonies, affiliations, mental manipulations, or socio-psychobiological acrobatics.

Humble acknowledgement of Truth, or the Lord, glowed in their eyes, as egos evaporated in Him, love radiated out of their faces; they marveled, they were in awe and wonder at what was happening inside them, and yes, I knew their thoughts and feelings, for, to be sure, we were one.

I felt no curiosity about what I didn't know, nor did I question anything, for all around me was perfect, as His design would surely be expected to be, and I was part of the design, pure in my heart, open, washed clean, free of dilemmas, warm all over and light as a cosmic dancer in perfect harmony.

It was "time" for the experience to end, and slowly, like an escalator rolling in from another dimension, ego returned to me, bringing with it my thoughts, my ideas, my values, my desires, and my psychological sense of self, in short, my mortal mind.

My mortal mind.

35: VRAJALEELA

I make no effort to pass myself off as "enlightened," or "special," or "spiritually advanced," or anything beyond the human being I am, that other people are, including those in the streets, in the taverns, the churches, the universities, the prisons, on constructions sites, in politics, regardless of social status, background, nationality, religious persuasion, education or accomplishments.

Only Truth can establish Truth. What is within establishes what is within, it doesn't come from lectures, from what is written, and I acknowledge my limitations, my biased perceptions. In my social role, I behave as if I were the creator of my life destiny, but, if I act as if these were mine beyond my limited life role, I create ego attachments, and yes, gentle reader, remember that whatever 'I' write is also from mind, all ego, the very ego that constitutes a barrier!

My character is structured a certain way, and operates accordingly, but my character, along with my biological body, is not the real me, it is impermanent, and my man-made values are also transient, all being there for my part in the Great Play, the Vrajaleela. Beyond my mental attachments, as I see it, sin, vice, virtue, good, bad, right, wrong are not relevant, except as off-shoots of ego-driven man-made values, important of course on the social scene,-as is individual personal responsibility-and friends and enemies alike are manifestations of God, in my life to help me come to my Self.

"You are simple and loving and so he draws you to him."
If we don't enjoy here...where? when?

Thousands of years ago, on the plains of India, a war was fought. An account of that war, known as the Kurukshetra War, is in the Bhagavad Gita, one of the major spiritual writings of India, and I, as an outsider to India, claim no knowledge of Indian history, but I know that, universally, war is waged, and I believe that war without reflects war within, and in India I learned that the Kurukshetra War symbolizes the war within, the war between the senses and the mind, which presents a dilemma, in that it offers a choice between two undesirable outcomes.

If the senses win, I'll overindulge to the point of loss of control and self-destruction, but, on the other hand, if the mind wins, I'll be into psychological over-control, inhibition and constriction, neither of which brings happiness. Am I my senses? Am I ego? Of course not. Nor am I a 'psychobiological agent.' Who I am is much deeper, more permanent, than that, a manifestation of the Creator, as all beings are, and if I make Him into some Being entirely outside of myself, which these days I do not, I'll use ploys to negotiate what I want, I'll try to please Him, either by praying directly for what I want, or else by acting in whatever dilemma-ridden manner I used to get what I wanted from my parents, and if He fails to respond, I'll get angry, and, in suppressing my anger, I might judge those who follow religious practices other than my own as a bunch of phonies and hypocrites, not up to my lofty standards, morally inferior to me.

I see so much in life that is beautiful, whether I am in the mountains, on the plains, by the sea, or in some big city in the midst of noisy machines. Sometimes I watch, alone, in silence, feeling the beauty, eyes open, eyes closed, many times being where I imagine I am, and many nights I revisit old haunts, interspersed with periods of deep dreamless sleep in which my Creator revitalizes me.

What if I were to carry a grudge? Grudge-bearers destroy in fantasy, they wish harm upon others, in ways disguised, and if I were to indulge in grudge-bearing, I'd be trying to destroy my own 'dark side,' the side where the grudge would be buried, the secret side, I'd be trying to destroy in others what I'd despise in myself, an aspect of myself I'd be hiding from myself, and projecting on to others, and of course, to the degree that I wouldn't know what I was doing, refusing to examine myself, the destruction would go on indefinitely.

It's not hard to imagine chronic grudge-bearing as at least a partial precursor to psychosomatic maladies, or to stress-induced disease, or to participation in violence, civilian or military, easily justified by egoistic imagination, justified, yes, but not relieved in this way.

If I'm at war within and blind to it, I'm drawn into each and every war between quarreling factions all over the world, taking sides, claiming moral superiority, naturally on the side of the virtuous, concealing my anger from myself. Regardless of insight and of modification of one's behavior, the core war within cannot be won by brute force, it cannot be won by science, it cannot be won by religious rituals, it cannot be won by psychological manipulations, it cannot be won by psychiatric ceremonies, it cannot be won by persuasion, and, bottom line, winning isn't relevant! What is?

Do your duty and remember Him. He will do the rest. Patience is the only virtue. Remember Nam. Surrender ego and...

Truth being intellectually non-analyzable, non-debatable to a conclusion, Truth being existence itself,-and Dadaji as Truth, being Truth, the core, the whole, the life itself, Creation-beyond biology, beyond dilemma, beyond mind, and all that as a flash of intuition, exactly what I had been waiting for all these years, but, to be sure, no intellectual understanding.

Love and complete surrender to Supreme Being, Creator.

We, or at least those of us who are curious in an introspective way, want so much to know how we become the human beings we are. We want to know what motivates us. We want to know why we behave in ways we do. We want to bring intellectual order on to aspects of the universe. It allows us to feel in control. Once we feel in control, we feel better. I reject an understanding of the human being that is simply psychobiological. I know that, at the core, we are not confined to mind, brain or body, that our true identity is divine, and that kind of knowing is not readily reducible to words. The attempt to reduce everything to words diminishes the experience of being into an intellectual formulation that it isn't, and we lose thereby. Any intellectual order I formulate may be of my own fantasy. Who am I to say that human nature has an intellectual foundation? Why should it? Or, of course, why shouldn't it? All mind! Much of perception is beyond the rational, and all I do is express myself in a limited way, knowing that putting certain experiences into words reduces them to what they cannot be. Words, being of mind, are inadequate. Words reflect mental processes. What? Is silence then golden? Not always of course.

Of course, I believe in studying the human being, socially, psychologically and biologically, if it is done in a humane way, *without torturing living beings in the process,* which rules out much laboratory work.

"Maybe you'll come back into a next life as a liberated, playful man; perhaps, as you have said about yourself, a lay philosopher-at-large, a wise observer-participant in, but not a meddler in, the Grand Play."

"Liberation is a social psychological term. It's elusive, it isn't primary, it's not in my power to bring about in myself or in another, and indeed I might negate it by pursuing it as if it were some goal at work, requiring shoulder to the wheel, but it may happen spontaneously, from within, not subject to rituals or ceremonies, and, certainly, insight helps, and honesty in daily life."

At one time, I wanted to find a method, perhaps a ritual, or a demonstrable formula, similar to, or at least analogous to, methods we used in psychiatry, that would work in my spiritual life, only to find that I was making a false assumption, for there was nothing specific to do to be loved. I was already loved. No need for me to do anything. Well, I do remember the Divine presence within, I see the Divine presence in all of life, I see the Divinity in my enemies, but then again, I forget, and, as often as I forget, I remember. There are devout sincere people in each and every one of the world's religions; God, in His own way, draws all of us on this earth to Him, and, sooner or later, in this life or another, we will arrive.

It is true that, as a result of going to India, I questioned aspects of my own life and my way of life, and my beliefs, but my purpose is not to speak against anybody's spiritual practices, for we do the best we can with what knowledge we have, and our approaches appear to diverge only because of our human propensity for ego-centric wants, fears, divisiveness and conflict, which also accounts for organization into groups in spiritual pursuits, organization that creates problems, separation, conflict, debate, arguments and quarreling, some of which become violent. How do 'I' know who is 'right' and who is 'wrong,' who is 'good' and who is 'bad,' except as my splintered biased mind judges, or misjudges?

I happened to go to India. As a result of my going there and meeting with Dadaji, and I did spend many hours in his presence,-he also visited me many times in my house, visits identified as sleep visions-I underwent a major change in my worldview, in my way of identifying myself, and in clarifying exactly what I want out of life. The one I went to see in India is no longer there. The fact that I went to India in no way suggests that others should or should not visit India, or that anyone else should or should not question what they believe in, or that anyone else should or should not see things the way I see them. I have nothing spiritual to teach to another. I have no prescription for another.

I came to value the identity of Jesus and his core teachings all the more because of what I learned in India. Jesus lived Truth, he was beyond psychological dilemmas, desires and fears, or at least he transcended them, he had beyond-mind experiences, he was beyond the dualistic style of thinking, that endless struggle between opposites such as vice and virtue, good and bad, right and wrong; he spoke of the presence of the Father, as if he knew the Father as he walked the earth, and it appears that most people who heard him failed to understand what he was talking about...Do I? Understanding is limited.

Man is a helpless being.

"I saw a television program recently," Marjorie said, "in which a talk-show host interviewed a world-renowned scientist. What were the greatest problems facing the world today? According to the scientist, the greatest problems facing us are global warming, the threat of nuclear and biological war, and overpopulation."

"The great scientist said nothing new," I said, "if that's what he said. Anyway, these are not the greatest problems in life as I see it. Many years ago, in a Highland glen, on a construction site, a man called Pagoda told me that his notion of himself, that is, his ego or his mind, got in his way of knowing. I didn't have a clue what he meant, but I never forgot what he said. Now I know what he meant, but just think of how long it took in my case.

"The greatest problem facing me in my life is my failure to remember and live in a consistent way who I am, who I am at the core, who we all are, the presence of God within me, in all living beings, and whether I accept egoistic rewards, which give immediate brief gratification, or whether I live, whether I am, what is permanent, which is Truth."

Of course, as the great scientist suggested, a global crisis may come to pass, even global destruction, what with modern weapons designed by his fellow scientists, the possible lethal application of chemical and biological discoveries, the destructive long-term effects of industrial processes, all ego; not to mention gigantic natural disasters, unpredictable, the universe waking up, reacting, yawning, stretching its limbs, warming up, freezing over, our planet transforming its precious resources, then, restoring a balance of nature, destiny running its course. And if the planet crashes, those of us who are alive will know existential crisis, a re-arrangement of priorities, spiritual renewal, and a new world, as the planet finds a fresh balance, as it surely will.

On the other hand, there are some intelligent, scientifically minded people who believe that ahead of us lies an age of release from hunger, pain, suffering and disease, brought about as a result of future scientific accomplishments, some of which will take us to fresh and abundant sources of energy, such as from sun, wind, fresh water, salt water, with no undesirable side-effects.

Maybe many of us in our hearts want the same thing, which is the peace of mind that comes from union of the 'seeker' with the 'sought,' who, as it turns out, are one and the same, the 'seeker' being the 'sought.' We do not 'find' God, as we sometimes say, for He already has us, as He is within us from the beginning, and in our realization, He 'finds' Himself, so to speak, in love, but, in our mortal minds we identify His love as if it were our love for Him, and so we say that we find God or love God. But that union doesn't come from reading the egoistic productions of writers like me.

I remember Name, the Lord's Name, *Nam*, in my daily life in all I do and say, except when I forget, and then I remember, knowing that I am in this life so as to know the Lord in my daily life, to enjoy His Grand Play, to taste His love, working in His name, living my destiny, being, remembering Nam, using my intellectualizing, my passion for learning, my insecurities, my compassion and my creativity to grasp the bottom line in complexity, to see myself in others, to love wherever I go, aware of the divinity within, transcending barriers of race, religion, language, geography, property, wealth, species and accomplishments, perhaps one day internalizing the whole in a playful way, but, then again, it is not my place to suggest to others why they are in this life. For me to suggest such a thing to others would be pompous.

It is not pompous, however, to suggest that, if I insist on seeing myself as a member of one of separate incompatible groups of people, if I refuse to acknowledge what I have in common with others, if I compete destructively against others, fighting over limited resources, if I struggle endlessly over mastery, there will be consequences. What consequences? Alienation, for one, and what else? A 'dark side,' with all that that implies, including projection on to others, blaming, fault finding, splintering, quarreling, self-enslavement to ideology in the name of freedom.

I came into the lives of certain others, they came into mine, we all had and still have unfinished business to attend to, I attend to mine, but I need the input of others, family members, friends, associates, enemies, yes, enemies too, help me come to my Self in a non-intellectual non-linear complex way that I put to writing at peril of reductionism, for I make life appear linear so that my mind can grasp it. Do I forgive my enemies? With knowing, the question seems unnecessary, but then again, it must be asked, seeing that we exist so much in mental perception. The word 'forgiveness' implies a self-righteous sense of moral superiority, a one-upmanship: All mind; all ego. Who am I to presume to forgive another?

"How do you know this?"

"Good question. I don't know anything, except what I see through my own idiosyncratic perception; slivers, splinters, dots of light in the dark, and, as I have said, remember that whatever I say or write is partial, egoistic."

"Well, then, what if you're wrong?"

"It's my way of looking at things, but I am only one simple human being. 'Wrong' brings up the idea of 'right.' That's dualistic thinking all over again. I want to avoid debate in these matters. It doesn't help. Reflective conversation is one thing, debate is another. Debate divides. I'm not capable of grasping Truth. Who am I to try? Someone else will look at life and see it similarly to the way I see it, or entirely differently, and indeed, I could be self-righteous, I could be duplicitous."

"What about psychiatry?"

"Without psychiatry, society as we know it would collapse. The hypotheses of psychiatry are part of our worldview and mythology. If we didn't believe in them, they would self-extinguish, to be replaced by some other hypotheses that we would believe in. These hypotheses are, however, useful in practice, and, certainly, modern neurological-biological innovations, computer generated imagery, neurologically active chemicals, and the understanding of and future application of genetics are, and will continue to be, helpful.

"My own earliest recollection in this life role is of me standing up alone for the first time, as a new arrival on stage, gazing around me with awe and delight."

"I'm different from you. I'm more social, more light-hearted, I like golf, I like Mah Jongg, I like flowers and fresh fruit, I like light conversation that has no profound meaning. You like to contemplate."

* * *

I am here to enjoy His Vraja-Leela, His Grand Play, revealed in this world, as manifestations of Him, and taste His love, but I am to avoid exploitation, either as perpetrator or as victim.

Dadaji, in his earthly manifestation, was beyond dilemma, beyond mind, had no ego like the rest of us, but I, with my egoistic psychological processes, might see him as separate, as I might see separation all around me.

According to Dadaji, the language of the heart is one, religion is one, human beings are one at the core all over the world-which is not to deny transient man-made cultural, psychological and social differences-and true worship is thinking, feeling, acting, working and enjoying in His name, accepting God as the doer, in humility.

Dadaji took on the appearance of an ordinary man, allowing me-and others-to see him as an ordinary man, so that he could relate, but he was far from ordinary, and indeed, I believe he remains inside each and every one of us, in love, with no quid pro quo, no exchange, all natural, relaxed, requesting no rites of passage, no steps to master, no tests to pass, no coercive maneuvers, but, even knowing that to be so, at times I tend to imagine that I must perform to satisfy. I use the present tense in referring to Dadaji, because that is the way I see him, but, as for judging him in any way, that is beyond me, and I make to effort to do so. Who am I to judge the core of Creation? Can I even judge myself?

We each have unique destinies, for no two minds are the same, nor do we, as I see it, direct our own destinies, which is His play of creation, and indeed, even our human psychological processes are established by our Creator, who ultimately brings us to Him, in one life or another, but, of course, we must finish whatever life issues we came to fulfill, and we will. If, however, I stubbornly cling to egoistic mind, with no attempt at ego abandonment, I'll incarcerate myself in a self-made torture chamber in which I see no exit, and that I blame on others or circumstances.

When He exits from my body, my Self returns to Him, and my mind in part-mind is also from God-may return to Him, if necessary, to attach to another body in another life in order to finish desires that came with me from the beginning of creation.

"Remember," Abhi said to me one day, "that a beam of sunlight pierces darkness instantly, rather than gradually."

And another day, to repeat: "Now I get what I need, without sense of wants or expectations. You will feel it also. This is called natural living in Him, living where there are no complaints, and everything is loving and beautiful. In the future, all will be like this. It is difficult to be simple, but you are simple. It is His choice."

* * *

And, as I thoughtfully contemplate the past or the future in the present, I peer into the now, and an old man in Canada in his house in the forest-a metaphor in the East for wisdom-reveals to me whatever dilemma-ridden drama recurs in my life, in simple words like fodder on the floor where the horses can get to it.

In my own bunk house round-the-wood-stove kind of way, he might say, I am innocent, as I imagine that little boy on his bicycle is innocent, and so I express myself, I stand up for innocence, for simplicity, accepting mystery in a simple way, and my place in it, my heart empty, a load off, pristine pure.

ISBN 141203244-X